EVERY DAY IS A HOLIDAY...

EVERY MEAL IS A FEAST!

MSgt A. A. Bufalo USMC (Ret)

ISBN 978-0-9745793-8-2

First Printing – October 2006
Printed in the United States of America

www.AllAmericanBooks.com

Every Day is a Holiday, Every Meal is a Feast!

OTHER BOOKS BY ANDY BUFALO

SWIFT, SILENT & SURROUNDED
Sea Stories and Politically Incorrect Common Sense

THE OLDER WE GET, THE BETTER WE WERE
MORE Sea Stories and Politically Incorrect Common Sense

NOT AS LEAN, NOT AS LEAN, STILL A MARINE
Even MORE Sea Stories and Politically Incorrect Common Sense

THE ONLY EASY DAY WAS YESTERDAY
Fighting the War on Terrorism

TO ERR IS HUMAN, TO FORGIVE DIVINE
However, Neither is Marine Corps Policy
A Book of Marine Corps Humor

HARD CORPS
The Legends of the Marine Corps

AMBASSADORS IN BLUE
In Every Clime and Place
Marine Security Guards Protecting Our Embassies Around the World

SALTY LANGUAGE
An Unabridged Dictionary of Marine Corps Slang, Terms &Jargon

THE LORE OF THE CORPS
Quotations By, About & For Marines

Every Day is a Holiday, Every Meal is a Feast!

IN MEMORY OF

Brigadier Stephen W. J. Saunders
Duke of Edinburgh's Royal Regiment
(Berkshire & Wiltshire)
"Duty First"

Every Day is a Holiday, Every Meal is a Feast!

PREFACE

I never expected to compile ONE book of sea stories, and here I am putting the finishing touches on volume number *four*. Time sure flies when you are having fun. I say fun, because I never tire of the exploits of those who have worn, or are wearing, the uniform of our beloved Corps - and just when I think there can be no more stories to tell, some Devil Dog out there does something unbelievable. I guess I didn't realize what I was getting into when I decided to become the "unofficial historian" of the Marine Corps!

During the time I was compiling this edition I was saddened to learn of the death of Brigadier Stephen Saunders, to whom this book is dedicated. I first met then-Colonel Saunders when I invited him to be guest of honor at a Mess Night commemorating the 4th of July during the time I was assigned to the MSG Detachment in Canberra, Australia. He was the Military Attaché at the British High Commission there, and I thought it would be appropriate to have a "Redcoat" as our guest on the day we celebrated our independence from England. The irony wasn't lost on Colonel Saunders, and we ended up having an evening to remember!

I learned of the Brigadier's assassination by Greek terrorists quite by accident and somewhat after the fact, but even so it was quite a shock. I dedicate this book to him as evidence of the strong ties between our respective countries, and as a way to convey my condolences to his widow and family. His unfortunate and unnecessary death shows the world *yet again* that the world's nations must put aside their petty differences and stand together in the face of terrorism until it is eradicated. As Brigadier Saunders himself might say, "Duty First!"

TABLE OF CONTENTS

Every Day is a Holiday, Every Meal is a Feast!

A MARINE 24/7

Chet Lynn

"Marines are different. They have a different outlook on life."

When I was serving on Okinawa I heard about a Sergeant Major who was so dedicated to the Corps he had never taken one single day of leave in his entire twenty-plus years of service. I found that hard to believe at the time, but I guess he wasn't the only one like that.

Hockaday possessed not one item of civilian clothing. Most of the time this had proven to be no great disadvantage, until the day he was assigned to the 2nd Marines, a regiment with a rather socially-minded officers' mess. It came to pass that the regimental commander decided there would be a gathering of the officers and their spouses as a matter of "calls made and returned," and the uniform was specified as "appropriate civilian attire." In this case, coat and tie was deemed "appropriate."

Hockaday stated that he believed Summer Service 'A' would also be appropriate, but was informed that it would be deeply appreciated (or words to that effect) if he would comply with the desires of the regimental commander. After some thought Hockaday referred himself to the Marine Corps Manual and conducted research in order to discover what, if any, uniform items might be worn with civilian attire - and found that virtually *any* item of uniform which did not have some device identifying it as military could be worn.

On the day in question Hockaday presented himself to the

assembled regimental officers and spouses and proceeded through the receiving line - attired in spit shined cordovan dress shoes, regulation black socks, khaki trousers, starched long sleeve khaki shirt with no ribbons or badges thereon, a multi-colored necktie which looked as if the local foundling home had used it as a spit-up rag, and a sort of rust-colored sport coat I am sure he located in a local thrift shop.

After passing through a suddenly quiet and bemused receiving line Hockaday proceeded to the bar, where he had the two ritually imposed drinks and made his departure - stopping only to drop his card into the bowl provided for that purpose. As he left the officers' club he passed a large dumpster, into which he deposited the coat and necktie before boarding his Marine Green TR7 with camouflage covered upholstery and departing the area.

That was the first, last and *only* time Hockaday was ever observed in civilian attire.

Chet Lynn was a Marine. In a sense, that says it all. He joined the Corps as a teenager in the late 1940s, made the long walk out from the Chosin Reservoir in 1950, took a commission when still young enough to look like a child, and rose to lieutenant colonel before retiring.

A VETERAN'S DAY
Recollection

Major Phil Seymour

"Music is the shorthand of emotion." - Leo Tolstoy

It's odd how a particular smell or sound has the power to transport one back to the events of decades past. The "Marines' Hymn" has such a power for me, largely due to events on a night almost forty years ago in a land half a world away.

Certainly for any present, former, or retired Marine, the Marines' Hymn is the one melody which evokes thoughts of Marine Corps Birthday Ball celebrations shared with friends in disparate regions of the four corners of the globe. But the 12th of October, 1967 was not a time for celebration or for toasting to the Corps with one's friends. Instead it was a moment in time - otherwise insignificant - during which a company of Marines fought for its very existence and for which the Hymn played a significant role.

In early October of 1967 I was a sergeant with C Company, First Battalion, First Marine Regiment of the First Marine Division (C 1/1 for short, or simply "Charlie Company"). Since arriving "in country" (South Vietnam) the previous December, Charlie Company had been conducting "search and destroy" operations in an area about twenty-odd miles south of Da Nang. But, on October 6th both 1/1 and our sister unit, the Second Battalion, First Marine Regiment (2/1), were ordered north to the area adjacent to the so-called Demilitarized Zone (DMZ) which separated North and South

Vietnam. We boarded trucks for the twenty-mile drive up Highway 1 to the Da Nang Air Base, and there transferred to KC-130 aircraft for the short hop north to Dong Ha Air Base. After touching down, we trucked to nearby Quang Tri and dug in for an indefinite stay.

We had little time to enjoy our new surroundings. The area adjacent to the DMZ was under the operational control of the Third Marine Division, but also operating in this area were both the 9th North Vietnamese Army Regiment and the 808th Viet Cong Main Force Battalion. They had positioned numerous anti-aircraft guns on the hilltops in this area near their base-camps. These guns were responsible for an alarming number of "shoot downs" of U.S. aircraft, principally helicopters flying over the thick jungle canopy of the Hai Lang rain forest. So it was that elements of the Third Marine Division, with 1/1 and 2/1 attached, would set out on "Operation Medina" to try to locate and neutralize these guns and the NVA force which freely operated in the area.

At 1100 on October 11th Charlie Company boarded fourteen U.S. Army UH-1 "Huey" helicopters for a twenty minute, zigzag treetop flight into a Landing Zone on the edge of the jungle. Charlie Company had been designated the "point" company, and the remainder of 1/1 and 2/1's seven companies would land and follow us about a thousand meters to our rear. In theory Charlie Company would encounter the enemy forces first, thus preventing the greater force to our rear from stumbling into an ambush with potentially dire results. It was not lost on us that we were out in front, and largely on our own, if the worst was to happen.

Once all of our Marines were on the ground, we moved off the LZ through head high elephant grass toward the jungle's edge. Entering the enveloping jungle, little daylight filtered through the three separate layers of dense canopy.

With the sun's rays unable to penetrate the thick foliage, virtually everything we touched was covered with slimy, rotting vegetable matter. The ground was crawling with land leeches. These, in particular, made for an interesting night. Whether on watch, or trying to catch some much needed sleep, each of us sought to ward off the persistent crawling and sucking of these leeches. Sleep was in short supply that night.

Before first light on the morning of the 12th, those fortunate enough to find sleep were awakened by their less fortunate brethren. Largely by feel in the darkness, each Marine found a score or more black leeches adhering to their bodies. With only minutes to spare before moving out, each of us busied ourselves burning off the attached leeches - and thoughts of a C-ration breakfast would have to wait until later.

That morning dawned as had each morning since the end of the monsoon season several months before - hot and very humid. Our progress through the thick jungle was slow, typically measured in yards rather than miles. The "point" man had to hack a narrow path fifteen or twenty yards ahead, while those behind quietly waited. Everyone faced outboard, alternating left and right, though none of us could see much beyond ten feet through the foliage. On signal to move out, everyone picked up his gear and moved forty or fifty feet forward, only to halt once again and face outboard. This went on through the morning and into the early afternoon. Finally, at around 1400, our point man emerged onto a trail - a very well used NVA trail! After consulting by radio with our Battalion Commander, who was more than a thousand meters to our rear, our Commanding Officer, Captain Bill Major, decided to risk moving onto this trail. Each of us was concerned about the possibility of an ambush, but the alternative was to remain in the jungle and not reach our objective before nightfall. This would in all likelihood subject us to plunging fire from the NVA unit we knew to be encamped on the mountaintop above.

Movement certainly was both swifter and quieter once on the trail, but as we approached the base of the heavily forested hillock the jungle ahead erupted in sustained bursts of heavy and light machinegun fire down the long axis of our ranks. Those closest to the ambush site were also subjected to several incoming grenades. The entire lead squad was down, and those immediately behind scrambled for whatever cover they could find. Being about midway back and not in immediate danger from the fire ahead, I and those in my platoon began to deploy rapidly off the trail to either side and moved ahead toward the steady fire, now both incoming and outgoing. Moving into position, we laid down suppressing fire against those in the ambush position. After ten minutes or so of heavy contact the incoming fire ceased, as the NVA manning the guns on the rise to our front pulled back to the safety of their comrades on the hill above. They left behind two 12.7mm heavy machine guns however, as well as several of their more seriously wounded and dead soldiers.

We set up a 360-degree defensive perimeter while our Navy corpsmen attended to the wounded. Those killed in action were beyond help at that point and were moved off the trail where they were hastily covered with green rubberized ponchos. Our CO immediately radioed for an emergency medical evacuation to remove our casualties as quickly as possible. Several Marines began cutting down small trees with their machetes in order to transform our little hillock into a barely usable landing zone for the incoming helos. C-4 plastic explosive was used on the larger, more stubborn trees.

Not long after, an incoming radio call advised that the

helos were in close proximity and needed some sort of illumination to define the four corners of our landing zone. With the NVA occupying the high ground above us, we elected to light the "heat tabs" that fuel our C-rations. Barely fifty feet across, our makeshift LZ was smaller than the pilots would have desired - but they came in nevertheless. Unable to actually land due to the many tree stumps in the LZ, the first CH-34 "Chinook" helicopter slowly descended into a close hover just above ground level. The more severely wounded were loaded aboard. Upon its departure, three more helos descended in turn. As the fifth helo began its descent, a torrent of automatic rifle fire erupted to our immediate front. The North Vietnamese had launched a company-sized unit into an attack on our lines, but fortunately our strength as a reinforced company was more than adequate to repel the hundred or so attackers.

As incoming rounds skipped across our shallow defensive position, a series of whistles sounded off to our left flank as a second NVA company joined the assault. The volume of fire, both incoming and outgoing, was intense. Soon after this second assault began, the intensity of the fire waned momentarily while both attackers and defenders paused to jam another magazine into their respective weapons. It was during this pause that a storm of grenades rained in on our small LZ. Almost immediately, a third blast of whistles signaled the appearance of two more companies on our previously unmolested rear and right flanks. With more than four hundred fresh, well-armed North Vietnamese soldiers completely encircling us, our CO realized reinforcements would be needed - and very soon. He radioed our Battalion Commander, who was then establishing a defensive position on a hilltop about a thousand meters to our rear. Also on that hilltop was Delta Company's CO, Captain John Gallagher, who immediately ordered his men to saddle up and begin the long trek through the jungle toward the sound of battle below.

Charlie Company's Marines moved off the landing zone into the dense foliage surrounding the small knob of a hill that would serve both as a command post for our Company Commander and as a collection point for the rapidly increasing number of casualties. Those whose wounds were not immediately life threatening remained on the line and continued to aid in the company's defense. With darkness rapidly falling, an Air Force C-47 aircraft arrived above our position and began dropping illumination flares. It, and several more that followed, remained on station throughout the night. Without their continuous illumination, I doubt we could have held out as long as we did.

Among those who had been wounded in the initial onslaught was machine gunner Corporal Jimmy Leonard. He remained at his position, however, providing covering fire with his M-60 machine gun. As this trail overlooked one of the few "open" fields of fire through the underbrush, the NVA also chose to set up one of their machineguns just down the hill from Leonard's gun. Leonard fired first, and killed both the enemy gunner and his assistant gunner. Two other NVA soldiers moved in to re-man this machinegun; Leonard killed these two as well. By the time the enemy gun was finally destroyed, Leonard had wiped out seven two-man gun teams.

The NVA attacks were coming in waves now from all sides. The attackers were part of a freshly deployed unit and, as we learned later, each man was equipped with the venerable AK-47 assault rifle. Each weapon employed a thirty round magazine, which allowed its owner to put out an incredible amount of firepower. We, in turn, were carrying the new M-16 rifles with their twenty round magazines. Although we did not consider these weapons as reliable as either our old M-14 rifles (which we had relinquished back in March) or our opponents' AK-47s, the M-16's smaller, lighter 5.56mm cartridge did have one saving grace - it permitted us to carry twice the amount of ammunition as when carrying our old M-14s with their larger, heavier 7.62mm cartridge. In our present predicament, this would prove to be the difference between life and death.

The battle raged around us interminably. One could not distinguish individual rifle shots. The roar of several dozen automatic weapons - both ours and theirs - simultaneously firing on full automatic shut out all other sound. So too did the dozens of grenades exploding both farther down the hill and amidst our positions. Nobody truly had any idea what was happening anywhere except around his own position. Scores of NVA soldiers repeatedly advanced up the slope toward our positions, firing on full automatic as they came. As their rifles' magazines emptied, the volume of fire diminished somewhat as they paused to insert another full magazine before continuing their advance. For our part, we poured fire into their ranks, also on full automatic. Before withdrawing, the NVA soldiers armed and tossed their fragmentation grenades into our lines. Our grenades followed their withdrawal.

With the battle in its fourth hour, our ammunition was almost gone. We began scavenging for grenades and fresh magazines from our casualties, and for weapons and grenades from the several NVA soldiers who had been killed within our lines. We had gone to the field with 172 Marines, a number far greater than Charlie Company's typical strength of less than one hundred men. Now, as the number of our "effectives" dwindled to seventy or less, our resistance became more of an individual effort than the concerted effort of before. We had long since fixed our bayonets, as had the North Vietnamese soldiers to our front.

The NVA soldiers were penetrating our thinning lines with regularity now. Before withdrawing back down the hill, many of them lobbed grenades into our perimeter. Many of these landed among the wounded men lying within the cleared area at the top of the hill. The sound of grenades falling and exploding had become commonplace. Lance Corporal Bill Perkins, a combat photographer attached to Charlie Company for this operation, saw one of these grenades land among several wounded men. He yelled, "Grenade!" and threw himself on top of the explosive as it detonated, thereby giving his life in order to save the several men in close proximity. Perkins' family later received his posthumous Medal of Honor for his selfless actions that night.

As our strength dwindled further, we were forced to contract our lines back up the hill to the very edge of the clearing. With our ammunition all but exhausted, we had little option but to meet the advancing enemy with just our bayoneted rifles and machetes. Our resistance became less effective as our numbers diminished.

The attackers continued their assaults on our positions, though they appeared as spent as we felt. We attempted to time our forays into their ranks when they - or most of them - were reloading their weapons. We lost men, and they lost men as well. After penetrating their ragged lines we had to drag our wounded back up the hill, and often engaged the same enemy soldiers making their way back down.

After several forays into the attacker's ranks, each with less effectiveness than the previous attempt, our numbers had dwindled to just over thirty men still able to fight. It was apparent to each of us, as well as to the many wounded lying about both in the cleared LZ and in the jungle below, that our ability to provide an effective defense was at an end. We could not keep the NVA soldiers from completely overrunning our position for much longer. It was then that First Lieutenant Jack Ruffer, a former enlisted man who had since received a commission (commonly referred to as a "Mustang"), began singing the Marines' Hymn. Other Marines, both wounded and as yet unscathed, picked up the Hymn as well. It was a last ditch effort to "rally the troops" for one last rush down the hill. With the Hymn still echoing through the hills and valleys, those few of us still on our feet moved back into the underbrush toward the advancing shadows. The singing of the Hymn felt somehow reassuring and familiar. It also provided a sense of peace and continuity with those Marines from wars past.

Captain John Gallagher's Delta Company also heard the singing. They began pushing up the trail we had come down the previous afternoon, and almost immediately encountered the North Vietnamese encircling our position. His men blasted a hole in their lines and spread into and over our small LZ. I had not been aware that Delta Company was on the move for our relief. Nor can I recall the emotions I experienced when I first realized they had made it through the enemy force surrounding us. On reflection, I believe it was a mixture of pure exhaustion and unadulterated relief! I do recall making it back to the LZ, where I dropped my rifle to the ground, followed by my cartridge belt and helmet. I then sank to my knees. I had nothing left.

Delta Company's timely arrival had turned the tide of this engagement just that quickly. Had they arrived ten or fifteen minutes later, I question whether they would have found anyone still alive. As it was, all of our officers and staff

NCOs had been wounded or killed. Four of our seven Navy corpsmen had been wounded while tending to fallen Marines. And, of the 172 Marines who had begun this operation just two days before, only thirty remained. As for the enemy's losses, we only counted twenty-one bodies - all within our perimeter. The blood trails surrounding our little hill attested to a considerably higher toll however, as their practice was to drag off their wounded and dead. For our part, we were just glad the worst was over!

Our contact with the North Vietnamese did not end with Delta Company's arrival, but for us everything following that night was anticlimactic. We were not aware that our singing of the Hymn had penetrated beyond our own little LZ on that tiny hill. But after rejoining our other two battalions at their hilltop position several days later, I had the opportunity to talk with several friends in another company. They informed me that, on the night of 12-13 October, they and the others on that hilltop had listened to the sound of the engagement below and watched the light green NVA "tracer" rounds mix with our red tracer ammunition flying about in all directions from our position a thousand meters off. They recounted how they had listened as the Hymn's familiar refrain echoed above the sound of the firing. They said they all had been moved by this event, as had we. To this day - almost forty years later - I am still moved by both the Hymn's words and by its tune. To me, it brings back recollections of the Marines I served with, both in the Hai Lang Forest that night, and throughout my thirty-year career as a U.S. Marine.

Our town's recent 4th of July parade featured the Second Marine Aircraft Wing's band. I was once again moved to tears as they passed by playing that familiar Hymn. And, I suspect, were I to ask other Marine veterans of the Persian

Gulf Conflict, Vietnam, Korea, or World War II, they too would echo my sentiments for their own very personal reasons. I suspect too that our town's old soldiers, sailors, airmen, and Coast Guard personnel stand a bit taller when their service songs are heard. These simple tunes have deep meaning for these veterans as well.

My story is only one of countless thousands of such stories, some less dramatic, some more so. On this (and every) Veterans' Day, please pause a moment and remember those men and women who were not so fortunate to survive and cannot not be with us today to relate their own personal stories. Instead they reside in cemeteries around the world, and their exploits are known but to God. We are here today because they are not. They freely gave their lives so that we could live ours. Please honor them with a thought or a prayer. God bless.

RAISE YOU GLASS
And Remember

Chris Taylor

"They Came in Peace" - A stretcher bearing a wreath and the sign *"24 MAU: They Came in Peace"* was put up soon after the recovery operation on the site of the bombed-out BLT headquarters building began in Beirut.

I've just returned from a two-week trip to the Gulf region and Lebanon, and thought I would relay an experience from Beirut...

I had meetings with the Prime Minister and President of Lebanon scheduled, but they were delayed because the government was trying to select a new Cabinet before Ramadan, so both Prime Minister Hariri and President Lahoud were kind enough to have each of their Deputies meet with me. President Lahoud's representative, a General (who will remain nameless) and I had a great talk about the history of the region - past, present, and future. We were touring Beirut, and I very politely and almost sheepishly asked if he would take me past the site of the Marine Barracks, and he said, "Okay." On the way we drove through much of the city. The "Old Town" area is wonderfully rebuilt amongst Phoenician ruins, and the rest of the city is on its way to greater growth. Against that backdrop were still the remains of buildings with countless rounds in their walls, and holes from RPG and artillery attacks. We also drove through the Shia area, which is scheduled to be demolished and rebuilt because it is in stark contrast to the rest of the city. And it is still filled with extremists.

14

We drove toward the airport, and as we got very close he simply pulled off to the side of the highway and turned off the vehicle. I sat there for a few seconds, and finally asked if we were waiting for someone else. He replied, "No, you said you wanted to see the site, and here it is." I was a bit surprised. I think I expected to see something more than an overpass near the airport. Maybe I wanted to see an open area, maybe I wanted to see some sort of marker for those brave Marines and Sailors who fell that day.

The General saw my puzzled look and said, "Chris, you must understand our two perspectives. You asked to come here because it was of great importance to you as a Marine and to your history, but Lebanon has been at war for twenty years or more, and to be honest, it was one of many bombings either by Islamic Jihadists, or by the Israelis, or by the Syrians. It is better for the Lebanese to not commemorate such attacks for two reasons - one, we must move forward from war, and two, we would have memorials on every corner in the city."

I thought about that for a long minute. I realized, in a very personal way, that terrorism affects the world's people in many ways, and creates very different perceptions, and that our warriors were victims of extremism some twenty-one years ago as well. I understood the General's point, and he made it politely and honorably. So, I stood there for a few more minutes and slowly saluted (internally) those brave warriors from October 23, 1983. Ironically, when I reported to L 3/3 in 1986, my first fireteam leader was a young Lance Corporal who had been in Beirut that day, and so were many of the NCOs in the company and battalion.

I am not sure that I have some specific point with this note, other than to relay the experience of standing on the hallowed ground of yet another place where Marine warriors sought to defend freedom for all, and as usually happens in such struggles, many died. This is not a statement in support of any policy, other than that of freedom and democracy for all.

Raise your glass tonight at dinner with some friends, and remember...

Chris Taylor is a former Force Recon Marine who now works with an international security firm in the private sector.

FORTUNATE SON

William McGurn

"I feel shame because it took my son's joining the Marine Corps to make me take notice of who is defending me."
- Frank Schaeffer

Forgive Mindy Evnin if she's not up for cake and candles today. Even if she knows how important this birthday was for her son.

On this day in a Philadelphia tavern, the Continental Congress gave birth to the Marine Corps almost a full year before the Declaration of Independence. More than two centuries later in Fallujah, America still looks to the Marines to do the job no one else can.

And no one knows better than Mindy Evnin the price. On a dusty Iraqi roadside in April of 2003 her son, Corporal Mark Evnin, gave his life wearing that same uniform - but you hear only admiration for the Corps from Mindy.

Until the Marine recruiter came to her home the day after Thanksgiving during Mark's senior year at South Burlington High in Vermont, his mother didn't know what her son would do with his life. And once he did know, it was sometimes hard to explain to her social circles.

"At a book club where the other mothers were all talking about which colleges their children were going off to," said she, "I shared that Mark wanted to go to *sniper* school."

Mark's recruiter had given Mindy a Marine bumper sticker - which, he noted, she had no right to affix to her car until Mark had made it through boot camp. As she confessed over lunch in Manhattan, "I told Mark I wasn't sure then I could *ever* put it on my car."

Gradually, however, as she watched the changes in her son and his pride in his achievements, she realized that the little boy who wore fatigues to Hebrew school was finally where he was meant to be - with his fellow Marines.

While in Iraq a *San Francisco Chronicle* correspondent embedded with Mark's unit let him use his satellite phone to call home. Two days later, Corporal Mark Evnin was killed in action while returning fire in an Iraqi ambush.

And that's when Mindy *really* learned about the Marines. When Mark's buddies came back from Iraq, they wrote her as they might their own moms, and Mindy flew out to the base at 29 Palms, California, to spend some time with them. The young Marine recruiter who was in Burlington when Mark was killed recently invited Mindy to his wedding - and insisted on seating her in the row reserved for his family.

The sergeant major whom Corporal Evnin was driving when he was killed invited Mindy to his wedding. And on the first anniversary of Mark's death, Marines sent her a bouquet of crimson-and-gold. (Actually, they had them delivered the day before, so she wouldn't be disturbed on that painful day).

Mindy's done her own work. She was particularly taken with a book by novelist Frank Schaeffer, *Faith of Our Sons: A Father's Wartime Diary,* written after his son joined a Marine Corps that was initially as alien to him as the Navajo.

"I was able to relate to him," she said, "because he described himself as a Volvo-driving eastern-establishment parent who did not know anyone in the military before his son enlisted, and whose friends wondered what was wrong with his son's private-school education that allowed this to happen."

Like Frank Schaeffer, Mindy was well aware of the

Marine reputation for ferocity in battle. Nothing either has learned since changes that. But they have also learned what few outside the Corps seem to appreciate - that Marines' heroics have mostly to do with the courage and pluck shown in looking out for one's fellow Marine.

So the next time you hear of a hopelessly polarized America, remember Corporal Mark Evnin, USMC, and the life he freely gave for something larger than himself.

And on the Corps' birthday, with Marines fighting for freedom around the world, remember too the Jewish mother in Vermont, a self-described product of the '60s, whose car now sports a bumper sticker that not so long ago would have been inconceivable... "Proud Parent of a U.S. Marine."

William McGurn, a veteran of the *Wall Street Journal* editorial page, *National Review* and the *Far East Economic Review*, is now writing a weekly Post column. This story originally appeared on November 10, 2004.

HALFTIME SALUTE

Anonymous U.S. Marine

"Marines don't have an attitude problem - we are just *that* good." — From a bumper sticker

I recently attended a Kansas City Chiefs football game at Arrowhead Stadium. It was their annual Veteran's Day salute, so members of all the services were asked to participate in the festivities.

A color guard for the National Anthem was provided by the Buffalo Soldiers Association. They looked very sharp in their 1800's era U.S. Army Cavalry uniforms. Following that the U.S. Navy parachute team put on an impressive display that brought great cheers from the 78,000 football fans in attendance. Shortly after that we were treated to the truly awesome sight of an Air Force B-2 Stealth bomber flyover, as well as a few other aircraft. All of these sights were truly appreciated by the crowd (especially the B-2) who let it be known by their cheers. I expected that was all that we would see of the military that day.

I thought we would see a high school or college marching band during halftime. Few watch these shows anyway, because they have to use the head or grab another beer (or two) during the intermission.

Shortly before halftime, however, I looked down on the sidelines near the end zone and saw the Silent Drill Platoon forming up. As the halftime started the players left the field, and the announcer came on the public address system and advised us of the Platoons' upcoming performance. Many of us Marines have seen these performances in the past, and they are always awe-inspiring. Even so, I did not expect the large "civilian" crowd of football fans would be as appreciative of the Silent Drill Platoon as they had been of the high-tech B-2, or the daring of the Navy parachute team. I, however, was on the edge of my seat. As the Platoon marched onto the field it was very noticeable that the crowd was growing quieter. Soon the Platoon was fully into their demonstration, and the stadium was silent.

From high in the upper reaches of the stands where my seats were, I was able to hear the 'snap and pop' of hand striking rifle. Both big screen scoreboards displayed close-ups of the Marines as they went through their routine. As they completed their platoon demonstration and lined up for the inspection, the crowd began cheering as the Marines twirled their rifles in an impossible fashion. Then came the inspection. Again the crowd fell silent and watched intently as rifles were thrown, caught, twirled, inspected and thrown some more. Each well practiced feat brought a "wow" or "did you see that?" from those sitting behind me or next to me.

I sat there in my silent pride as I watched my brother Marines exit the field. A young girl behind me asked her mother a question about how the Marines had learned to do the things they had just done. The mother replied "They practice long and hard - and they're Marines, so they're the best!"

HAND SALUTE!

Bob Smith

"Old Marines should have arthritic elbows from snapping salutes." – Colonel 'Bull' Meecham in Pat Conroy's novel 'The Great Santini'

I've known many enlisted guys who hated to salute officers. They would duck out of the path of an oncoming officer, or go completely out of their way to avoid saluting one. This was not the case for me.

Early in my enlistment and before going to Vietnam I was returning from the laundry with my clean starched 'utilities,' when suddenly a Brigadier General appeared in my peripheral vision headed in my direction. I had both hands full, so I gave way and came to attention - but I didn't salute.

A little while later the Sergeant Major flagged me down and read me the riot act for not saluting the general. After a major ass chewing, the Sergeant Major told me something which stayed with me the rest of my enlistment. He said, "I know saluting can sometimes be a pain in the ass, but if you look at this way it will become very enjoyable. As an enlisted man, you are required to salute all officers - regardless of rank or branch of service. The very same regulation requires that an officer return every salute, in the same manner as presented. If an enlisted person does not feel as though the returned salute was appropriate based on regulation, you can require another exchange. This places you, the enlisted man, in control of every salute exchange - the snappier your salute is, the snappier the *return* salute has to be."

I thought about this for a while, and it made sense - and from that point on I really enjoyed saluting officers.

Later on, when I became an MP, I developed a sort of "wave through salute system" for traffic duty. It was a sure-fire system whereby you could keep the traffic flowing, and at the same time never screw up and miss saluting an officer. It was your basic wave-through, except I would bring my hand up and finish with a salute.

Hell, I had everyone saluting me - sailors, officers' wives, officers' kids, even civilian base workers! And when the civilian workers initiated their first "Sentry of the Month" program, I received the honors.

So, my best advice to the active duty Marines out there is to salute sharply, and salute often. The hand salute is the enlisted persons' most powerful tool for both showing and commanding respect.

I salute you all!

FALLEN MARINES

Major Zarnik

"They shall not grow old, as we who are left grow old. Age shall not weary them, nor the years condemn. At the going down of the sun, and in the morning, we will remember them." – Australian Ode to War Dead

I just wanted to share with all of you my most recent Air Force Reserve trip. As most of you know I have decided to go back into the Air Force Reserves as a part time reservist, and after six months of training I have recently been promoted to Lieutenant Colonel and become fully mission qualified as the Aircraft Commander of a KC-135R Strato-tanker aircraft.

On Friday of last week, my crew and I were tasked with a mission to provide air refueling support in order to tanker six F-16's over to Incirlik Air Base in Turkey. We were then to tanker back to the States six more F-16's that were due maintenance. It started out as a fairly standard mission - one that I have done many times as an active duty Captain in my former jet - the KC-10A Extender.

We dragged the F-16's to Moron Air Base in Spain where we spent the night, and then finished the first part of our mission the next day by successfully delivering them to Incirlik. When I got on the ground in Turkey, I received a message to call the Tanker Airlift Control Center because my mission would change. Instead of tankering the F-16's that were due maintenance, I was cut new orders to fly to Kuwait City and pick up twenty-two "HR's" and return them to Dover Air Force Base in Delaware.

It had been a while since I had heard the term "HR" used, and I pondered what the acronym could possibly stand for. Then it dawned on me that it stood for "human remains." There were twenty-two fallen comrades who had just been killed in the most recent attacks in Fallujah and Baghdad, Iraq over the last week.

I immediately alerted the crew of the mission change. Although they were exhausted due to an ocean crossing, the time change, and minimum ground time in Spain for crew rest, we all agreed it was more important to get these men back to their families as soon as possible.

We were scheduled to crew rest in Incirlik, Turkey for the evening, and start the mission the next day. Instead, we decided to extend/continue our day and fly to Kuwait in order to pick up our precious cargo. While on the flight over to Kuwait I knew that there were protocol procedures for accepting and caring for human remains - however in my thirteen years of active duty service I had never once referred to this regulation. As I read the regulation on the flight over, I felt prepared and ready to do the mission. My game plan was to pick up the HR's, turn around to fly to Mildenhal Air Base in England, spend the night there, and fly back the next day. This was the quickest way to get them home, considering the maximum crew duty day that I could subject my crew to legally and physically. I really pushed them to the limits, but no one complained at all.

I thought that I was prepared for the acceptance of these men until we landed at Kuwait International Airport. I taxied the jet over to a staging area where the honor guard was waiting to load our troops. I stopped the jet, and the entire crew was required to stay on board. We opened the cargo door, and according to procedure I had the crew line up in the back of the aircraft in formation at attention. As the cargo loader brought up the first pallet of caskets, I ordered the crew to "Present Arms." Normally we would snap a salute at this command, however when you are dealing with a fallen service-member the salute is at a slow three second pace. As I stood there and finally saw the first four of twenty-two caskets draped with American Flags, the reality hit me.

As the Marine Corps honor guard delivered the first pallet on board, I ordered the crew to "Order Arms" - where they rendered an equally slow three second return to the attention position. I then commanded the crew to assume an at-ease position and directed them to properly place the pallet. Protocol requires the caskets be loaded so that when it comes time to exit the aircraft they will go head first. We did this same procedure for each and every pallet, until we could not fit any more.

I felt a deep knot in the pit in my stomach because there were more caskets to be brought home which would have to wait for the next jet to come through. I tried to do everything in my power to carry more, but had no more space on board. When we were finally loaded with our precious cargo and fueled for the trip back to England, a Marine Corps Colonel from first battalion came on board our jet to talk to us. I gathered the crew to listen to his words of wisdom.

He introduced himself, and said that it is the tradition of the Marines to leave no man behind - and it makes their job easier knowing there were men like us to help them complete this task. He was very grateful for our help, and the strings that we were pulling in order to get this mission done in the most expeditious manner possible.

He then said: "Major Zarnik - these are MY MARINES, and I am giving them to you. Please take great care of them, as I know you will." I responded by telling him that they were my highest priority, and that although this was one of the saddest days of my life we were all up for the challenge and would go above and beyond to take care of his Marines. "Semper Fi, Sir!" A smile came to his face, and he added a loud and thunderous, "Ooh- Rah!"

He then asked me to please pass along to the families that these men were extremely brave and had made the ultimate sacrifice for their country, and that we appreciate and empathize with what they are going through at this time of grievance. With that, he departed the jet and we were on our way to England.

I had a lot of time to think about the men I had the privilege to carry. I had a chance to read the manifest on each and every one of them. I read about their religious preferences, their marital status, the injuries that were their cause of death. All of them were under age twenty-seven. Most of them had wives and children. They had all been killed by an "IED," which I can only deduce is an (improvised) explosive device. Mostly fatal head injuries, and injuries to the chest area.

I could not even imagine the bravery they must have displayed, and the agony suffered in this God forsaken war. My respect and admiration for these men and what they are doing to help others in a foreign land is beyond calculation. I know that they are all with God now, and in a better place.

The stop in Mildenhal was uneventful, and then we pressed on to Dover where we would meet the receiving Marine Corps honor guard. When we arrived, we applied the same procedures in reverse. The head of each casket was to come out first. This was a sign of respect rather than defeat. As the honor guard carried each and every American flag covered casket off the jet, they delivered them to waiting families with military hearses. I was extremely impressed with how diligent the Honor Guard was in the performance the seemingly endless task of delivering caskets to families without fail and with precision.

There was not a dry eye on our crew, or in the crowd. The Chaplain then said a prayer, followed by a speech from Lieutenant Colonel Klaus of the Second Battalion. In his speech, he reiterated condolences to the families similar to those passed along by the Colonel from First Battalion back in Kuwait.

I then went out to speak with the families, as I felt it was my duty to help console them in this difficult time. Although I would probably be one of the last military contacts they would have for a while - the military tends to take care of its own. I wanted to make sure they did not feel abandoned - and more than that, were appreciated for their sacrifice.

It was the most difficult thing I have ever done in my life. I listened to the stories of each and every person I came in contact with, and they all displayed a sense of pride during an obviously difficult time. The Marine Corps had obviously prepared their families well for this potential outcome.

So, why do I write this story to you all? I just wanted to put a little personal attention to the numbers you hear about and see in the media. It is almost like we are desensitized by the "numbers" of our fallen comrades coming out of Iraq. I heard one commentator say that "it is just a number." Are you kidding me? These are our American Marines, not numbers! It is truly a sad situation that I hope will end soon.

Hug and embrace your loved ones a little closer and know there are men out there defending you and trying to make this a better world. Pray for their families, and when you hear the latest statistics and numbers of our troops killed in combat remember this story. It is the only way to personalize these figures and have them truly mean something to us all.

A MOTHER'S WAR

Cynthia Gorney

"Being deeply loved by someone gives you strength; loving someone deeply gives you courage." - Lao Tzu

I sometimes wonder how my Mom would have handled losing me in combat. I always made it a point to remind her that I loved the Corps and what it stood for, and think it lightens the load somewhat if your parents know you are doing something in which you strongly believe. Now that I am a parent myself, it can better appreciate how it must feel. Michael Moore once asked interviewer Bill O'Reilly, 'Would you send your son to fight in Iraq?' My answer to that question would have been no – I wouldn't 'send' him (or her) anywhere. But I would respect and support their choice to serve, if that's what they wanted to do. I don't know about anybody else, but my mother didn't 'send' me to Parris Island, anymore than she volunteered me for recon, jump school or demolitions training. I made those choices.

They were talking about military burial benefits as the waitress took the salad plates away, and one of them had come up with something perversely humorous even on this subject, so they had been laughing. Now there was a brief, comfortable silence. They had one of the back rooms at Boone Tavern in downtown Columbia, Missouri - where they usually go. It was a Friday night in February, and because one woman had other plans there were only five of them, which made the big, round table seem too large. Instead of spacing themselves around it they had taken seats

29

along one side, closer to one another.

Patricia said, "I had a doorbell moment this week."

Tracy Della Vecchia looked up quickly and watched Patricia's face. Tracy's son had gone to high school with Patricia's son, so Tracy and Patricia knew of each other during the years when all the teenagers would hole up drinking beer in the barn on Tracy's property. But now their sons were twenty-two and in the same Marine unit in Iraq, and Tracy knows things about Patricia that she has never known about another person before. Tracy knows that clipped to Patricia's refrigerator is a list of things to remember in case the telephone rings in the middle of the night and it's Patricia's son calling from a camp somewhere just to talk. Tracy knows that the grandfather clock in Patricia's house chimes nine times when the other clocks say it's noon, because the grandfather clock is set to Baghdad time. Tracy knows that Patricia has figured out how to tell if someone is in her driveway by squinting at the reflection off a certain glass-covered picture in the dining room, so that if it should ever be two men in uniform, Patricia will know they have arrived before they start ringing the bell and before she is obliged to look directly at them and hear what they have come to say.

"It was last night," said Patricia, who asked that her last name not be used. "Around 8 PM I was home by myself. I was not expecting the doorbell."

Patricia said she finally saw that it was an older gentleman, alone. "Probably canvassing for leukemia or something," she said. She said she never did open the door for him, and the other women said, no, of course not, and Tracy told the story about the blue car at dawn. She was telling it for my benefit - the others nodded as she spoke, like church women hearing a familiar passage of Scripture. "This

30

was Derrick's first deployment, in 2003, right after the war started," Tracy said. "I was a basket case. Five-thirty in the morning, I'm not sleeping anyway, I go downstairs and make coffee. You've seen my house - nobody ever comes down my driveway. But a car comes down my driveway. A Lincoln Town Car."

"Crown Victoria," Sharon Curry said.

"Sorry," Tracy said. "A dark blue Crown Vic. Thank you, Sharon. And it's got these little antennas. And I'm sure someone's coming to tell me my son has died. I'm sure of it. And I literally fall down on my knees. I'm saying to myself, 'You've got to answer the door, you've got to answer the door.' I'm yelling for my husband, but nothing's coming out of my mouth. I'm crawling toward the door. The car turns around the driveway circle. It stops for a minute. I think, 'Okay, he's going to get out. He's going to come tell me now.' And - he drives away. I come busting out the door. 'Wait! Wait!' But he didn't stop. So I called 911 - 'There's somebody at my door! My son's in Iraq!' Turns out it's the fire district. There was smoke coming from someplace. They were going up and down driveways trying to find out where it was from."

Tracy has a wide, beautiful face, with pale skin and thick black hair that curls down her back, and her expression was complicated, at once anguished and amused, in a way I was beginning to recognize. She lives and works on fifteen acres outside town in a two-story house, where she runs a website called marineparents.com, which she built after she understood that her nineteen-year-old son, who had enlisted two years earlier in the Marines, was going to be sent to war. The website has sprouted message boards, chat rooms and multiple layers of explanatory information, turning it into a national gathering place for adults whose sole connection is their role as parents of Marines. Tracy tries to devote part of each day to her web-design business, but most of her waking hours are now spent attending to marineparents.com, hunched in a silent office before a computer in which pride and grief and bewilderment and rage seem to be crashing around all the time, so that sometimes Tracy just pushes back from the desk and walks outside to smoke a cigarette and look at her pond. She signs her e-mail messages "Semper Fi." She is forty-three, and once thought she would become a hippie. When her son was small and received toy guns as presents, she threw them into the trash.

That son, Derrick Jensen, has spent three birthdays in a row deployed in Iraq. There are about 140,000 American troops stationed in Iraq, and 23,000 of them are Marines. As this article appears, Corporal Jensen should be somewhere near Fallujah. He is an infantry radio operator, which sounded to Tracy like a good, safe job until she found out that radio operators carry big antennas, which make them easier targets. She let me stay at her house for a while this winter, partly because I am a reporter and happen to have a twenty-two-year-old son who is not in the military. Tracy thought people like me might want to know something about what it's like to live all the time with that kind of information about your child, to go to sleep knowing it and wake up knowing it and drive around town knowing it, which makes it possible to be standing in the Wal-Mart dog-food aisle on an ordinary afternoon and without reason or warning be knocked breathless again by the sudden imagining of sniper fire or an explosion beneath a Humvee. Still, Derrick has been shipped home twice since President Bush delivered his May 2003 speech in front of the "Mission Accomplished" banner on the deck of an aircraft carrier, and shipped back twice. He has had one occasion of near death that Tracy knows about in some detail. There are others, she assumes, that Derrick has so far kept to himself. "During the first deployment," Tracy said to me once as we were sitting in her car, a lipstick-red PT Cruiser with a yellow "Keep My Son Safe" ribbon magnet on the back, "the only emotion I could imagine him having was fear."

Tracy's closest friends in the world right now are other parents whose sons and daughters have served in Iraq or are serving there now. Some of these parents think the war is righteous, some think it was wrongheaded from the outset and some, like Tracy, have made fierce internal bargains with themselves about what they will and will not think about as long as their children and their children's comrades remain in uniform and in harm's way. The women Tracy meets every week for dinner, each of whom has a son in the Marines or the Army, have a "no politics" rule around their table - this was one of two things I remember Tracy telling me the first time she took me to a gathering of the mothers. The other thing was that draped over a banister in Tracy's house was an unwashed T-shirt Derrick had dropped during his last visit home. I thought Tracy was apologizing for her housekeeping, which I had already seen was much better than mine, but she cleared her throat and said what I needed to understand was that she hadn't washed the T-shirt because if the Marine Corps has to send you your deceased child's personal effects, it launders the clothing first. "That means there's no smell," Tracy said.

She let this hover between us for a minute. "I've heard from so many parents who were crushed when they opened that bag, because they had thought they'd be able to smell their son," Tracy said.

One morning in February, Tracy got up at 4:30 AM, made coffee, filled a commuter mug and climbed into her car with a suitcase to drive east to St. Louis. The highway was nearly deserted, an occasional McDonald's or Super 8 Motel sign looming in the darkness. Tracy hadn't slept well. She had been brooding for days about what she was on her way to do. "Luigi keeps telling me, 'Breathe,'" she said. Luigi is Tracy's husband. He is Italian, and moved to Missouri from Naples four years ago after he and Tracy met while teamed up on a Web-design project. Tracy had divorced Derrick's father a couple of years before that, and had been raising Derrick and his younger sister by herself on the Columbia property when Derrick marked his seventeenth birthday by signing up for the Marines.

He left for boot camp in the summer of 2001, two months after his high-school graduation. The timing is significant, the way Tracy recounts the story, although then she always sighs and says there was really nothing she would have done differently even if she had known what was coming. In August of that year the World Trade Center had not yet been attacked, nor was the American military in active combat anywhere that Tracy knew of. In any case, Derrick had been declaring since he was four that he wanted to become a Marine. "Who knows where it started with him?" Tracy told me. "He had Marine posters in his room. When he was a little kid, he read *The Punisher* comic books, and *The Punisher* was a former Marine. We have pictures of him crawling on his belly through the grass, arms extended as guns. Chubby-cheeked cherub, out there playing war."

Tracy stared straight at the road. We were still an hour from the St. Louis airport, where we were going to fly to Chicago and wait for someone to pick us up and take us to a place called Elk Grove Village. "When he drew, he drew battlefields," Tracy said. "Tanks.... Action pictures.... Explosions."

Tracy was raised in a military family, moving in childhood from one base town to another until her parents finally resettled in Missouri, their home state. Her father, a twenty-year Air Force communications expert before his 1979 switch to civilian life, served several stints in Vietnam during the closing years of that war. But Tracy's anti-gun period wasn't strident or directed at her own upbringing. The way she thinks about it now, she was just a late-era counterculture sympathizer who became a young mother in Columbia, which is where the main University of Missouri campus is, and which is sociologically as close to Berkeley as Missouri gets. "That whole flowers-in-your-hair, wear-gauze, dance-to-the-Grateful Dead sort of thing," Tracy said and smiled. The Vietnam flak jacket was kept in a closet at her father's house, where Derrick was allowed to admire it whenever he visited, and by the time he was finishing high school Tracy had come to believe that her restless, hard-partying, sleep-until-midafternoon teenage son was probably right about the direction and discipline the Marine Corps was going to give him.

She delivered Derrick herself to Kansas City, from which his next stop would be the Marine boot camp in San Diego. "I'm thinking, 'Well, he's going to go play war,'" Tracy said. "Okay. That's what he's done all his life."

One of the first illustrations Tracy had put on marineparents.com was a pair of Derrick snapshots, both taken inside Tracy's car. In the first photo he's on his way to Kansas City, open-mouthed, seat back in full recline, sacked out at 2 PM. In the second, he's on his way home three months later for the break between boot camp and the early combat training the Marine Corps calls School of Infantry. It's 2 AM, and Derrick is in uniform, wide awake, shoulders rigid, bolt upright in his seat. Tracy captioned the two photos

"The Transformation." "I was like, 'If you're tired, you can put the seat back and go to sleep.' 'No, Ma'am! I'm fine!'" All of Missouri seemed be-ribboned with post-9/11 American flags by then, Tracy remembers, and she can still do comically vivid impressions of the unfamiliar person suddenly occupying her son's room - leaping up to make his bed at six every morning, sticking his arm out at the tattoo parlor for the "U.S.M.C." across the biceps, eating straight-backed at the kitchen table with elbow held at right angle and both feet squarely on the floor - and also of the insomniac emotional mess the calamitous times had made of her. She was intensely proud of Derrick, convinced that genuine peril faced the United States and terrified about what would happen next. "After 9/11 the news was on nonstop twenty-four hours a day, seven days a week," Tracy said. "And I swear, if I could have, I would have gone to San Diego, grabbed my son by the ear and said, 'Buddy, you made a mistake. Let's go home now.'"

On the flight to Chicago Tracy read a book she had just bought called *"McCoy's Marines,"* which is an account by John Koopman, a reporter for *The San Francisco Chronicle,* of his weeks embedded with a Marine unit during the 2003 assault on Iraq. The unit happened to have been Derrick's, and when Tracy got off the plane her eyes were red and swollen and she hurried into the bathroom to rinse her face. In one passage of Koopman's book the Marines' commanding officer tells his men, just before combat against an Iraqi tank division called the 51st, "We're going to slaughter the 51st Mechanized Division. We're going to kill them, and make an example out of them." In another, word is spread that Iraqi suicide drivers have begun carrying bombs in ambulances. "The order comes down - 'You see an ambulance driving fast toward you, shoot it,'" Koopman writes.

Tracy had put on a black leather coat for the trip to Elk Grove Village, which made her look even taller and more imposing than usual. "You know," she said, as we were standing outside watching for the car that was coming for us, "when your kid grows up to be an architect or something, you think you'll be able to know what they do - to know something about it."

She lit a cigarette. "I know he's done things he never imagined he'd do," she said. "And you don't ask the question. I can't bring myself to. You don't ask it. And he never tells."

A white Toyota with two crosses hanging from the mirror pulled up at the curb. A woman with layered, lightened hair got out, shook Tracy's hand, and said she was the niece of Georgette Frank, whom Tracy had come to know on the website and who was now awaiting our arrival at the Veterans of Foreign Wars hall. We drove through a bleak-looking industrial stretch for a while, country music on the radio, and finally Tracy asked what Georgette looked like. I knew Tracy had an idea about this. She had decided that Georgette must be a big woman, like Tracy - probably bigger, Tracy thought, and with great wide shoulders. Georgette Frank and her husband, Roy, had organized the marineparents.com event Tracy had come to help supervise, a daylong volunteers' assembly-line to pack up boxes for Marines in Iraq, and although she had never met Georgette in person or even seen a picture of her, Tracy still kept in the website archives the year-old posting from the night the two Marines in dress uniforms came to the Franks' house in Elk Grove Village:

TOPIC AUTHOR: HISMOM

POSTED ON: 04/08/2004 21:52:10

MESSAGE: My dear friends - the Marines just left us - LCPL Phil our beloved son was killed in action yesterday - please keep my husband, daughter and me in your prayers. Please pray for my nieces and nephews as well. Our Phil was so loved by all our family. My heart is breaking - help me.

REPLY AUTHOR: TDV

REPLIED ON: 04/08/2004 21:56:25

MESSAGE: Georgette, I pray for God to be with you and your family. Your son is our hero. Please let us know how we can help. My love and prayers are here for you and your family. God bless and Semper Fi, Tracy.

There was a 22:23:31 posting that night directed to Georgette too – "words mostly fail me. This is a parent's worst fear" - and one at 00:39:08 and at 1:21:41 and at 1:55:55. All night, into dawn the next day, and long into the following weeks, Tracy read messages from 'Cindi' and 'Justinsbud' and 'vermontmom' and scores of other devastated women. Men's names turned up here and there, but mostly they were women, and Tracy pictured them alone at their keyboards, all over the country, typing and crying and trying to think of what to say to Georgette. Tracy had built the website in part because she guessed this would happen, that people would want a place where they could sit in the dark making an effort to hold one another up, and although Georgette was neither the first bereaved marineparents.com parent nor the last, she maintained a kind of sorrowful grace on the message boards that Tracy found extraordinarily brave. Months after Phil was killed, shot by an Iraqi sniper during the insurgency in Fallujah, Georgette was still a regular on the site, helping out, consoling other parents. She closed each of her postings, "I remain - as always – hismom."

At some point in recent weeks, as the planning was peaking for this volunteers' packaging day in Elk Grove Village, it occurred to Tracy that she was afraid of meeting Georgette. By this time they had talked long distance quite a bit, so she knew that Georgette's bearing on the telephone was as kind and dignified as her presence online. But when Tracy began envisioning the encounter itself, she was panicky about doing the wrong thing. Working from Columbia, deep inside her elaborate web of intimate connections online, Tracy had yet to come into the physical presence of someone whose Marine child was dead. She had caught herself entertaining the idea that there was some grim dress-rehearsal aspect to the situation, as if Georgette were being presented to Tracy as an example of how to press on admirably through grief, and she was sure she was going to fall apart the first time Georgette walked up to say hello. "I keep playing these scenarios out," Tracy told me one night. "How do I act? What do I do? If I cry, that will make her cry, and will bring the pain back up to her? And the inability to have anything to offer, except, 'Here's a hug.'"

Now Georgette's niece, glancing curiously at Tracy, said her aunt was very small. "Like five feet tall," Georgette's niece said.

"Really!" Tracy said. She sank back in the passenger seat, trying to imagine Georgette small. The Toyota pulled into the parking lot of the V.F.W. hall, and Tracy got out with her suitcase and bumped it slowly up the stairs. She stopped at the top of the landing, taking a deep breath, smoothing her hair with her fingers. There was a lot of activity visible inside, men and women in blue jeans crowding around long tables that were covered with open boxes. Tracy stepped in and set her suitcase down. A voice called out across the room, "There she is," and striding toward Tracy came a tiny woman with gold hoop earrings and a black USMC T-shirt tucked into her jeans. She had to reach up to get her arms around Tracy's shoulders as they embraced. They stood that way for a long time, swaying slightly, like slow dancers who have forgotten to move their feet.

"Blouse" means shirt when a Marine is referring to his uniform, and "cover" means hat. A "rack" is a bed. "Trash" is personal possessions. "Nasty" means anything pertaining to the civilian world, as in a recruit's nasty relatives, with their nasty disorderly way of walking and speaking and wearing their nasty hair. These are some of the things Tracy learned, trolling the Internet, reading Marine books obsessively, once the war began and Derrick vanished into his first deployment. He telephoned once during that time, from Kuwait, to say that his unit was waiting to invade and that he was using a bank of telephones for Marines and that he had exactly one hour of liberty left. After that there was nothing for a long time, and Luigi made Tracy turn off the news because he kept finding her downstairs at 3 AM watching CNN or Fox News with both hands to her mouth. On the phone in Kuwait, Derrick's closing comment to Tracy was, "You know what, Mom? There's a Burger King across the street here, and I haven't had anything decent to eat in a month, and if you don't mind I'm going to use my last ten minutes to get myself a hamburger." She kept thinking about that as she read. She was gaining fluency in abbreviations and acronyms, both online and during the military families' monthly support-group meetings in Columbia. B.C.G.'s are birth-control glasses, Marine-issue eyeglasses, which replace nasty civilian models and are so ugly they prevent pregnancy because of their propensity for making women lose all interest in the wearer. An M.E.U. is a

Marine expeditionary unit, which is different from an M.E.F., a Marine expeditionary force, and an M.E.B., a Marine expeditionary brigade.

An R.P.G. is a rocket-propelled grenade. An I.E.D. is an improvised explosive device. A V.B.I.E.D. is a vehicle-borne improvised explosive device. A B.F.G. is a big (expletive) gun.

Barbara Schneider had a big-gun photo of her son, Stephen, which she began carrying around with her in a crumpled phone-bill envelope, along with a dozen other snapshots of him on patrol with his weapons and a folded map of Iraq she had printed off the Internet. Barbara was one of the five mothers Tracy had dinner with every week; they had all met at the monthly support group and liked one another at once, despite the profound differences in their political loyalties and their opinions of the war. Barbara, who has been divorced from Stephen's father for many years, is an ardent Democrat. She has a law degree, works for the University of Missouri, and makes a pained face when President Bush's name comes up. In high school, Barbara's son was a university-bound member of the debate team; when he joined the Marine Corps Reserves in August of 2002, he told his mother that he didn't see why having been admitted to college should entitle him to some sort of dispensation from responsibility. "He really thinks he has an obligation to this country," Barbara told me one morning. "And he also thinks that if this country is sending nineteen and twenty-year-old boys to war, why not him? Why should they be fighting for him?"

Barbara pulled the phone-bill envelope out of her purse and held it over the coffee-shop table between us - not brandishing it, exactly, but almost. Stephen was deployed to Iraq in March of 2004, eleven months after the United States invaded Baghdad; in September, two-thirds of the way through his tour of duty, the American military death toll topped one thousand. "When I ran into people around town, in this coffee shop, or someone from soccer or Scouts, I would whip out my envelope," Barbara said. "It was really for people to know they knew someone there. I would make people look at it. I would just say, 'This is Stephen.' It's so easy for people to go about their lives or their business. Saddam Hussein had been found, and people would say to me, 'I thought that was pretty much over.'"

By the time Stephen had left Missouri for his military training, Barbara already knew a fair amount about protest organizations that shared her assessment of the Iraq invasion, which is that it was precipitous and ill conceived and would ultimately do more harm than good. There was 'Military Families Speak Out,' a national antiwar alliance whose logo entwines a yellow support-the-troops ribbon with a 60's-era peace symbol. There were demonstrators every Saturday morning outside the Columbia post office downtown, where a longstanding weekly pacifist vigil has been updated, since the invasion, with banners reading "End the Occupation" and "President Bush: Thou Shalt Not Kill." But Barbara had talked to Stephen at length and had seen that he had his own view of the situation and was determined to serve. She was glad the protesters were there - she didn't agree with the parents in the monthly support-group meetings who called them traitors - but her own admiration for her son, she concluded, would keep her from picking up a banner and standing on the lawn in front of the post office.

"It's a tough one," Barbara said. The snapshots lay fanned out on the table - Stephen in cammies on a shot-up rooftop, Stephen's hand pointing to a thermometer registering 130 degrees - and I wondered aloud how a parent really manages what Barbara had resolved to do, to support her young adult son's decision to accept discipline and orders from an institution she believes is doing the wrong thing. She sighed. We stared at the pictures. Stephen came home in October; he's a senior in college now, but his commitment to the Marine Corps will keep him on potential call-up rosters until 2010. "I don't completely understand Stephen's position," Barbara said. "But I have so much respect for him that it seems like it's an appropriate resolution. And I'm experiencing this as a mother, not as a male. I never had to wrestle with 'Am I obligated to serve my country in the military?'"

Barbara's office is on the university campus, and walking to and from work among students, she has been ruminating recently about the Vietnam War. "I knew a lot of people in the Vietnam era who were wrestling with whether or not they would go," she said. "It seemed to me that even the people who didn't want to serve wrestled with it in their mind. We thought about it. We talked about it. Everyone talked about it, and discussed it, and what I sense missing now is that same need to…" She hesitated, searching for the right word. "To grapple with it," she said.

This is one luxury an all-volunteer military provides, especially for those with adequate education and privilege - this option of sidestepping the enlistment question entirely, and with it a certain kind of difficult decision-making about matters like duty, resistance, justifiable violence, conscientious objection. "So you can be lazy and not think about it," Barbara said. "And that's what a lot of young people are doing. It makes me angry." She considered for a second, and then said, no, that was not quite right. "What makes me angry," Barbara said, "is how can a young person be in favor of this war, and not feel they have some obligation to participate in it? That boggles my mind."

Tracy had boxes to send Derrick one morning, so we carried them to the PT Cruiser, and she backed out of the carport to head up the long gravel road past the pond. Two geese glided on the quiet brown water. A Marine Corps flag and a faded yellow ribbon hung from a tree near the house. Inside the boxes were cans of smoked baby clams, Starkist prepackaged tuna-and-crackers lunch kits, beef-jerky packets and enough Girl Scout cookies, Tracy guessed, for a couple of dozen Marines. Tracy knows Derrick doesn't like Girl Scout cookies much, but she was enjoying the image of him ripping open the boxes and rolling his eyes and looking around his barracks for someone to give them to. "'Here!'" - Tracy doing what I knew to be a spot-on rendition of the exasperated, affectionate voice of a twenty-two-year-old male being fussed over by his mother – "'these are from my mom. You know how my mom is.'"

There was a book on the back seat of the car, not yet wrapped in shipping paper, titled *"The Seven Principles for Making Marriage Work."* The book had shown up in Tracy's mail after Patricia read about it on the Internet and thought it might be helpful for Derrick and Missy, the young woman Derrick married, rather suddenly, during his last home leave. Derrick was introduced to Missy at a friend's apartment eight weeks before they decided to marry. She is a composed, good-looking twenty-one-year-old who was raising her two-year-old daughter, working as a receptionist and living at her mother's house in Columbia when Derrick told Tracy that he had fallen in love and that at one point he and his new girlfriend had talked on the telephone for twenty-eight hours straight. The wedding was in January - church ceremony, Missy in bridal white, Derrick in a tailed tuxedo. They spent ten days together, in a hotel near a

Marine base in Southern California, before Derrick left again for Iraq. Framed bride-and-groom photos now decorate Tracy's house and Missy's mother's, where Missy and her little girl are still living; at Tracy's, the photo hangs right over her desk, as if it were a chart she needed to memorize. Once, at one of the Boone Tavern dinners, the women were deep into a conversation about war veterans' culture shock when I saw Tracy rub her forehead, thinking of Derrick and Missy:

PATRICIA: It's like everybody's staring at them. Especially when they're first back.

TRACY: Derrick wanted normalcy. He'd done two tours already at that point. When they started saying, "Let's get married," that felt like a normal life to him.

BARBARA: There's got to be a sense of – 'this is life, this is it, right here.' That you can't be planning for five years down the way. These guys have been in a war zone. We haven't had that happen to us.

TRACY: The wedding budget was going through the roof when the kids were getting married. I was really upset for a while. And then I'm thinking: Today Derrick can walk down the aisle. What if nine months from now he can't? What if he's sitting in a wheelchair? And I started writing checks.

Now Tracy looked sheepish as she explained why the book was still unwrapped. "I started to write something in it and pop it in the mail," she said. "And then I thought, 'Wait a minute.'" It embarrassed her that she had to instruct herself that the inscription ought to come from Missy, not from her; delivering the marriage book to the oil-change facility where Missy works was one of Tracy's errands for the day. She would have thought she had learned enough, watching the mother-wife tension that occasionally snarled into the open on marineparents.com message threads, to be above ever characterizing her son's great romance as a headache. She had come to love both Missy and the cheerful child who called her son 'Daddy Derrick,' but Tracy had figured out that she was capable of fretting for Derrick's marital happiness while simultaneously feeling crestfallen about the number of Iraq-to-Columbia telephone calls that now came to Missy instead of to her. This was not a charming quality to discover in herself.

Patrolling her Web site, most of which is accessible to anybody who learns to navigate it, Tracy still sends admonitions to certain mothers she assumes haven't realized that their messages might be read by their own sons or by some Iraqi insurgent. "Does she really want to be calling her Marine son's wife a bitch on a public message board?" Tracy said. "I don't think so."

Tracy had dropped her cellphone into her purse before we left; she always has it with her when she walks out of the house, and today in particular she was expecting to spend some time helping to talk Georgette Frank through her commute home from work. Since the Elk Grove Village box-packing weekend, Georgette had taken to phoning every few days from her car: the Franks were approaching the first anniversary of their son's death, and Georgette had found that the forty minutes alone in the car at dusk was the hardest part of her day. The conversation starter was always something to do with marineparents.com, but both Tracy and Georgette understood what was really going on, and most recently Georgette had been venting to Tracy about "Eyes Wide Open," an anti-war installation that had been traveling from city to city for more than a year. (The Quaker American Friends Service Committee, which was sponsoring the exhibit, preferred to call it a "memorial to those who have fallen," but Georgette found that disingenuous). "Eyes

Wide Open" included displays on Iraqi casualties and the cost of the war, and the exhibit's centerpiece was row upon row of empty boots, each pair tagged with the name of a dead American service member. Georgette had not seen the exhibit - thank God she hadn't known when it was in Chicago, she said. But after someone told her that Phil's name was on a pair of boots, Georgette fired off a furious e-mail message to the organizers, demanding that his name be removed and adding that if ending the violence was their most pressing concern, perhaps they should direct their attention at the Iraqi insurgency. The organizers comply when relatives request removal of a name, but the episode rankled nonetheless. "Demeaning his death" was how she put it - as if Phil hadn't understood the risks when he joined the Marines, she would say; as if he had not died believing that he was helping to liberate a nation. She liked to quote something he said to his father the last time they saw him: "Where else can a guy like me be part of freeing twenty-five million people out from under the likes of Saddam Hussein?"

So far, Tracy was doing a better job of holding up her end of these conversations than she had thought she would. Sometimes she doesn't know whether to be gratified or unsettled by the agility with which she now moves among women with intensely different ideas about the war - Georgette, Barbara, Patricia, and all other the volunteer message-board monitors who are so dedicated to marineparents.com that they undergo weeks of training to learn which posts are acceptable and which are not. Acceptable: conversation, comfort, pleas for emotional support, practical information containing no threat to troop security. Unacceptable: troop security threats, libelous remarks, political arguments. These are Tracy's rules, not the Marines'; she takes advice from, but has no official tie to, the

47

Corps, and she has tried to make the website what she thought she needed most, a non-contentious community in which the panicked parent of a young Marine at war could find help making it from one day to the next. "You know, I've got this easy escape route," Tracy remarked as she pulled the PT Cruiser up to Missy's workplace. "I'm sitting here helping people. I don't have to look at the politics. 'Nope! Can't go there! No time for that!'"

I waited in the car while Tracy dropped off the marriage book. She was inside for a long time. When she came back, she was silent and emotional; I thought something had happened between her and Missy, but after Tracy put on her seat belt and gazed at the steering wheel for a minute, she started up the car and said: "She talked to Derrick this morning. They're about to go out on a mission. It's going to get really dangerous for the next few days."

We drove through Columbia and onto the county roads that lead to the Della Vecchias' house. The fields were still bleached and wintry-looking, although the air had begun to turn warm, and after a while Tracy mentioned an Italian political-commentary program she and Luigi were watching on satellite television the evening before. Luigi has been opposed to the Iraq invasion from the start, and Tracy knows enough Italian to have understood that the commentator was saying that an invading army cannot possibly maintain a legitimate advisory role inside the nation it is occupying. "'Recipe for disaster,'" Tracy said, translating the man's wording. Then, as she turned the car onto the gravel road, she glanced at my notebook and gave me a look that meant 'Don't push me on this.' "If we leave in less than three years' time, there will be a civil war," Tracy said. "Then we'll have that blood on our hands. And then we'll be even worse off than we are now."

The day before Easter, Tracy and her nineteen-year-old daughter, Lauren, went over to Missy's with a bag of egg-dyeing kits and two huge baskets full of Easter presents Lauren had bought for Missy's little girl, Kylie. They weren't expensive presents - there was a wind-up plastic chicken that dispensed jelly beans out its rear end, which broke Tracy up laughing. But she chided Lauren for having bought so much. "For heaven's sake, Lauren," Tracy said, "she's only two years old."

"Oh, let me have my fun," Lauren said lightly. "I want a real Easter." Lauren lives with her boyfriend in a nearby town and looks just like Tracy, except that her long curly hair is the color of butter. She and Tracy had been sparring off and on all day. Tracy was in a brittle mood, which Lauren attributed to back pain - Tracy had spent the morning sorting donations for Marine care packages, kneeling on her office floor over piles of toothbrushes, baby wipes, disposable razors, nail clippers, Q-Tips and black socks - and to uneasiness about whether Derrick was getting enough sleep. Every time Derrick telephoned home recently, Tracy said afterward that he sounded tired. The calls came every few days during most of this deployment; Derrick had been moved into some sort of building, Tracy knew, where the bunks were thin-mattressed metal and a nearby tent contained computers for e-mailing, telephones for placing international calls and, in a back corner, a webcam with which the men who wanted to could take turns making face-to-face contact with home.

Sometime during the egg-dyeing evening, Derrick was supposed to show up on a webcam connection, a two-way live visual accompanying an instant-message chat, and the computer and camera were set up and waiting at Missy's mother's house. I wondered whether that was making Tracy edgy too. Much has been made of the breadth and immediacy of communication in this war, the first large-scale American combat since the proliferation of cellphone technology and the Internet, and I was coming to appreciate how complex it might be for a parent simply to know that it's possible to be linked daily by telephone or e-mail, or even live camera, to a child stationed in a war zone. It must be like keeping an extra muscle clenched all the time, I thought: the cellphone always on; the nervous glance at the caller ID to see if the area code is an unfamiliar one that might signal an overseas patch-through; the steady weight of remembering what may and may not be said amid the double constraints of military security and universal protocol regarding the sorts of questions so often lurking in the backs of anxious parental brains. 'Are you all right? Are you telling me the truth about being all right? Will you promise me that you will not die before I can talk to you again? What is the most exactly perfect thing I can say to you right now?' "You feel entirely responsible, as a mother, for keeping the conversation going without asking stupid questions," Patricia said to me once. "My son had to teach me. 'Where are you, what did you do today, what are you doing tomorrow' - you can't ask these questions. You just say, 'Stay safe.'"

Missy's mother's house is on a cul-de-sac near town, and once we had settled in, Tracy ordered pizza and Missy's mother put a lot of eggs on to boil. The computer sat on a desk by the front door, where the screen could be seen from anywhere in the living room. There was a vigorously female bustle of activity for a while – Missy's mother, who is divorced, had also bought Easter presents for Kylie and kept holding up small lacy outfits she had found at Wal-Mart - and then Missy said, "Whoa, there he is." She darted to the desk and plopped down in front of the screen, where a three-inch-square image of Derrick's face had just appeared. His movements were jerky, and his skin looked sepulchral in the dim greenish webcam lighting, but he was smiling. A tent pole was visible behind him. The instant-message box on the computer screen read, "hi sweetheart."

Tracy stood in the living room, watching Missy type, and then wheeled around to go back into the kitchen and paint another egg. At first she had left the egg-decorating to Lauren and Missy, who were having a good time making delicate, elaborate designs with the miniature dyeing-kit paintbrushes. Finally Tracy had taken up a brush herself, saying somewhat savagely: "It's Easter. He needs to see an Easter egg." The eggs were filling the cardboard tray by the kitchen sink, dripping small pools of pastel. Missy kept typing and chuckling and showing Kylie how to wave into the webcam. After half an hour or so, she pushed away from the computer and yelled, "Hey, Tracy?"

TRACY: Are you going to be able to sleep more?

DERRICK: Have to go to work in like an hour.

TRACY: Do you need anything besides food?

DERRICK: Yeah tell me about it.

TRACY: Are the insects starting to come out yet? Or is it still too cold?

DERRICK: Still too cold.

TRACY: Good . . . no bugs.

DERRICK: I'm in a barracks now.

TRACY: Missy made a better egg than mine. Mine has hearts & dots. Missy has a house, bushes, swing set and clouds on her egg.

Now Tracy was laughing and called Missy over to hold up her house-and-bushes egg in front of the webcam. The sky on the egg was golden, and there were turquoise clouds and a deep purple sunset.

51

DERRICK: Looks good.

TRACY: Damn. I wanted to be the best.

Tracy's fingers paused above the keyboard. Derrick seemed to have bent over, and she gazed at the top of his blurry, murky, green-tinted, close-cropped head. It was 5 AM in Fallujah.

TRACY: I say 'ho dang' now instead of swear words. Kylie taught me.

DERRICK: That is good, but if she keeps telling you the right thing to say she will never get to Harvard.

TRACY: Take care of YOU. Keep God with you buddy, and watch out for your brothers, okay? Love you.

That night I lay in the downstairs room where Tracy was putting me up, the bedroom that used to be Derrick's, and studied the silhouettes of the objects left behind: a few sports trophies, a high-school-graduation mortarboard, a half-dozen stuffed animals rescued from end-of-childhood discard and squashed into a high corner on the shelves. I was thinking about a DVD that a Marine in Derrick's unit had titled *"Operation Iraqi Freedom"* and sent back to Missouri a couple of weeks before. The DVD set a half-hour of raging heavy-metal music against a pulsing video-and-stills lineup the young Marine had assembled quite expertly. Bodies, exploded torso, helicopters, bodies, desert hills, bodies, bomb cloud, bodies, sunset, kneeling prisoners, bodies, a man struggling in the street until his head snaps back and he drops - the only internal coherence in the whole DVD was one brief sequence in which a half-dozen bored-looking Marines took turns electrocuting a trapped gecko, and the first time Tracy watched it from start to finish I could see her sag in her chair. Derrick belongs to the Marine unit that helped pull down Saddam Hussein's statue in April of 2003, and sometimes Tracy can still make herself visualize the cheering people in the square, or the women and children waving at the Humvees as they rolled through Baghdad that month, or the photos of the jocular-looking troops with their arms slung around one another's shoulders. But there's such a paucity of bearable images available to a parent whose child is at war, and it seemed to me, as I tried to fall asleep in Derrick's bedroom, that even the lucky parents - the grateful ones, the ones whose sons and daughters come home intact - must have to learn how to carry the burden both of imagining what happened over there, what was seen and done and experienced, and of understanding how much they will never really know.

"It's the pieces you don't see that they've got to work through," Tracy had said. One section of her website is called "Post War Coping Strategies & Help"; it includes links to veterans' stress-disorder assistance and to articles with titles like *"The War of Emotions"* and *"The Other Battle: Coming Home."* It would be nice not to have to make use of any of these resources, either for Derrick or for herself, after he leaves Iraq this summer for what Tracy fervently hopes will be the last time. "One of the things Derrick said to me was, 'I never want to pull a trigger again,'" Tracy said. "And when I think about that, my prayers then turn to: 'Please, God, give him the strength to pull the trigger when he needs to. Please, God, give him the strength to know when it's the right time to do it.'"

When I woke the next morning it was barely light outside, but Tracy was already at her computer. She was smoking at her desk, which she usually doesn't do, and her face was bleak. "I got a D.O.D.," she said.

A D.O.D. is what Tracy calls a death notice from the Department of Defense. These notices come to her as e-mailed press releases, each with a headline that identifies the service the deceased American belonged to; when she sees "Marine Casualty," Tracy passes the official information directly to the message boards of marineparents.com, so she can make accurate the latest fearful online rumors started by an unverified posting or a televised news report. I looked over Tracy's shoulder at the message on her computer screen. "Corporal Bryan J. Richardson, 23, of Summersville, West Virginia, died March 25 as a result of hostile action in Al Anbar Province, Iraq."

I asked Tracy how long she had known that there was a new Marine death. "Since yesterday morning," she said. "CNN said something about it, but they were vague, and everybody was in a panic. The message boards were popping. The posts yesterday were full of it. But there was no D.O.D., not until now."

She had walked around with it all day in other words; she had known, at Missy's, but she hadn't known the details, only that it wasn't Derrick, first because the Marines had not come to her house, and then because Derrick was there, on Missy's computer screen, examining his wife's painted egg. Tracy had said nothing because that's what she has taught herself to do, between the initial rumors and the arrival of the D.O.D.'s: say nothing, pray, wait for Derrick to call, sprint around the website to see whether it's the child of someone she has come to know. Tracy was typing now – "Let's remember him and his family in our prayers" - and I asked whether she was thinking about Corporal Bryan J. Richardson's house in Summersville, West Virginia, and she said, yes, she was. "The knocking on the door," she said.

Tracy jammed her cigarette into the ashtray, hard.

"And the way I'd react: You've got the wrong house. I just talked to my son. This can't be right. Denial is the first thing. And knowing there's just complete and total despair in somebody's home right now. This is their Easter."

She started to cry. "And I feel so grateful, and then so guilty," she said. "Nobody's going to say, 'Thank God, it wasn't my son.' But that's what we're all thinking."

Cynthia Gorney is associate dean of the Graduate School of Journalism at the University of California at Berkeley. This story originally appeared in *The New York Times* on May 29, 2005.

ABOUT THE MARINES

"I almost feel pity for the poor stupid thugs in Fallujah who had dared tangle with the Marines. You jerks haven't got a chance. Just call Dr. Kevorkian and get it over with." - An Anonymous State Department Employee

A State Department Employee's thoughts on Marines:

Maybe it's the Christmas season. Maybe I'm just getting old. Maybe I've been working overseas in some pretty mean places just too long, and would rather be driving a turbo-charged American muscle car across the Nevada desert (we all have different fantasies, right?) Maybe it's the constant news crawl on my TV set announcing another dead American in Iraq or Afghanistan. I don't know, but for the last few days I can't stop thinking about how much we owe the young Marines who protect our Embassy and how angry I get every time I hear that a Marine has died in Iraq. And today was particularly bad, as CNN reports that seven Marines died in clashes against terrorists.

I don't want to denigrate any of our other fine armed services, but at State we have had a long and special relationship with the USMC. Since 1948, some of the best Marines get seconded to us to protect our diplomatic missions abroad. In addition, of course, both before and since 1948, it's the Marines who come yank us out when it all goes to hell or, as in Somalia and Liberia, to save the Embassy from a howling mob.

In our Embassy in this rather tough corner of the Far Abroad we get daily threats of all types, almost daily demonstrations in front of the fort-like Chancery, shuttle about in armored cars, and have weekly "duck-and-cover" drills. We've had some nasty and very lethal bombings - we know that the bad guys are out there. They have us under surveillance, and they have lots of time, explosives, and guns.

We also have a detachment of MSGs (Marine Security Guards), all of them very young (18-23) led by a quiet but tough "old" Staff Sergeant (I doubt he's thirty) tasked with protecting the Chancery building and ensuring that we follow good security practices (Note: One of the most dreaded events in the Foreign Service is to walk into your office and find a "pink slip" on your desk left by an MSG who the previous night found a classified cable left in an outbox, a safe not properly spun shut, or some piece of classified gear left unsecured. Those "pink slips" are career killers. Of course, in the old Soviet GRU, one of these "security violations" was *literally* a killer . . . it meant the death penalty.)

Most days, however, you're hardly aware that an MSG is there: Just a shadowy figure standing inside a glass box, buzzing you through the hard line. Normally you sweep past him (and increasingly her) absorbed in your own thoughts, blabbing away on your cell phone, adjusting your tie, fumbling with papers, or just plain too rude and self-important to say "Good morning." When you have events at your house you rarely think of inviting the Marines. But despite all that they remain cheerful, upbeat, and exceedingly polite, and exude a quiet confidence that comes from great training and dedication.

Among the MSGs at this post we have two fresh from combat in Iraq, and they are itching to go back. These youngsters, one nineteen, the other twenty-one (both younger than my kids!), seem genuinely puzzled when we civilians ask, "So what was it like?" They can't seem to believe anybody would be interested in, much less amazed by, hearing about coming under mortar attack or driving a truck at high speed down some "Hogan's Alley-type" street lined with crazed and armed Jihadists. They relate it in a shy, matter-of-fact manner, full of military jargon. And they want to go there, again.

Watching these guys as they pulled toys out of the big "Marines' Toys for Tots" box in the Embassy lobby and hearing their cheerful shouts of "Oh, cool! Check this one out!" I couldn't help but think, "They're kids. They're just kids. Probably not much older than the orphans to whom they'll give those toys." I kept thinking about my own kids, living safely in the States, and the fact that they're older than these kids, these Marines.

But then I went with the "kids" out to the gun range. Suddenly they became deadly serious. The "kids" disappear - no goofing around. Strict discipline and concern for safety kicks in. They certainly know firearms, and treat them with respect and care. It was quite a sight to see the former "kids" deliberately, methodically pumping out rounds from their M-4s - single shot, three-shot bursts, full auto - punching out quarter-size groups in targets I can barely see. They don't look like kids anymore. They look like Hollywood's idea of Marines - like the actors John Wayne "led" in *Sands of Iwo Jima.* Now my thinking shifts to, "I wouldn't want to go up against these guys." And for a brief, very brief moment, I almost feel pity for the poor stupid thugs in Fallujah who had dared tangle with the Marines: "You jerks haven't got a chance. Just call Dr. Kevorkian and get it over with."

We all have had our days when we rant and rail against America's youth. I have heard my father's voice emanating from my own mouth: hopeless, hedonistic, rock addled, etc. I take it all back. I don't know what the Corps does to those orange-haired kids I see hanging out in the malls when I go home to the States, but whatever it is, keep doing it. The Europeans and their imitators in Ottawa, New York, Boston, and Hollywood paint their faces white and prance around in the "theater of the street" calling for peace. They wave their oh-so clever *"Bushitler"* posters. And over their lattes they decry the primitive "Red State" Americans. I know it's way too much to ask of such smart and sophisticated people, but maybe they should take a moment to remember that it's these kids, these Marines from small-town America, who put their own lives on the line to make all that noise and color of freedom possible. These kids, these Marines are the wall holding back the fascists of this century, and keeping the rest of us free.

Life isn't fair. The odds are not even. But I don't think these Marines would have it any other way.

HOLLYWOOD HYPOCRISY

Amy King

"Hollywood is a place that attracts people with massive holes in their souls." - Julia Phillips

I believe everyone is entitled to their opinion, but having said that I have a big problem with hypocrites who say one thing and do another. A good example is actor Burt Lancaster, who made his fortune starring in a lot of 'action' films. For many years he has been vocally 'anti-gun,' but if you Google "Burt Lancaster movie poster" on the internet one of the first to come up shows Mr. Lancaster firing a .50-caliber machinegun with belts of ammo criss-crossing his torso (the movie: "From Here to Eternity"). Apparently he is anti-gun, but not so much so as to turn down a fat check for shooting things up on-screen. I would have a lot more respect for Burt's position if he had stuck to his beliefs and simply said, "No, I won't do it." But I shouldn't pick on him too much, since he certainly isn't the only Hollywood type to sell out for the big bucks. Here Marine wife Amy King tells us about a modern-day Hollywood hypocrite:

I think Hollywood has once again hit the term 'hypocrisy' right on the head. Harrison Ford is to star in what will be Hollywood's first feature film about the current Iraq war. Producers Michael Shamberg and Stacey Sher have bought the option for *No True Glory: The Battle for Fallujah*, a nonfiction written by Slate reporter Bing West. The book is due to be published in May, and tells the story of an assault on Iraqi insurgents in Fallujah from the perspective of U.S. Marines. Variety reports that Ford is already attached to play

General Jim Mattis, who was in charge of the attack.

Here's what Harrison Ford had to say about the American-led war in Iraq LAST summer. I especially like the line about everyone going for the big hit. Pretty omniscient, huh?

"Harrison Ford has voiced his concerns over the American-led war in Iraq. The veteran actor said armed conflict was not the solution to Iraq's problems. Speaking in the Spanish capital of Madrid to launch his latest film, 'Hollywood Homicide,' Ford also took a swipe at U.S. gun laws and the 'big hit' nature of the country's film industry. Ford said, 'I'm very disturbed about the direction American foreign policy is going. I think something needs to be done to help alleviate the conditions which have created a disenfranchised and angry faction in the Middle East. I don't think military intervention is the correct solution. I regret what we as a country have done so far.' And, despite having starred in the original Star Wars trilogy, Ford also attacked Hollywood for making too many films more akin to 'video games' than real life. He added, 'It seems everybody is going for the big hit, for the most return.' And although he has appeared in action films, he said America's liberal gun laws had greatly contributed to the country's crime problems."

Having met the *real* General Mattis on more than one occasion, I can honestly say *no one* will ever capture that man's essence and personality. He is truly one of a kind.

Hopefully since Bing West is the author, the story will give a positive perspective on the Battles of Fallujah which occurred in April and November.

I personally intend to write a letter to Mr. Ford and ask if he's had a change of heart about his previous stance, or if he just feels comfortable making money off the blood of United States Marines, Soldiers, Sailors and their families.

AT EASE GENERAL MATTIS

Ralph Kinney Bennett

"The first time you blow someone away is not an insignificant event. That said, there are some assholes in the world that just *need* to be shot." – *Major General Jim Mattis, USMC, Iraq*

I'd heard of U.S. Marine General Jim Mattis from other Marines over the years, and from news coverage of his own exploits. He was the blunt, bachelor general who had served nine tours of duty in the Middle East, including combat in Afghanistan and Iraq.

He was the commander of the 1st Marine Division in the longest, fastest thrust of a division in Corps history - that dash to Baghdad in 2003.

I knew he wasn't just an officer; he was a *leader*. And a fighter. Not a statesman. Not an orator. No, God love him, he's a fighter.

In the military it has always been true that what you see is not always what you get. The "salad" on the uniform chest often bears closer inspection. It may be the fruit of the career of a gifted bureaucrat, a crypto-politician, a superb manager, or a combination of these.

Nothing wrong with that. Our vast military establishment needs all of the above in varying ways and to varying degrees. But it also needs leaders who are fighters. Those who will kick down the door. Those who will get the job done. As we have observed here before, all the niceties of democracy and civilization depend from time to time on a few men who will go down dark streets and do uncivilized and possibly undemocratic things we would rather not think about, let alone talk about.

Well, General Mattis talked about it. A little.

It was in San Diego last week, at a conference hosted by the Armed Forces Communications and Electronics Association and the U.S. Naval Institute. There were lots of military types in the room. They were discussing what changes our military must make to battle terrorists in future wars.

General Mattis pointed out to fellow conferees that, capable as we are of fighting "modern wars," we are having trouble adapting to "historic forms of warfare" brought back by the terrorists in Iraq and Afghanistan.

The general warned, "Don't patronize this enemy. They mean business. They mean every word they say. Don't imagine an enemy somewhere in the future and you're going to transform so you can fight him. They're killing us now. Their will is not broken."

Of course, General Mattis knows whereof he speaks. He's been there, doing that. And it was while reflecting on this that he made the following remark:

"Actually, its quite fun to fight 'em, you know. It's a hell of a hoot. It's fun to shoot some people. I'll be right up front with you. I like brawling."

The general then made clear who "some people" are. "You go into Afghanistan. You've got guys who slapped women around for five years because they didn't wear a veil. You know guys like that ain't got no manhood left anyway. So it's a hell of a lot of fun to shoot them."

These remarks sent a predictable shudder through the press. A story from *The Washington Post* news service noted that the general's blunt words had "sparked criticism from military ethicists."

Military ethicists.

At Secretary of Defense Donald Rumsfeld's press conference Thursday, which centered on serious issues like the Iraqi vote and continuing security difficulties, the first question from the press was a fussy inquiry about the "appropriateness" of General Mattis' remarks.

Rumsfeld and Marine General Peter Pace, vice-chairman of the Joint Chiefs, somehow refrained from bitch slapping the reporter and moved on to more important matters.

Marine Commandant General Michael Hagee, to his immense credit, called General Mattis "one of this country's bravest and most experienced military leaders" and noted that he had merely been trying to "reflect the unfortunate and harsh realities of war."

To close the matter, General Hagee said, "I have counseled (Mattis) concerning his remarks, and he agrees he should have chosen his words more carefully."

It turns out there actually *are* "military ethicists." One of them, Jeff McCausland, director of the Leadership in Conflict Initiative (at Dickinson College, in Carlisle, Pennsylvania) called General Mattis' remarks "unprofessional and inappropriate" and noted that they send a "terrible message" to those serving under him.

If any "terrible message" has been sent, it has been by the bombings and butchery of the terrorists and Islamofanatics. These are General Mattis' "guy's like that," who treat women as beneath contempt, gleefully slit throats and behead innocents before cameras, stop buses on lonely roads and execute the young men inside, and murder in the streets for the world to see.

It is the civilized part of us that is always a little uneasy with our General Pattons, but in the end most of us cut them some slack. We know deep in our hearts what they really mean. There's a rough and half humorous hyperbole in

General Mattis' words - the language that cops know, and firemen, when they talk among themselves.

But I see an old fashioned gallantry, too, in those words. They are his blunt affirmation that he has fought in a war worth fighting against an uncivilized enemy that deserves to be destroyed. They tell us that he fights with élan and, I think, high purpose.

At ease, General Mattis. Your country salutes you... and needs you.

INTIMATE KILLING

Major General Robert H. Scales

"We must all remember that leaders like General Mattis and the men he commands are the rarest commodities that a protected society like ours can produce." - MajGen Robert H. Scales, USA

On Wednesday, I had the pleasure of moderating a panel on the future of warfare. Marine Lieutenant General Jim Mattis was one of the panelists. During his remarks he made a statement about the pleasure that young soldiers and Marines feel when killing in close combat, a statement that seems to have gotten him in trouble with the fourth estate - prompting an apology, and some counseling by the Marine Corps' Commandant.

First, a confession: I know General Mattis. He is a central figure in the book I coauthored with Williamson Murray, *"The Iraq War: A Military History."* For those of you who might have the image of a knuckle-dragging troglodyte, let me assure you that he is one of the most urbane and polished men I have known. He can quote Homer as well as Sun Tzu, and has over seven thousand books in his personal library.

Jim is the product of three decades of schooling and practice in the art of war. No one on active duty knows more about the subject. He is an infantryman, a close-combat Marine. He is one of those very few who willingly practices the art of what social scientists term "intimate killing." Those of us who have engaged in the act understand what he was trying to explain to an audience of defense technologists and contractors.

Intimate killing is a primal aspect of warfare unchanged since the beginning of civilization. It involves a clash of two warriors, one on one, armed with virtually identical weapons. The decision goes to the soldier with the right stuff, the one with the greater cunning, strength, guile, ruthlessness and will to win.

For a moment put yourself in the place of a young Marine fighting house to house in the mean streets of Fallujah. Burdened with over sixty pounds of gear, sweat dripping constantly into your face, you can't stop shaking from the fear of what the enemy has in store for you around the next corner. Just ahead is a darkened house with doors and windows closed and shuttered. The only sound is the crunching of your boots on the trash and broken glass as you move in slow motion to surround the dwelling. You watch as the sergeant signals you to cover a side entrance. Through the faint haze you can see your buddy kick in the door and immediately come face to face with an insurgent who greets him with a burst of AK-47 fire that tears a hole in his chest. Your buddy doesn't die. The terrorist wants him to live just long enough for his buddies to rush in for a rescue and become additional trophies to be laid at the altar of heaven.

Now, it's your turn. You use your superior discipline and skill to approach the insurgent, and you're detected just at the last second. Both of you raise your weapons simultaneously and open fire in a crushing tear of bullets that scatter and ricochet wildly across the room. One bullet finds the bad guy and he falls in a bloody lump, just inches from your boots.

What exactly do you "feel" at this moment? Relief, to be sure, but also something else that cannot be explained to anyone who hasn't committed an act of intimate killing. It's not joy, exactly, more like exhilaration and an enormous sense of self-satisfaction that in one of the most primal challenges - where all the satellites, planes, ships and smart weapons are of no use whatever - when you prevailed, one on one, over a diabolically evil enemy.

Who should be offended by the emotions of "joy" or whatever one feels at the moment of a successful kill? It's a fair fight, you win and the bad guy loses. It's that simple. One more terrorist will not threaten your unit or your buddies. Remember, this isn't a reality show. There are no retakes. Donald Trump doesn't fire you, and the price for second place is death.

My point simply is this: We must celebrate the fact that we have men like Jim Mattis willing to devote (and give) their lives when necessary to commit an act that most of those in our society would be horrified to even contemplate. If you are offended by these emotions, then seriously consider joining an Army or Marine infantry unit so that you can demonstrate how to kill an enemy in a more *humane* and politically correct manner.

Until such an unlikely day occurs, we must all remember that leaders like General Mattis and the men he commands are the rarest commodities that a protected society like ours can produce. All they want is the opportunity to serve a country that truly appreciates the difficulty and dangers inherent in the duties they perform, duties very few are willing even to contemplate.

Retired Army Major General Robert H. Scales is a former commander of the Army War College.

THE TRUTH ABOUT WAR

Ralph Peters

"Americans traditionally love to fight. All *real* Americans love the sting of battle." – General George S. Patton

In San Diego on Tuesday, I had the privilege of sitting beside Lieutenant General Jim Mattis, a Marine who knows how to fight. We were on a panel discussing future war, and General Mattis, a Marine to the marrow of his bones, spoke honestly about the thrill of combat.

Mattis has commanded at every level. In Desert Storm, he led a battalion. In Afghanistan and then in Iraq, he led with inspiration and courage. Everyone on our panel had opinions about war, but that no-nonsense Marine knew more about it than the rest of us combined.

In the course of a blunt discussion of how our military has to prepare for future fights, the general spoke with a frankness that won the hearts of the uniformed members of the audience. Instead of trotting out politically correct clichés, Mattis told the truth:

"You go into Afghanistan, you got guys who slap women around for five years because they didn't wear a veil... it's a hell of a lot of fun to shoot them."

The language wasn't elegant. But we don't need prissy military leaders. We need generals who talk straight and shoot straight, men who inspire. And I guarantee you that any real Marine or soldier would follow General Mattis.

What was the media's reaction? A B-team news crew saw a chance to grab a headline at the military's expense (surprise, surprise). Lifting the general's remarks out of context, the media hyenas played it as if they were shocked to learn that people die in war.

Combat veterans are supposed to be tormented souls, you understand. Those who fight our wars are supposed to return home irreparably damaged. Hollywood's ideal of a Marine is the retired colonel in the film "American Beauty," who turns out to be a repressed homosexual and a murderer. Veterans are supposed to writhe on their beds all night, covered in sweat, unable to escape their nightmares.

War does scar some men. Most vets, though, just get on with their lives - scratch a veteran looking for pity, and more often than not you'll find a supply clerk who never got near a battlefield. And some who serve - the soldiers and Marines who win our wars - run to the sound of the guns, anxious to close with the enemy and kill him. They may not love war itself, but they find combat magnetic and exhilarating. They like to fight.

That's fine in movies featuring Brad Pitt as a mythical Greek hero. But God forbid that a modern-day Marine should admit that he loves his work.

Well, Marines don't serve full careers because they hate their jobs. In peace or war, the military experience is incredibly rich and rewarding. And sometimes dangerous. Goes with the territory. But for most of the young infantrymen in Iraq, their combat experience will remain the highpoint of their lives. Nothing afterward will be as intense or exciting. And they will never make closer friends than they did in their rifle squad.

General Mattis may have been unusual in his honesty, but he certainly isn't unusual in our history. We picture Robert E. Lee as a saintly father figure, but Lee remarked that it's good that war is so terrible, since otherwise men would grow to love it too much. He was speaking of himself. Andy

Jackson certainly loved a fight, and Stonewall Jackson never shied from one. Sherman and Grant only found themselves in war.

We lionize those who embraced war in the past, but condemn those who defend us in the present. George S. Patton was far blunter than Jim Mattis - but Patton lived in the days before the media was omnipresent and biased against our military.

The hypocrisy is stunning. General Mattis told the truth about a fundamental human activity - war - and was treated as though he had dropped a nuclear weapon on an orphanage. Yet when some bozo on a talk show confesses to an addiction or a perversion in front of millions of viewers, he's lionized as "courageous" for speaking out.

Sorry. It's men like Jim Mattis who are courageous. The rest of us barely glimpse the meaning of the word.

We've come to a sad state when a Marine who has risked his life repeatedly to keep our country safe can't speak his mind, while any professor who wants to blame America for 9/11 is defended by legions of free-speech advocates. If a man like Mattis hasn't earned the right to say what he really believes, who has?

Had General Mattis collapsed in tears and begged for pity for the torments war inflicted on him, the media would have adored him. Instead, he spoke as Marines do in the headquarters tent or the barracks, on the battlefield or among comrades. And young journalists who never faced anything more dangerous than a drunken night in Tijuana tried to create a scandal.

Fortunately, Lieutenant General Mattis has three big things going for him: The respect of those who serve; the Marine Corps, which won't abandon a valiant fighter to please self-righteous pundits whose only battle is with their waistlines; and the fact that we're at war. We need *more* men like Mattis, not fewer. The public needs to hear the truth about war, not just the crybaby nonsense of those who never deigned to serve our country.

In my own far humbler career, the leaders I admired were those who had the killer instinct. The warriors knew who they were. We would have followed them anywhere. They weren't slick Pentagon staffers anxious to go to work for defense contractors. They were the men who lived and breathed the warrior's life.

Table manners don't win wars. Winning our nation's battles demands disciplined ferocity, raw physical courage - and integrity. Jim Mattis has those qualities in spades.

Semper Fi, General.

Ralph Peters is a retired Army officer and the author of "Beyond Baghdad: Postmodern War and Peace."

BUMPER OF MY SUV

Chely Wright

"And yes, I do have questions, I get to ask them because I'm free. That's why I've got a sticker for the U.S. Marines, on the bumper of my S.U.V." – From the song *'Bumper of My SUV'* by Chely Wright

In June of 2003 I was one of many entertainers, athletes, and actors who traveled to the Middle East to entertain the troops. It was a moving, powerful experience as we were the first to enter Iraq in our effort to reach out to the troops to say "thank you" after the fall of a dictatorial regime. Truly inspirational for *me*, due to the fact that my brother had just served in Iraqi Freedom. Our tour missed him by ten days. Chris is a Marine, and as I write this today he is approaching his fifteenth year. Before he was deployed to the Persian Gulf, my brother sent me a small Marine Corps sticker. I proudly marched down to my vehicle in my garage and slapped that thing on the back. Most of my motivation for doing that was pride, but a bit of my reasoning was simply that I was scared. My brother was going off to war. I wanted to show my support. I have never in my lifetime had a bumper sticker of *any* kind displayed on a vehicle that I own, but this seemed appropriate. So... after I returned from that initial trip into Iraq, I was driving down a main drag in Nashville called West End when something happened... something obviously moving enough for me to drive straight home and write this song. What you will hear in the song *"The Bumper Of My S.U.V."* is the absolute truth. No exaggerations, no poetic license, and truly how it made me feel. I had no intention of ever playing this song for anyone.

So... my band, crew and I took another trip to Iraq from September 13th-22nd in 2004. I had stumbled across this little home studio demo that I had done some sixteen months earlier. Truthfully, I had forgotten about it, but was curious, so I burned a copy from the hard drive of my home studio. I played it for a couple of guys in my crew, and a couple of other friends. They all commented that I *must* perform this song in the Middle East during our tour through Kuwait and Iraq. About twenty minutes prior to the first show of the tour, I sat down with my band leader and we wrote out a rudimentary chart. I didn't even sing it all the way through to rehearse it with him. I just said, "Have this ready to do... just you and I, on stage." Well, we did it. And we continued to do it on every show. I had 3-4 hour autograph signings after each show, and I'll bet seven out of ten Soldiers, Sailors, Airmen, Marines, Reservists and such ask me to "Please record *'The Bumper of My S.U.V.'* song. It would mean so much to us if you would. Thank you for that song, and for acknowledging that we're not a bunch of warmongers. Many of us believe that we are doing great things, and furthermore... we're just doing our jobs." I thanked them all for their kind words, and promised that I would record it and send it back to AFN (Armed Forces Network) who, by the way, had been playing my home studio version a *lot*. All the more reason to send them a proper recording of this song. I am in no way trying to exploit the situation in the Middle East by "writing a country song about it and 'cashing in.'" I am simply keeping my promise to about 4,000 young men and women who personally asked a favor of me... and I humbly said yes. So, here it is. Half of the revenue made from the sale of the single will be donated to *Stars For Stripes*, the nonprofit organization that took us on this trip, and is committed to taking entertainment to the guys and gals who need it the most.

I've got a bright red sticker on the back of my car,
Says: "United States Marines."
And yesterday a lady in a mini-van,
Held up her middle finger at me.

Does she think she knows what I stand for,
Or the things that I believe?
Just by looking at a sticker for the U.S. Marines,
On the bumper of my S.U.V.

See, my brother Chris, he's been in,
For more than fourteen years now.
Our Dad was in the Navy during Vietnam,
Did his duty, then he got out.
And my Grandpa earned his Purple Heart,
On the beach of Normandy.
That's why I've got a sticker for the U.S. Marines,
On the bumper of my S.U.V.

But that doesn't mean that I want war:
I'm not Republican or Democrat.
But I've gone all around this crazy world,
Just to try to better understand.
And yes, I do have questions:
I get to ask them because I'm free.
That's why I've got a sticker for the U.S. Marines,
On the bumper of my S.U.V.

'Cause I've been to Hiroshima,
And I've been to the DMZ.
I've walked on the sand in Baghdad,
Still don't have all of the answers I need.

But I guess I wanna know where she's been,
Before she judges and gestures to me,
'Cause she don't like my sticker for the U.S. Marines,
On the bumper of my S.U.V.

So I hope that lady in her mini-van,
Turns on her radio and hears this from me.
As she picks up her kids, from their private school,
And drives home safely on our city streets.
Or to the building where her church group meets:
Yeah, that's why I've got a sticker for the U.S. Marines,
On the bumper of my S.U.V.

CLASHING CULTURES

Ralph Peters

"It's easy to 'dominate your battle space' if you don't have anyone to battle." - Ralph Peters

Last month, I sat in the office of Colonel Jon "Dog" Davis, a veteran Marine aviator. While at war, the Corps' pilots had seen a rise in their accident rate. Davis was determined to do something about it.

I wanted to be sympathetic, so I said, "Well, you're flying some very old aircraft."

Davis, a taut, no-nonsense Marine, looked me in the eye and said, "They may be old, but they're good. That's no excuse."

As commander of the Marine Aviation Weapons and Tactics Squadron One out in Yuma, Arizona, Davis could have nodded and gone along, blaming the jets and helicopters. But he's a Marine. And Marines don't make excuses. They do their best with what the taxpayers give them. And their best is pretty damn good.

Contrast that with a recent conversation I had with two Air Force generals. I had written columns critical of the platinum-plated F/A-22, the most expensive fighter in history, and an aircraft without a mission. So the Air Force decided to lobby me.

Those two generals spun the numbers until the stone-cold truth was buried under a mantra of "air dominance," imaginary combat roles and financial slight-of-hand. Still, I wanted to be fair. I took them seriously and investigated their claims.

Not one thing they said held up under scrutiny.

Morally bankrupt, the Air Force is willing to turn a blind eye to the pressing needs of soldiers and Marines at war in order to get more of its $300-million-apiece junk fighters. With newer, far more costly aircraft than the Marines possess, the Air Force pleads that it just can't defend our country without devouring the nation's defense budget.

Meanwhile, Marine aviators fly combat missions in aging jets and ancient helicopters, doing their best for America - and refusing to beg, lie, cheat or blame their gear.

I had gone out to Yuma to speak to Dog Davis' Marines about future war. The truth is they should have been lecturing to *me*. There is nothing more inspiring than being around United States Marines (yes, a retired Army officer wrote that). The Corps does more with its limited resources than any other branch of government. The Marines are a bargain rivaled only by our under-funded Coast Guard.

Even the military installations are different. A Marine base is well-maintained and perfectly groomed, but utterly without frills. Guest quarters are Motel 6, not the St. Regis. Air Force bases are the country clubs of 'la vie militaire.'

Meanwhile, the Air Force twiddles its thumbs and dreams of war with China. Its leaders would even revive the Soviet Union, if they could. Just to have something to do.

If you go into the Pentagon these days, you'll find only half of the building is at war. The Army and Marine staffs (the latter in the Navy Annex) put in brutal hours and barely see their families. The Navy, at least, is grappling with the changed strategic environment. Meanwhile, the Air Force staff haunts the Pentagon espresso bar and lobbies for more money.

The Air Force hasn't forgotten how to fight. But it only wants to fight the other services.

Recently, the blue-suiters have been floating one of the most disgraceful propositions I've ever encountered in Washington (and that's saying something).

I heard the con directly from one of the Air Force generals who tried to sell me on the worthless F/A-22. The poison goes like this: "The Air Force and Navy can dominate their battle space. Why can't the Army and Marines?"

Let me translate that: At a time when soldiers and Marines are fighting and dying in Iraq, Afghanistan and elsewhere, the Air Force shamefully implies that our ground forces are incompetent, hinting that, if the Air Force ran the world, we'd get better results.

How low can a service go? Not a single Air Force fighter pilot has lost his life in combat in Iraq. But the Air Force is willing to slander those who do our nation's fighting and dying.

As for the vile proposition itself, well, it's easy to "dominate your battle space" if you don't have anyone to battle. Our fighter-jock Air Force doesn't have an enemy (Air Force special-ops and transport crews, as well as ground-liaison personnel, serve magnificently - but the generals regard them as second-class citizens).

While courage is certainly required, Air Force and Navy combat challenges are engineering problems, matters of physics and geometry. Our Marines, by contrast, face brutally human, knife-fight conflicts that require human solutions.

The Air Force is about metal. The Marines deal in flesh and blood - in problems that don't have clear or easy solutions.

Hey, if the Air Force knows of a simple, by-the-numbers way to win the War on Terror, combat insurgents in urban terrain and help battered populations rebuild their countries, the generals in blue ought to share the wisdom. (They've certainly been paid enough for it.)

But the Air Force doesn't *have* any solutions. Just institutional greed. Their strategy? Trash our troops. Lie about capabilities and costs. Belittle the genuine dangers facing our country, while creating imaginary threats. Keep the F/A-22 buy alive, no matter what it takes.

A little while ago I wrote that our Air Force needed to be saved from itself. Now I'm no longer sure salvation's possible.

If you want to see how to fly and fight, call in the Marines.

Ralph Peters is the author of *Beyond Baghdad: Postmodern War and Peace.*

GIG 'EM AGGIES!

"It is time for us to stand and cheer for the doer, the achiever, the one who recognizes the challenge and does something about it." - Vince Lombardi

He's just a walk-on. Number thirty-eight in your program, zero in your heart. Means nothing to you. Just another sadly spotless jersey on the sideline.

So how is it that Josh Amstutz is the toughest, bravest and most inspirational member of Texas A & M's football team?

Well, look at his right leg. There are two scars left by a bullet that passed through it almost two years ago, a gift from an Iraqi sniper. How he runs on it as well as he does is anybody's guess.

Look at his jaw. It was stern and square enough for the Marine honor guard that flanked President Clinton during ceremonial events at the White House, and led George W. Bush down Pennsylvania Avenue on Inauguration Day.

Look at his eyes. They're practically Aggie maroon-and-white. What other twenty-three-year-old Purple Heart winner would volunteer as scout-team meat five days a week just so he can stand on the sidelines on Saturdays in the fall yelping, "Gig 'em Aggies?"

"I can't believe I'm on the team," says Amstutz, an A&M sophomore with freshman eligibility. "One practice it was pretty hot, and everybody was complaining. But I thought to myself, 'Hey, this isn't bad. It beats being in 120 degrees in Iraq in a hazardous chemical protective suit. And at least nobody's shooting at me.'"

You want to bitch about the training table? There were days when all he had to eat was one dried meal. "The scary part," he says, "was we got so hungry, we started liking it." In fact, when he was recuperating in the hospital after he got shot, a doctor saw him take a cookie off of his tray and hide it under his pillow.

"What are you doing?" the doctor asked.

"Saving food for later, Sir," Amstutz admitted.

"Son," said the doctor, "you don't have to do that anymore."

You want to rag about the road hotel? This is a guy who dug a hole for his bed every night, "as deep as you could get it before you fell asleep." And every time praying you weren't digging your own grave.

You want to whine about the pressure of big time college football? Amstutz had to kill people. "All my teammates ask me that question, but it's not something I want to talk about," he says. But he carried a machine gun and an M-16 with a grenade launcher, and concedes that he did kill other men.

Through it all, he never gave up his football dream. Gave up? Hell, it's what kept him going.

As a tight end at Jasper High in Indiana, catching passes from eventual LSU standout Matt Mauck, he actually had two goals: become a United States Marine, and play college football. How could he know that one dream would almost wipe out the other?

Amstutz reported to boot camp three days after he graduated from Jasper in 1999, and he became such a dogged Marine - he could stand for hours and hours without so much as twitching - that he was assigned to the White House eight weeks out of boot camp. "The only bad thing about the White House is the crazy squirrels there," he says. "They jump around in the trees, and the branches slap you in the face and you can't do a thing about it."

While in D.C., he met Fox TV intern and Texas A&M

alum Jessica Fontenot and eventually married her. On a trip out west with Fontenot in November of 2001, Amstutz witnessed one of the great spectacles in college football: a Texas A&M game in College Station. "I knew right then I wanted to play for the Aggies," he says.

But 9/11 made him itch to *fight*. Before being shipped out to the Middle East, Amstutz said goodbye to his father-in-law, who was dying of cancer. "I won't be here when you get back," Jessica's dad said, "So come home and take care of my little girl."

That suddenly looked doubtful on April 8th of 2003, when Amstutz's unit was checking out a tip that there was a weapons cache in a school. "Bullets started whizzing by like in *Saving Private Ryan*," he remembers. One went clean through his leg, just above the knee. He dragged himself to a medic, who told him that he was lucky. The bullet got only muscle.

Yet he wouldn't give up his dream of playing football. For a year he put all of his Marine determination into rehabbing that leg and added forty pounds to his post-Iraq weight if 155. Having served his four years of active duty, he enrolled in a junior college in the fall of '03, transferred to A&M this year, and in August was one of about sixty students to try out for a half dozen walk-on spots. He made the team as a safety - *Rudy* with a bullet.

"When I first met him, he told me, 'It's an honor to be in the same locker room with you,'" says the Aggies NFL-bound wide receiver, Terrence Murphy. "But now that I know his story, I think the same exact thing about *him*."

Amstutz hasn't been in a game yet, but if he could get in for just one play, "I'd want to cover a kickoff. That's my dream. I wouldn't want any big glory thing. Just one kickoff."

On New Year's Day the Aggies play Tennessee at the Cotton Bowl.

Hey, Coach Dennis Franchione, can't you put him in? After all, he went in for *you*.

Excerpted from a Sports Illustrated article by Rick Reilly.

THE MIGHTY HERK

"Aeroplanes are interesting toys, but are of no military value." – Marshall Ferdinand Foch, circa 1911

The sense of humor of the American fighting man is amazing. Is it a defense mechanism, the venting of sentiments suppressed by living in a politically correct environment, a reflection of aberrant youth genes now in blossom, or an attempt to deny the realities of not knowing if your next meal is with your family, or the angels? This is from the 1st Marine Aircraft Wing:

There I was at six thousand feet over central Iraq, going two hundred eighty knots and we're dropping faster than Paris Hilton's panties. It's a typical September evening in the Persian Gulf; hotter than a rectal thermometer, and I'm sweating like a priest at a Cub Scout meeting. But that's neither here nor there. The night is moonless over Baghdad tonight, and blacker than a Steven King novel. But it's 2004, folks, and I'm sporting the latest in night-combat technology - namely, hand-me-down night vision goggles (NVGs) thrown out by the fighter boys.

Additionally, my 1962 Lockheed C-130E Hercules is equipped with an obsolete, yet semi-effective, missile warning system (MWS). The MWS conveniently makes a nice soothing tone in your headset just before the missile explodes into your airplane. Who says you can't polish a turd?

At any rate, the NVGs are illuminating Baghdad International Airport like the Las Vegas Strip during a Mike Tyson fight. These NVGs are the cat's ass. But I've digressed.

The preferred method of approach tonight is the random shallow. This tactical maneuver allows the pilot to ingress the landing zone in an unpredictable manner, thus exploiting the supposedly secured perimeter of the airfield in an attempt to avoid enemy surface-to-air-missiles and small arms fire. Personally I wouldn't bet my pink ass on that theory, but the approach is fun as hell, and that's the *real* reason we fly it.

We get a visual on the runway at three miles out, drop down to one thousand feet above the ground, still maintaining two hundred eighty knots. Now the fun starts. It's pilot appreciation time as I descend the mighty Herk to six hundred feet and smoothly, yet very deliberately, yank into a sixty degree left bank, turning the aircraft ninety degrees offset from runway heading. As soon as we roll out of the turn, I reverse turn to the right a full two hundred seventy degrees in order to roll out aligned with the runway. Some aeronautical genius coined this maneuver the "Ninety/Two-Seventy." Chopping the power during the turn, I pull back on the yoke just to the point my nether regions start to sag, bleeding off energy in order to configure the pig for landing.

"Flaps Fifty!, Landing Gear Down!, Before Landing Checklist!" I look over at the copilot, and he's shaking like a cat shitting on a sheet of ice. Looking further back at the navigator, even through the NVGs, I can clearly see a wet spot spreading around his crotch. Finally, I glance at my steely-eyed flight engineer. His eyebrows rise in unison as a grin forms on his face. I can tell he's thinking the same thing I am... "Where do we find such fine young men?"

"Flaps One Hundred!" I bark at the shaking cat. Now it's all aimpoint and airspeed. Aviation 101, with the exception there are no lights, I'm on NVGs, it's Baghdad, and now tracers are starting to crisscross the black sky. Naturally, and not at all surprisingly, I grease the Goodyear's on brick-one of runway 33 left, bring the throttles to ground idle, and then force the props to full reverse pitch. Tonight, the sound of freedom is my four Hamilton Standard propellers chewing through the thick, putrid Baghdad air. The huge, one-hundred-thirty-thousand pound, lumbering whisper pig comes to a lurching stop in less than two thousand feet. Let's see a Viper do *that!*

We exit the runway to a welcoming committee of government issued Army grunts. It's time to download their beans and bullets and letters from their sweethearts, look for war booty, and of course, urinate on Saddam's home. Walking down the crew entry steps with my lowest-bidder, Beretta 92F, 9-millimeter strapped smartly to my side, I look around and thank God, not Allah, that I'm an American and I'm on the winning team. Then I thank God I'm not in the Army!

Knowing once again I've cheated death, I ask myself, "What in the hell am I doing in this mess?" Is it Duty, Honor, and Country? You bet your ass. Or could it possibly be for the glory, the swag, and not to mention, chicks dig the Air Medal. There's probably some truth there too. But now is not the time to derive the complexities of the superior, cerebral properties of the human portion of the aviator-man-machine model. It is, however, time to get out of this shit-hole. Hey co-pilot , clean yourself up! And how's about the "Before Starting Engines Checklist."

God, I love this job!

HOW JOHN WAYNE
Saved the Corps

Author Unknown

"If you do something I don't like I'm gonna jump, and when I land it'll hurt. I'll ride you until you can't stand up. When you do, you'll be Marines." – John Wayne as 'Sergeant Stryker' in *The Sands of Iwo Jima*

A lot of people like to dump on John Wayne because he played a lot of heroic parts in the movies, but never actually served in the military. Even so, he may have done more to guarantee the continued existence of the Marine Corps (and thereby the security of our Nation) than most people:

Today is John Wayne's 98th birthday. He was born on May 26, 1907 in Winterset, Iowa, weighing thirteen pounds. His birthplace is a museum, and a few years ago I took my son Brandon to visit it. There was a guest book, opened to a page with an entry, in the entrant's handwriting... Name: Ronald Reagan. Address: 1600 Pennsylvania Ave., Washington DC.

To celebrate the birthday of a truly great American, let me tell you how John Wayne saved the Marine Corps. In the aftermath of World War II, amid a psychological letdown after years of war and bloodshed, the huge demobilization of servicemen, the desire to slash military spending, and the antipathy towards the military by left-wingers in the Democratic Party, there was a call by a number of Senators and Congressmen to abolish the Marine Corps.

In this, they were supported by the Doolittle Board,

created by the Truman Administration, which called for the Marine Corps to be "disbanded" as a separate military force, and "unified" with the Army (yes, the board was headed by an *Army* general, Jimmy Doolittle).

A group of enterprising Marines - you can always depend on Marines to be enterprising - with Hollywood connections thought a movie made around the most famous photograph of World War II, Joe Rosenthal's shot of the Marines raising the flag on Mount Suribachi on Iwo Jima, could help sway public opinion against their disbandment.

They approached legendary director Allan Dwan, who agreed to commission a script. The movie was to be called *"The Sands of Iwo Jima,"* and everybody agreed there was only one man who could play the lead role of Sergeant Stryker - John Wayne.

To their great surprise, Wayne turned it down. He didn't like the script, and he wasn't enamored of the character of Stryker. The Marines came to the rescue again. The Marine Corps Commandant, General Clifton B. Cates, got on an airplane and flew from Washington to California to personally request Wayne make the picture. When General Cates explained the stakes involved - the very existence of the Marine Corps - Wayne immediately changed his mind, promising the general he would do everything in his power to have the movie be a success.

The Sands of Iwo Jima was released in 1949 and quickly became a runaway blockbuster, with millions of moviegoers packing every theatre showing it. Wayne was nominated for a Best Actor Oscar, establishing him as Hollywood's Number One box-office star. The Doolittle Board folded its tent, and no politician on Capitol Hill ever again said a word about disbanding the Marines.

So let's all say "Semper Fi" to the memory of John

Wayne.

To further celebrate his birthday, here's a treat and some advice.

The treat is this: A biography of John Wayne was written by Ronald Reagan in the October 1979 issue of Reader's Digest.

The advice is this: Don't ever trust a man who doesn't *like* John Wayne!

HOW THE MARINES ARE DIFFERENT

Colonel Daniel F. Bolger, U.S. Army

"All (Marines) speak the language of the rifle and bayonet, of muddy boots and long, hot marches. It's never 'us and them,' only 'us.' That is the secret of the Corps." -Colonel Daniel F. Bolger, USA

A homage to the Corps from an Army colonel....

"What makes Marine infantry special?" Asking the question *that* way misses the most fundamental point about the United States Marine Corps. In the Marines, *everyone* - sergeant, mechanic, cannoneer, supply man, clerk, aviator, cook - is a rifleman first. The entire Corps, all 170,000 or so on the active rolls, plus the reserves, are *all* infantry. All speak the language of the rifle and bayonet, of muddy boots and long, hot marches. It's never 'us and them,' only 'us.' *That* is the secret of the Corps.

If Army infantry amounts to a stern monastic order standing apart, on the edge of the wider secular soldier world, Marine infantry more resembles the central totem worshiped by the entire tribe. Marines have specialized, as have all modern military organizations. And despite the all-too-real rigors of boot camp, annual rifle qualification, and high physical standards, a Marine aircraft crew-chief or radio repairman wouldn't make a good 0311 on a squad assault. But those Marine technical types know that they serve the humble grunt, the man who will look the enemy in the eye within close to belly-ripping range. Moreover, all Marines

91

think of themselves as grunts at heart, just a bit out of practice at the moment. That connection creates a great strength throughout the Corps. It explains why Marine commanders routinely, even casually, combine widely disparate kinds of capabilities into small units... Marines send junior officers and NCOs out from their line rifle companies and expect results. They get them, too.

Even a single Marine has on-call the firepower of the air wing, the Navy, and all of the United States. Or at least he thinks he does. A Marine acts accordingly. He is expected to take charge, to improvise, to adapt, to overcome. A Marine gets by with ancient aircraft (the ratty CH-46E Frog, for example), hand-me-down weapons (such as the old M-60 tanks used in the Gulf War), and whatever else he can bum off the Army or cajole out of the Navy. Marines get the job done regardless, because they are Marines. They make a virtue out of necessity. The men, not the gear, make the difference. Now and again, the Marines want to send *men*, not bullets.

This leads to a self-assurance that sometimes comes across as disregard for detailed staff-college quality planning and short shrift for high-level supervision. Senior Army officers in particular sometimes find the Marines amateurish, cavalier, and overly trusting in just wading in and letting the junior leaders sort it out. In the extreme, a few soldiers have looked at the Corps as some weird, inferior, ersatz ground-war establishment, a bad knockoff of the real thing. "A small, bitched-up Army talking Navy lingo," opined Army Brigadier General Frank Armstrong in one of the most brutal inter-service assessments. That was going too far. But deep down, many Army professionals tended to wonder about the Marines. Grab a defended beach? Definitely. Seize a hill? Sure, if you don't mind paying a little. But take charge of a really big land operation? Not if we can help it.

Anyone who has watched an amphibious landing unfold would be careful with that kind of thinking. The Marines actually have a lot in common with their elite Army infantry brothers, if not with all the various Army headquarters and service echelons. True, Marine orders do tend to be, well... brief. But so do those of the airborne, the air assault, the light-fighters, and the rangers, for the same good reason: Hard, realistic training teaches soldiers how to fight by doing, over and over, so they need not keep writing about it, regurgitating basics every time. More enlightened soldiers consider that goodness. A three-inch thick order, a big CP, and lots of meetings do not victory make. The Marines consciously reject all that. And why not? Despite the occasional Tarawa or Beirut, it works. A Corps infused with a rifleman ethos has few barriers to intra-service cooperation. The Army talks a great deal about combined arms and does it down to about battalion level, often with great wailing and gnashing of teeth. Marines do it all the way down to the individual Marine. Soldiers have defined military occupational specialties, and guard their prerogatives like union shop stewards. Finance clerks don't do machine guns. Mechanics skip foot marches to fix trucks. Intel analysts work in air-conditioned trailers; they don't patrol. Marines, though, are just Marines. They all consider themselves trigger pullers. They even *like* it, as might be expected of an elite body.

Excerpted from Colonel Daniel F. Bolger's book *USA Death Ground: Today's American Infantry in Battle*.

IN THE FIGHT

Matt Friedeman, PhD

"Appreciation, smiles, handclaps - they can go a long way when a nation is at war, regardless of what the media and some Europeans might think." - Matt Friedeman, PhD

A few 'anti-war' types complained that the Budweiser commercial shown during the Super Bowl (where Americans in an airport clap as returning Iraq War veterans walk by) was 'unrealistic' and further charged that the brewery was 'pandering to warmongers.' I must have seen a <u>different</u> commercial than they did. The one I saw was about showing the troops that we appreciate their service and sacrifice. I have to wonder - would they have preferred to see them spit upon, ala the Vietnam era?

Rick from Winona, Mississippi, called my state-wide talk radio program this week. Sometimes, you get a phone call that ought to be read in the broader market.

On the program that day we were discussing the report that some Europeans were disgusted with the Super Bowl commercial of American soldiers getting applause in an airport. The critics thought it too extreme in its patriotism, and a possible incitement to further war.

At any rate, Rick (he asked us not to use his full name) called to talk about his experience in coming back recently from the fields of war. His words (and they are worth your time reading, only lightly edited):

"I heard you talking about the Super Bowl commercial. I'm a Marine, a Recon Marine. I just got back from overseas, the second week of December, actually. I was injured overseas, so that's why I'm home now. The whole time I was [there, in recovery] we watched the news to see what was going on. We saw the protests, and we saw what the media was saying about what's going on, and we were worried about what we were actually going to face when we came home. We didn't know what to expect, to be honest with you. From the news media we were seeing, the *whole country* was basically telling us we're a bunch of jerks. I thank God that the troops that are over there don't see the news coverage. I thank God every day, because there'd be ten times the number getting killed, just because it would so de-motivate them.

Back to the story: there were seven other soldiers that came home with me that day. We flew into JFK, and we were talking on the way back: 'What's going to happen? What will we be facing? Is it going to be like the Vietnam era? Are there going to be people spitting at us?' We didn't know. We had that much trepidation about it.

When we got into JFK, we stepped out of the breezeway into the main terminal, and directly in front of us was an elderly gentleman carrying a bag. And he immediately stopped, set his bag down, and the first thing we all thought was, 'Oh, Lord, here we go already.' He just stopped and looked at us for a second, and then tears came to his eyes - and he *saluted* us. And – I'm breaking up now [editor's note: with tears] - every one of us just started crying like babies. Everybody in the terminal - I kid you not, at least two to three hundred people - just started clapping, spontaneously. To me, it was so much more worth it when we realized that people over here actually get what we were doing. We weren't over there because it's fun. We're over there doing a job.

When I saw the Super Bowl commercial I just started bawling like a baby again, because that was something totally unexpected. We had no idea that people actually appreciated what we're doing, from what we see on the news. We thought we were going to come back and get eggs thrown at us. It was so refreshing to know that what we were seeing on the news is just a bunch of garbage that's being concocted by the media, that 99.9 percent of the country doesn't believe that way.

I have a couple of more months of recovery. I got hit with a concussion and have some internal damage, but I'm feeling up, doing well, and hopefully I can get back over there with my boys."

It caused some tears in this talk show host's eyes to know there were tears in *his*. Appreciation, smiles, handclaps - they can go a long way when a nation is at war, regardless of what the media and

some Europeans might think.

This story originally appeared on February 10, 2005

MAKING A DIFFERENCE

"The world has no room for cowards. We must all be ready somehow to toil, to suffer, to die. And yours is not the less noble because no drum beats before you when you go out into your daily battlefields, and no crowds shout about your coming when you return from your daily victory or defeat." - Robert Lewis Stevenson

Our troops do so much for us. Many thanks to those who give back to them. Marine Mom Lori, with two sons in the Corps, passes along this heartwarming story of generosity and appreciation:

My oldest son, Josh, came back from Iraq doubting (as in "I'm just a &%$*in' POGUE") that he had accomplished anything worthwhile. No matter what I've said to him, he's been wondering if the time away from his new wife, and the rest of us, was wasted. He, like so many warriors, came back to a surprising amount of negative news and questions from people who delighted in asking incredibly stupid and insensitive questions. Even after some bad firefights, he thought he hadn't "really served."

Josh and his wife finally found an apartment. He's been back from Iraq since October, and they've been staying with friends. Not cheap by Oklahoma standards ($950 for a small two-bedroom) but at least it'll be home. They spent the morning packing their few belongings. They didn't have much money left after the rent and deposits, but decided they'd spend a bit on some used furniture and eat sparingly until payday.

They found a small used furniture store. Inside, they

spotted a green leather couch and a nice coffee table. Josh figured that could do double duty as a place to eat, and they'd wait to find a table for the dining room. While his wife wandered around looking for dishes, Josh approached the clerk and told him they'd like to buy the sofa and table and told him he'd have to go back to the apartment, empty the Explorer, and then come back for the furniture. The man asked him, "Are you new to town?" Josh said "Kind of, Sir... I just got back from Iraq. It's our first apartment."

The man was silent a moment, then thanked Josh for his service, and told my son to look around and see if they could find anything else they might need. The man told him that the items were on sale for half price. Josh was pleasantly surprised, and decided they might be able to add a few more things, since they were getting the furniture for less than they originally thought. They looked around for a while, deciding on a few more things like dishes, a chair, a few lamps and something to hang on the living room wall.

Josh approached the man and asked what their total was. That man looked at my son and said "Go over to the register, give us twenty dollars, and we'll call it even."

Josh was stunned. He stammered "Are you sure? I... I... Thank you so much!" The man said "Don't you *dare* thank me. *Thank you* for what you boys are doing for *us*." Then he said he'd help take the furniture to the apartment for them. Color my boy even more amazed. At this point my daughter-in-law was in tears.

It gets better. After following the kids to the apartment and helping Josh unload, that man who had just given my son a new outlook on his experience post-combat earned even more of my eternal gratitude. My daughter-in-law went to get her purse from the car to pay him for helping them. She got back to the curb as he drove off, waving. Josh was sitting on the curb with his head between his legs. Dakota thought he was praying. He was, but his face was white as a sheet when he looked up. Dakota said, "Babe, what's the matter?" Josh, sporting a serious case of 'eyeball sweat,' said: "He just handed me a hundred-dollar bill and told me to take you out for a nice dinner."

After they got over the nausea and shock, they called me to share this blessing. I bawled like a baby, of course, and then asked Josh if the man might have been a Marine, or a veteran. He said, "Oh my Gawd, I should have asked!" (Uh, yeah. Duh.)

My son, who'd spent the last several months doubting the worth of human nature after combat around Fallujah and Ramadi, kept babbling, "He *must* have been an angel, Mom. He had to be, he just had to. That guy was an angel sent by God." (Of that, I have no doubts!)

I told him, "Yes, honey, he could have been... he could also be "just" one of the grateful Americans I keep insisting are around. I *told* you they exist. And I *told* you that you *do* make a difference. You may now allow me to say 'I *told* you so!'" In a tearful, but smug-mama voice, of course.

The kids were at a loss wondering what they could do to thank this wonderful man. I suggested buying a USMC OIF flag, having his unit sign it, and presenting it to that dear, sweet man with many thanks. I plan to thank him as well - with a letter letting him know just what he's done for my son's faith and confidence (and mine). That man might never really fathom what his gesture meant to my family, but I'm going to bust my ass trying to tell him.

My Marine now realizes that what he did *does* make a difference. And hey, we moms just *love* being right!

A QUESTION OF
Semantics

"We are getting into semantics again. If we use words, there is a very grave danger they will be misinterpreted."
- H. R. Haldeman

The Korean War, in which the Marine Corps fought and won some of its most brutal battles, was not without its gallows humor. During one such conflict a ROK (Republic of Korea) commander, whose unit was fighting along with the Marines, called the legendary Chesty Puller to report a major Chinese attack in his sector. "How many Chinese are attacking you?" asked Puller.

"Many, many Chinese!" replied the excited Korean officer.

Puller digested this for a moment, and then asked for another count - and got the same answer "Many, many Chinese!"

"Goddammit!" swore Puller, "Put my Marine liaison officer on the radio."

In a minute, an American voice came over the air: "Yes sir?"

"Lieutenant," growled Chesty, "exactly how many Chinese you got up there?"

"Colonel, we got a whole *shitload* of Chinese up here!"

"Thank God." exclaimed Puller, "At least there's *someone* up there who knows how to count!"

MILITARY ANTHEMS
And the Marines' Hymn

Pat Dugan

"A pessimist sees the difficulty in every opportunity; an optimist sees the opportunity in every difficulty." - Winston Churchill

Sir Winston Churchill, British Prime Minister, became an ardent admirer of the U.S. Marine Corps. In the company of guests of state, he often demonstrated his respect for U.S. Marines by reciting, from memory, all three stanzas of The Marines' Hymn.

The U.S. Army, the U.S. Navy, and the U.S. Air Force all have their own songs.

For the U.S. Navy, *Anchors Aweig*h was written in 1906 by Lieutenant Charles Zimmerman and midshipman Alfred Miles. Initially the song was a tribute to the Naval Academy Class of 1907. Various people revised it later, trying to weed out the nonsense. Another midshipman, Royal Lovell, penned the final stanza in 1926.

Anchors Aweigh has a snappy little tune, but no one knows what the words imply. The original first stanza in 1906 had dealt solely with the game of football. Even today, the song offers a bittersweet "farewell to college joys." The lyrics end by "wishing you a happy voyage home." Many musical experts think that *Anchors Aweigh* is a ballad for football players who like sailboats. But, no one really knows for sure.

The U.S. Army adopted a snazzy tune for *The Caisson Song.* Unlike the words in the Navy's song, the words of the

Army's song make sense. According to each stanza, *The Caisson Song* clearly is a melody for rural motorists.

Edmund Gruber wrote the original lyrics in the Philippines during World War I. Naturally, since most of the fighting was 8000 miles away in Europe, Gruber made only a passing reference to warfare. Yet, he was careful to be "politically correct." He apparently sought the help of first grade students in composing the lyrics. The banal "Hi, hi, hee" is a dead giveaway. No one has a clue as to what it might mean. Still, at least it rhymes.

The U.S. Air Force did not exist in 1938. But, that year *Liberty Magazine* sponsored a contest for an official song for the Army Air Corps. The magazine received 757 entries. A group of Army Air Corps wives (yes, believe it or not, *wives*) selected the entry from Robert Crawford, *Off We Go Into the Wild Blue Yonder*. After World War II the Army Air Corps evolved into the U.S. Air Force. This fledgling flying club adopted *Off We Go* as their official song. It suited the illusionary nature of the new Wild-Blue-Yonder-Wonders with references to "those who love the vastness of the sky" and the fictitious "rainbow's pot of gold." The final stanza speaks of the "gray haired wonder," an admirable gesture of non-discrimination for the new civilized Air Force.

These three songs, *Anchors Aweigh*, *The Caisson Song*, and *Off We Go Into the Wild Blue Yonder*, are often played at public events. They obviously delight the members of the affected service: Navy, Army, or Air Force. When their song is played, sailors, soldiers, and zoomies leap to their feet and shout, cheer, clap their hands, and jive with the music. They have a jolly time, almost like a high school pep rally!

The U.S. Marine Corps is the United States' military band of brothers dedicated to war fighting. The proud Brotherhood of Marines is guided by principles, values, virtues, love of country, and its Warrior Culture. This brotherhood of American Patriots *has no song.* Instead, Marine Warriors have a *hymn.* When *The Marines' Hymn* is played, United States Marines stand at attention. They silently show their pride in their fellow Marines, their Corps, their Country, their heritage, and their hymn. *The Marines' Hymn* is a tribute to Warriors.

Marine Warriors stormed fortress Derna, raised the American flag, and gave us "the Shores of Tripoli." Marines fought their way into the castle at Chapultepec and gave us the "Halls of Montezuma." Marines exist for the purpose of war fighting. Fighting is their role in life. They "fight for right and freedom" and "to keep our honor clean." And they fight "in the air, on land, and sea."

The Marine Corps is Valhalla for Warriors. U.S. Marines need no song. They have a Hymn. Ironically, no one knows who wrote the Hymn, which was in widespread use by the mid-1800s. Colonel A.S. McLemore, USMC, spent several years trying to identify the origin of the tune. In 1878 he told the leader of the Marine Band that the tune had been adopted from the comic opera *Genevieve de Barbant*, by Jacques Offenback. Yet others believe the tune originated from a Spanish folk song. Whatever! Regardless of its origin, *The Marines' Hymn* has remained a revered icon of the United States Marine Corps for almost two hundred years.

In 1929 *The Marines' Hymn* became the official hymn of the Corps. Thirteen years later, in November of 1942, the Commandant approved a change in the words of the first verse, fourth line. Because of the increasing use of aircraft in the Corps, the words were changed to "In the air, on land, and sea." No other changes have been made since that time. When you have attained absolute perfection, there is no need for further modification!

MILITARY SPOUSES

Paige Swiney

"The only thing harder than being a Marine is being married to one." – Colonel "Irish" Egan

It was just another harried Wednesday afternoon trip to the commissary. My husband was off teaching young men to fly. My daughters were going about their daily activities knowing I would return to them at the appointed time, bearing, among other things, their favorite fruit snacks frozen pizza and all the little extras that never had to be written down on a grocery list.

My grocery list, by the way, was in my sixteen-month-old daughter's mouth, and I was lamenting the fact that the next four aisles of needed items would pass by while extracting the last of my list from my daughter's mouth, when I nearly ran over an old man. This man clearly had no appreciation for the fact that I had forty-five minutes left to finish the grocery shopping, pick up my four-year-old from tumbling class and get to school, where my twelve-year-old and her car pool mates would be waiting.

I knew men didn't belong in a commissary, and this old guy was no exception. He stood in front of the soap selection staring blankly, as if he'd never had to choose a bar of soap in his life. I was ready to bark an order at him, when I realized there was a tear on his face. Instantly, this grocery isle roadblock transformed into a human.... "Can I help you find something?" I asked.

He hesitated, and then told me he was looking for soap.

"Any one in particular?" I continued.

"Well, I'm trying to find my wife's brand of soap."

I started to loan him my cell phone to call her when he said, "She died a year ago, and I just want to smell her again."

Chills ran down my spine. I don't think the 22,000-pound Mother of All Bombs could have had the same impact. As tears welled up in my eyes, my half-eaten grocery list didn't seem so important. Neither did fruit snacks or frozen pizza. I spent the remainder of my time in the commissary that day listening to a man tell the story of how important his wife was to him - how she took care of their children while he served our country. A retired, decorated World War II pilot who flew over fifty missions to protect Americans still needed the protection of a woman who served him at home.

My life was forever changed that day. Every time my husband works too late or leaves before the crack of dawn, I try to remember the sense of importance I felt that day in the commissary. Sometimes the monotony of laundry, housecleaning, grocery shopping and taxi driving leaves military wives feeling empty - the kind of emptiness that is rarely fulfilled when our husbands come home and don't want to or can't talk about work. We need to be reminded at times, of the important role we fill for our family and for our country.

Over the years, I've talked a lot about military spouses… how special they are and the price they pay for freedom too. The funny thing is, most military spouses don't consider themselves different from other spouses. They do what they have to do, bound together not by blood or merely friendship, but with a shared spirit whose origin is in the very essence of what love truly is.

Is there truly a difference? I think there is. You have to decide for yourself. Other spouses get married and look forward to building equity in a home and putting down family roots. Military spouses get married and know they'll live in base housing or rent, and their roots must be short so they can be transplanted frequently. Other spouses decorate a home with flair and personality that will last a lifetime. Military spouses decorate a home with flare tempered with the knowledge that no two base houses have the same size windows or same size rooms. Curtains have to be flexible and multiple sets are a plus. Furniture must fit like puzzle pieces.

Other spouses have living rooms that are immaculate and seldom used. Military spouses have immaculate living room/dining room combos. The coffee table got a scratch or two moving from Okinawa, but it still looks pretty good. Other spouses say good-bye to their spouse for a business trip and know they won't see them for a week. They are lonely, but can survive. Military spouses say good-bye to their deploying spouse and know they won't see them for months, or for a remote, a year. They are lonely, but will survive.

Other spouses, when a washer hose blows off, call Maytag and then write a check out for having the hose reconnected. Military spouses will cut the water off and fix it themselves. Other spouses get used to saying "hello" to friends they see all the time. Military spouses get used to saying "good-bye" to friends made the last two years. Other spouses worry about whether their child will be class president next year. Military spouses worry about whether their child will be accepted in yet another school next year. And whether that school will be the worst in the city... again.

Other spouses can count on spouse participation in special events... birthdays, anniversaries, concerts, football games, graduation, and even the birth of a child. Military spouses only count on each other, because they realize that the flag has to come first if freedom is to survive. It has to be that way. Other spouses put up yellow ribbons when the troops are imperiled across the globe, and take them down when the troops come home. Military spouses wear yellow ribbons around their hearts and they never go away. Other spouses worry about being late for mom's Thanksgiving dinner. Military spouses worry about getting back from Japan in time for dad's funeral.

The television program showing an elderly lady putting a card down in front of a long, black wall that has names on it touches other spouses. The card simply says, "Happy Birthday, Sweetheart. You would have been sixty today." A military spouse is the lady with the card, and the wall is the Vietnam Memorial. I would never say military spouses are better than other spouses are. But I will say there *is* a difference. I will say, without hesitation, that military spouses pay just as high a price for freedom as do their active-duty husbands and wives. Perhaps the price they pay is even higher. Dying in service to our country isn't nearly as hard as loving someone who has died in service to our country, and having to live without them.

God bless our military spouses for all they freely give. And God bless America.

A DOSE OF PRIDE

Colonel John Ripley

"His name was Joe Enders, from south Philadelphia. He was a fierce warrior, a good Marine. If you ever tell a story about him George... say he was my friend." - Navajo 'Ben Yahzee' in the film '*Wind Talkers*'

Navajo code talkers took part in every assault the U.S. Marines conducted in the Pacific from 1942 to 1945. They served in all six Marine divisions, Marine Raider battalions and Marine parachute units, transmitting messages by telephone and radio in their native language – and it was a code that the Japanese never broke. Long unrecognized because of the continued value of their language as a classified code, the Navajo code talkers of World War II were finally honored for their contributions to the defense of our Nation on September 17, 1992, at the Pentagon. Thirty-five code talkers, all veterans of the U.S. Marine Corps, attended the dedication of the Navajo code talker exhibit.

All of this discussion on the Navajo Code Talkers brings to mind an incident I think you would enjoy hearing about. We don't need much reminding of the close bond we Marines have with this particular WWII group, but this will cement it even more, and I dare say you will not have heard of a similar story.

Several years ago my Vietnam battalion, 3/3, a very tight group
consisting of some legendary Marines we've all heard of, had its reunion here in Washington. We had met here before, but decided to come back because one of our members

agreed to be the honored guest and speaker for the banquet; a former Company Commander, now CMC, named Krulak.

All of the usual events were planned; a visit to the Vietnam Memorial (where, remarkably, the Park Service permitted us to have a Battalion formation with wreath-laying, etc. - a first), the Friday night parade, a visit to the Museum here, and other Marine Corps related events. I organized a separate, special event as the reunion coordinator. This was a personalized, Marine Corps oriented tour of the Arlington National Cemetery with our own private trams and exclusive access to off-route locations the general public doesn't see.

It's a pity that more people don't do this, as I have done for over thirty years for private groups. It is one of the most beautiful, moving, poignant and proud events you can imagine; impossible to describe. One of our purposes was to see and decorate the graves of the former 3/3 CO's all of us had at one time or another served under, and we are very well represented there.

Joe Muir, the first battalion commander, was KIA in Vietnam; Josh Dorsey, later to become the Senior Marine Advisor during my year as an advisor; Jim Marsh, a great Marine by anyone's standards; and Dutch Schultz, for whom all of the previous superlatives can be said. None of these Marines need embellishment or introduction, and they are all there in Arlington.

We were enroute to Jim Marsh's gravesite when we passed two quiet senior men in Navajo dress walking slowly on this very hot summer day. They waved politely, and I stopped the tram to offer assistance. They wanted to know the location of Ira Hayes' grave. We would be going there at our next stop after paying respects to Jim Marsh, but they preferred to walk. We carried on to Colonel Jim's gravesite (the columbarium) and spent some time there as most of us had either served with him or knew him.

Upon leaving this site, we proceeded to Ira Hayes' grave which was central between Dutch Schultz and Josh Dorsey. On arriving there we saw the two men we had passed earlier. Although they were tired from the long walk in the hot sun, it was easy for my party of two-hundred plus Marines to see that something had happened, just by looking into the faces of these old warriors. They had created an air of dignity and reverence that was thicker than armor. At first we would not disembark from the trams and go up the short hill to the grave because it was obvious that we were intruding on something solemn, something of great meaning. They had decorated the grave with stones, feathers and what looked like beads, painted sticks, etc. Seeing us there, they motioned us forward and we reluctantly, slowly approached; surrounding them and the grave. What happened next is hard to describe.

These men spoke English, somewhat imperfectly, but their meaning was clear. They knew we were Marines and were pleased that we would join them, for "it gives great honor to our brother Ira." Already my eyes were getting that familiar sting, and I wasn't alone. Then, for the next ten to twenty minutes, they went through a prayer ritual that was so beautiful, so moving and poignant, that we stood there transfixed and speechless. They picked up rocks from the headstone where they had placed them and gestured toward the sky, and then other artifacts as well. They swept their arms slowly around and over the grave while softly, respectfully incanting their prayers and singing; all in their own language. The meaning, however, came through profoundly to all of us.

By this time we - all of us - were sobbing openly, and then

the real surprise came. They began to look directly at us and ever so often we would hear "Semper Fidelis" or "Marines," and on one occasion "they look after Ira." We were all to pieces, and not the least bit ashamed. Indeed, we were damned honored that they would include us.

Like most of us I have attended more than my share of funerals, in and out of uniform, and each have been meaningful, dignified and memorable. But nothing in my entire life was like this, and all of us said so. We returned to our tram and carried on with the tour, but we were emotional basket cases. It took me weeks to recover, and the memory of that quiet, dignified moment on a lovely Arlington hillside will never leave me.

We belong to a proud Corps. I have often said that pride is the high octane fuel of the Marine Corps. If you can't be proud, you can't be a Marine. I thought about that as I stood there with those humble, respectful warriors, tears running down my cheeks, my shirt, and damn near to my shoes. Most Americans have no idea of the meaning of pride; the kind of pride that comes not from what you do, or who you are, but because you belong to something so much greater than the individual himself - our Corps. And it is this Corps that produced such men as Ira Hayes, and the two lonely warriors that came all the way from Arizona at no small expense just to pay homage to their fallen brother. God bless these wonderful Marines. They gave us Vietnam vets a dose of pride that will last a lifetime.

The preceding piece was written by Colonel John W. Ripley USMC (Ret), who was at the time Director of Marine Corps History & Museums.

IT'S MY TURN

"You've done your job, Mom. Now it is *my* turn to protect *you*." - Sergeant Byron Norwood, USMC

It was no accident when President Bush saw fit to quote two Marine NCOs during successive State of the Union addresses, because in doing so he told the American people what the <u>true</u> State of our Union was:

From 2005: "Our men and women in uniform are making sacrifices - and showing a sense of duty stronger than all fear. They know what it's like to fight house to house in a maze of streets, to wear heavy gear in the desert heat, to see a comrade killed by a roadside bomb. And those who know the costs also know the stakes. Marine Staff Sergeant Dan Clay was killed last month fighting in Fallujah. He left behind a letter to his family, but his words could just as well be addressed to every American. Here is what Dan wrote: 'I know what honor is. ... It has been an honor to protect and serve all of you. I faced death with the secure knowledge that you would not have to.... Never falter! Don't hesitate to honor and support those of us who have the honor of protecting that which is *worth* protecting.'"

From 2006: "Right now, Americans in uniform are serving at posts across the world, often taking great risks on my orders. We have given them training and equipment; and they have given us an example of idealism and character that makes every American proud. The volunteers of our military are unrelenting in battle, unwavering in loyalty, unmatched in honor and decency, and every day they're making our nation more secure. Some of our servicemen and women have survived terrible injuries, and this grateful country will do everything we can to help them recover. And we have said farewell to some very good men and women, who died for our freedom, and whose memory this nation will honor forever.

One name we honor is Marine Corps Sergeant Byron Norwood of Pflugerville, Texas, who was killed during the assault on Fallujah. His mom, Janet, sent me a letter and told me how much Byron loved being a Marine, and how proud he was to be on the front line against terror. She wrote, 'When Byron was home the last time, I said that I wanted to protect him like I had since he was born. He just hugged me and said, 'You've done your job, Mom. Now it is *my* turn to protect *you.*''

ONE OF THEIR OWN

Chief Warrant Officer Peter Zorba

"The one, absolute, unselfish friend that man can have in this selfish world, the one that never deserts him, the one that never proves ungrateful or treacherous, is his dog."
- George Graham Vest

Weather is beginning to climb up into the hundreds now. With the heat comes the dust and sandstorm season here. So many of our days are spent working and living in an orange haze of diffused sunshine, wind, heat and dust which gets everywhere and covers everything (aircraft, equipment, skin, teeth, weapons, even the food in the chow hall).

We're all glad to be at the two-month mark, though it feels more like our ninth. Hard to believe we were home at all sometimes ... that we haven't been here, doing what we do, day after day - night after night - all along. Still, morale is high, and both the Marines and the helicopters we're flying are doing well in spite of long hours and high operational tempo.

It must go hand in hand. The busier you are, the faster time goes. The faster time goes, the happier you are. Needless to say, most everyone tries to stay as busy as possible. The days are long, but the weeks are flying (no pun intended).

I want to tell you all a quick story, and if any of you know me at all... then you know I love a good story! But I think this story says something about the organization that I am a small part of here.

The last time I wrote I described the Marines, in particular the young men and women here with me that I am so proud to serve with. Many of you responded that you were touched by the knowledge, or at least depiction of those kids… those heroes, for that is what they are. But, I digress.

A couple of weeks ago I flew a night mission into Baghdad. Baghdad is a big city, and where we actually flew into, whether it would be a name you'd recognize from the news or not, doesn't really matter. Suffice to say that I fly into Baghdad almost every night, but this night's mission was a special ASR (assault support request).

A Marine K-9 had been killed and another dog wounded earlier in the day, and we were going there to pick up the dead K-9, the wounded K-9, and their Marine handlers. How these Marines were attacked, whether in contact with insurgents, a sniper or an improvised explosive device (IED), we never knew.

We took off from our base and flew through the dark, star-clustered Arabian night in an open combat spread. Radios crackled and disembodied voices rolled through my helmet. The lights of small towns scattered across the desert floor, illuminated with a green glow through my NVGs, (night vision goggles) as they passed below us and in and out of my gun sights.

At about midnight we were on short final into a small LZ with battle-scarred concrete walls, and a hardened outpost with a bullet-riddled watchtower. As we touched down, I hopped out the back of our helicopter and watched as our "Dash Two" landed about forty feet to our seven o'clock.

The LZ was dark, and no one was around. Through my NVGs I could see the Marines in the tower, and in the bunker at its base, watching us, not really thrilled to see us there, two phrogs spinning on the deck inside their perimeter. And why would they be, as we presented a wonderfully enhanced target for indirect fire (IDF) on their position. Not that they don't take IDF often enough, just that we were now an added bonus to anyone already predisposed to 'throwing' a few mortars or RPGs our way... and theirs!

We waited. Five minutes. Ten minutes. After fifteen minutes, with still no sign of anyone, or any dogs, the crew began to grow a little uneasy...

We're here, where the hell are they?"

"Goddamnit. Who the... is running this place?"

"Do you see anybody, gunner?"

"Negative, sir."

"... If we don't see anybody soon, let's get Dash Two out of here, so at least there's only one of us on the deck here in case we take incoming. You copy that (call sign)."

"Roger that. Copy all."

Just then the door of a small industrial looking building about a hundred meters away opened, and I could see Marines moving awkwardly towards us. They were carrying their rifles with their outside hands, and with the inside hand each held the edge of a body bag. Behind them followed another Marine with a shouldered rifle, MOLLIE pack, and his hands were on the back of the bag.

But this Marine's hands held the trailing edge of the body bag more like a priest would grasp a holy cloth or a child his mother's hem, not really supporting any weight, just holding on. As they loaded the body bag into our bird I took the young Marine's pack and stowed it, and then got him buckled in. The wounded K-9 and his handler were loaded into Dash Two, and I sat back down behind my .50-cal and called us clear of wires and trees as we lifted into the night sky.

Once airborne and on the go, out of the cultural lighting from over the town, I looked back to see a big Marine, head in his hands, sitting in darkness, bent over the body of his

116

dog.

That was a long flight. My pilot, a battle-hardened colonel, kept asking me "How's our boy doing?" as if he were a worried parent checking on his child. He handed me back a small package of chocolate chip cookies he'd been saving for the return to base. "Give 'em to our boy. He's had a rough day of it." I unhooked my gunner's belt and walked back to the young man. I put my hand on his shoulder, handed him the cookies and patted him on the back, smiling some compassionate, but dumb, smile there in the dark – at three hundred feet somewhere over Iraq. What else can you do?

When we touched back down at our base, the passenger/cargo terminal sent a vehicle out for the dogs. I helped the Marine with his gear, out away from our rotor arc, and then ran back up the ramp and into our bird just in time to grab one of the terminal guys as he was reaching for the body of our Marine, thinking it was just another piece of gear.

"Hey man - what the… are you doing?!" I yelled over the engine noise. "Leave him alone. We'll get him." The crew chief and I reverently bent over and gently lifted the body bag and carried it out of our plane. I had carried body bags before while here, and I was surprised by how light this one was.

I placed my arms under the dog's body and gently set him down in the vehicle. And then, out of sheer habit, I petted the poor pup on the shoulder… or maybe it was his hip. His body was still soft, even inside the thick black polyethylene bag. As I turned to head back to my plane, I was face to face with the fallen Marine's master.

The young corporal looked at me. He had seen me pet his dog, and I like to think he saw how reverently we carried his fallen comrade's body out of the plane, but maybe not. Red eyes and a sad, exhausted face were eclipsed by a smile of gratitude as he shook my hand and mouthed the words "thank you." Then he was gone, and we were back on the plane and set to lift.

Once back on our line after we had shut down, we all sat down in the back. It was quiet, and no one really spoke until the colonel asked, "Did you take care of our boy? Was he hurting too bad? Did you do right by the pup? Did we treat them both with the respect and honor they deserved?"

"Yes sir." I replied last year while we were here, the brevity code for friendly KIA was "Angels." I don't know what it is this time for OIF III, but it is a very fitting term. So I told the colonel "Yes, sir, the 'Angel' was carried with respect, and treated with dignity and compassion, as was his handler." The colonel liked this, and we all agreed that the dog was a Marine… as much as *any* of us.

But on another level, that kid had not only lost his partner, but he'd lost his dog, a dog that I am sure he loved and that loved him back. That had touched us all deep down somewhere, where you're still a kid yourself. We were proud to have been able to do what we did for this fellow Marine, this 'Angel,' and each of us would willingly do it again any time. That's what Marines do.

I guess what I am saying is we continually hear the question asked, "Why we are here?" I heard a Marine say yesterday, "Don't ask me why I am here. I don't make our country's policy, I execute policy." So I guess to me "why" is not really that important.

What *is* important is 'how' I am here. To me, this story illuminates that "how," by showing the nature of the Corps and what it is that makes Marines what they are – and, in turn, is made what it is by the Marines devoted to it and to each other.

I am part of an organization which believed it was important enough to send two helicopters and their crews into harm's way to retrieve the body of one of its fallen. It made no difference that the Marine killed in action was a dog and not a man, what *does* matter is that each one of us involved felt the same.

To us, not only was it a warranted and reasonable utilization of Marines, Marine Corps assets, and resources, but the risk to eight Marines and two aircraft was far outweighed by a pervading sense of honor, commitment and espirit de corps. Why else am I here, if not to go get a boy and his dog - both of whom are fellow Marines? Few things here have been as important as that mission to me, and to my crew as well. That's "how" we are.

Chief Warrant Officer Peter Zorba was a member of Squadron HMM-764, "The Moonlighters" when he wrote this in May of 2005.

AN AMERICAN TERM

James Kirschke

"All men are created equal – and then some become Marines."

Some years ago I was living with my family in northern Italy. While there, at a cafe, I had just finished making out a post card to a friend in California, a retired Sergeant named Vince Rios. He had served with the 5th Marines in Vietnam, where he had lost three limbs.

I had signed the postcard SEMPER FIDELIS near the end, and then underlined the words. An Italian engineer friend had noticed this, and kindly asked me if I had underlined 'Semper Fidelis' because it was a foreign term.

When I nodded, "Si," he responded, in the finest Italian demeanor, "Surely by their actions, the U.S. Marines have made 'Semper Fidelis' an *American* term," a comment which brought tears to my eyes.

The author served in Vietnam with Mike Company, 3rd Battalion 5th Marines.

120

SEMPER FIDELIS

LtCol Steve Richmond, USMC

"He died a Marine, holding his position, facing the enemy, rifle in hand. And I don't much care what he had written on his helmet." – Lieutenant Colonel Steve Richmond, USMC

I can still see the twin grooves the heels of his jungle boots made in the mud. Four friends were struggling to carry his body through the rain to the landing zone in the foothills of the Que Son Mountains. His legs dragged behind the poncho liner, while his head lolled back over the front edge, slack jawed in that peculiar open-mouthed way that only death brings. He and the others - those for whom I wrote condolence letters to families back home - have returned to my thoughts more frequently in recent times.

He wasn't a model Marine – certainly not by today's standards. He wore braided bracelets and necklaces of peace beads, and his graffiti-decorated helmet proclaimed his involvement with the black power activism prevalent at the time. I had seen him on more than one occasion at informal discipline hearings - one in particular comes to mind: He had threatened an MP at the entrance to the Freedom Hill Post Exchange compound, after that individual had objected to the ragged condition of his utilities and flak jacket - without duly regarding his locked-and-loaded M-16 and the two grenades hanging from the flak jacket.

He was almost illiterate, unable to comprehend the entries in his service record book. In the rear, he was a real handful - and when the time came to return to the bush, he was always vocal about not wanting to go back out. Going out the last

121

time he had been "short," only three weeks to go, and had complained bitterly that he should have had a rear-area job at Landing Zone Baldy for the last little bit of his tour. He probably personified the problems that most people talk about when they are discussing the degradation in discipline and morale so prevalent in the Marine Corps, and in all of the Armed Services, at the end of the Vietnam "experience."

Speaking in 1996 at the National Press Club, Secretary of the Navy John Dalton contrasted the "men he had put up with" as a naval officer during the late 1960s and 1970s with (1996's) "best military the U.S. has ever had." Echoing that refrain, a recent well-received book about the combat history of the Marine Corps speaks slightingly of the "reluctant draftees" of the Vietnam era... in 1970, in Vietnam...

That there were significant problems existing in the Marine Corps during Vietnam is irrefutable. But assuming that the blame for any of those problems falls on some invidious suspect category of enlisted Marines is absurd; the combat record of all Marines during that conflict is *not* a matter in question. More Marines were killed and wounded in Vietnam than in any other conflict in U.S. history. Whatever their garrison problems, Marines fought that dirty and bloody action for more than a decade, a sacrifice that by and large was unwelcome, and certainly unappreciated.

Although the Marine Corps made up about ten percent of the forces deployed in Vietnam, one in four names on that black granite wall in Washington under Mr. Lincoln's gaze belongs to a Marine. Uncommon Valor persisted as a common tribute.

All of these veterans deserve a better memory than the one presently in vogue - and those who may be required to lead the sons and daughters of the Vietnam generation in future combat would do well to reflect on their experience.

For now, I ask you to remember my Marine. As much as he complained, he went back out when the time came. The night the North Vietnamese hit us, he was there. When an RPG hit his hole, he did not cave. When his partner took a round and went down, he stood over him in the hole and fought it out.

It wasn't a glorious death... but he died a Marine, holding his position, facing the enemy, rifle in hand. And I don't much care what he had written on his helmet.

Lieutenant Colonel Richmond was an infantry officer, and later a Naval Aviator. While on active duty in Vietnam, he led a rifle platoon in the 1st Battalion, 26th Marines and commanded L Company, 3d Battalion, 7th Marines.

SHANGHAI STANDOFF

Jim Bennett

"Given the same amount of intelligence, timidity will do a thousand times more damage than audacity." - Karl von Clausewitz

On August 25, 1937 the world was plunging headlong into war and the United States was trying to stay out of it. Franklin D. Roosevelt was President, and the Fourth Marine Regiment was stationed in Shanghai, China. The Japanese had brutally conquered most of China, and in Shanghai only the international settlement was independent of Japanese oppression. A very good friend of mine, George Richardson, M.D., shared a letter from his father describing an incredible event on that day. The story goes like this:

On the 23rd of August, 1937, the Japanese consul general demanded of the Shanghai Municipal Counsel that the Japanese be allowed to have two additional voting seats on the counsel. This would have given them a voting majority over the American and British members, and allow the Japanese to install one of their own as Chief of Police in the International Settlement. The American chairman of the counsel refused their demands, since this would have given the Japs control over the International Settlement and annulled the Regulations of Shanghai which had been in effect since 1870. The information contained in a letter from Mr. George Green explained a state of war existed in China in all but the International Settlement. He was a member of an adhoc organization of bankers, lawyers, and insurance brokers calling themselves the 'American Troop' of the

'Shanghai Volunteer Corps' (SVC).

The only U.S. Military in the area was the 4th Marines, so the SVC patrolled around the Settlement and hoped to keep the Japanese out. On the 25th the American Troop started their 3 PM to 7 PM patrol on a well-known course where they were able to wave at friendly merchants as they traveled. Rounding a corner near the French concession, they suddenly found themselves faced with a column of Japanese with fixed bayonets marching southward, four abreast. They had already crossed the Soochow Creek Bridge that was the boundary - and there were about two thousand of them.

Since the Japanese had already crossed over the bridge, their intent was clear - to take over the police station and the International Settlement. If they were allowed to seize the settlement, it would be nearly impossible to eject them. Mr. Greene acted quickly to order the driver of his vehicle to turn broadside to the column of marching Jap soldiers and park it, and he ordered the men to dismount and fix bayonets in a line across the street to halt the procession. This they quickly did, halting the column and giving the giving the Captain time to get to a telephone and call Colonel Wilford Price, commander of the 4th Marine Regiment.

Mr. Greene then stood at the front of his troops with one other man and denied the Japanese further progress. The Japanese stopped and stood in place, evidently lacking the authority to initiate war with the Americans. The Japanese clearly had superior numbers, and could have killed every American there with one volley. The Jap Major advanced with two of his soldiers, who made threatening thrusts with their bayonets in an effort to intimidate the American volunteers. For half an hour the two combatant units faced each other at bayonet point, waiting for the inevitable crossing of the line. Finally they heard the siren of the

Marine Commander's staff car, which heralded the arrival of the U.S. Marines.

Colonel Price leaped from his car and quickly marched to the front of the volunteers and spoke to the Jap Officer. He berated him in the worst, most obscene filthy language he could muster, insulting him, his parents and the sexual orientation of the Japanese troops. The Jap Major got very red faced and said "Sir, I will have you know I speak English, and I understood every word you just said."

Colonel Price replied, "If you understand what I said, then you know what I *mean*. If you don't get your men out of my defense sector, you're going to be starting World War Two right here. Get moving. Now!"

While he was speaking, two tall burly Marines had flanked the two Jap soldiers who had been menacing Mr. Greene and his trooper. They were unarmed and stripped to the waist. Agilely grabbing the rifles of the two Japs, the two Americans then lifted them off their feet and threw them into the ranks of Japanese soldiers, where they disappeared. The two Marines then stood for a minute with their hands on their hips and glared at the Japanese as if to dare someone else to try intimidating them, before rejoined the rest of the Marines who were fast at work sand bagging machinegun emplacements.

With the arrival of the Marines, and with the thirty-six American Volunteers blocking his way to the international settlement, the Japanese Major realized he was in over his head, and ordered his troops to reverse march back across the bridge.

The Marine Colonel watched until the last Japanese soldier was across the bridge and said, "Carry on men!" to the American Volunteers. Then he remounted his staff car and left. The rest of the Marines were gone shortly after that. The

American Troop breathed a collective sigh of relief. No shots were fired, and no blood was spilled, in what had been a very dangerous confrontation. The most remarkable feature of this most remarkable event in history is those thirty-six American Volunteers - bankers, lawyers, and insurance brokers - couldn't have fired any shots, as they had not one bullet among them. They stood their ground with empty rifles against overwhelming numbers armed only with incredible courage.

THE MARINE FAMILY

Arthur Gunther

"If the Army and the Navy, ever look on Heaven's scenes, they will find the streets are guarded, by United States Marines!" – From The Marines' Hymn

You never know when the strength of a 'family' will be tested:

Imagine a family where the youngest brother is twenty-four and the oldest is actually a woman, age eighty-six.

Impossible? Not in the Marine Corps League, Rockland Detachment. The detachment held its tenth annual luncheon at the Platzl Brauhaus last week to mark, as usual, the birthday of the Marine Corps (then 226). The greeting room in this long-time Rockland lodge in Pomona was filled with one-hundred-twenty-five or so men and some women, all cheerfully offering "Happy Birthday!" as they met one another. It's the traditional greeting at the luncheon.

Gene Erickson, Frank O'Connor and Jim Davis smoothly organized the event, which, as you might expect, was a fraternal affair - with Marine veterans of service ranging from pre-World War II to the current time. On hand were Marie Bensiger, who is eighty-six years old and served with the Women Marines in World War II, and twenty-four-year-old Lance Corporal Jeb Heaney. Marie attended in her regulation dress uniform, complete with hat and shoes, which still fit her, a feat not duplicated by most of the males.

Marie Bensiger and Lance Corporal Heaney were just two of the Marine "brothers" at this moving tribute to the esprit de corps, the "Semper Fi" electricity that connects Marines of any generation or service. This year, given the September 11 attacks on the nation, Marine backs were a bit stiffer, even among those in their '70s and '80s. Dinner speeches included talk of valor by Marines and those in the Naval Militia at the World Trade Center site.

Tough Marines in the audience listening to the short, emotional, no-notes, from-the-heart remarks by those who have been working at the WTC site had tears in their eyes. Tears from those who once crawled through the hell of training down south, and from those who saw war's death and destruction, which cannot be described as horribly as they lived through it.

Especially poignant was the appearance by Patty Coughlin and Marie Anaya, whose husbands, NYPD Sergeant John Coughlin and NYFD Firefighter Calixto "Charlie" Anaya Jr., were heroes of September 11. Both were also former Marines who, before this latest war involving the nation, were usually at the annual Marine birthday luncheon.

The women were given plaques noting their husband's sacrifice, but were rendered even more than that: the standing salute of respect from the Marines.

Just a year ago, this "band of brothers," this Rockland Detachment of the Marine Corps League, could not have expected to give such a tribute. Yet the Marines then, young and old and in-between, also would not have been surprised that the call to service had yet again been sounded. That is the way the Semper Fidelis, "Always Faithful" motto, is fulfilled.

And *that* is why there are 226 years of Marine Corps history!

Originally published in *The Column Rule* on November 13, 2001

GOD BLESS THE MARINES

"Marines are different. They have a different outlook on life."

The following email was sent from a USAF Colonel who is a surgeon stationed in Iraq. It was sent to his Dad, who was a fighter pilot in Vietnam:

Dear Dad,

If I ever hear airmen griping and complaining, I jump into them pretty quickly now. Most people over here have nothing to gripe about compared to Marines. Marines are different. They have a different outlook on life.

One Marine Private was here for several days because he was a lower priority evacuation patient. He insisted on coming to attention and displaying proper military courtesy every morning when I came through on rounds. He was in a great deal of pain, and it was stressful to watch him work his way off the bed and onto his crutches. I told him he was excused and did not have to come to attention while he was a patient, and he informed me that he was a good Marine, and would "address Air Force Colonels standing on my feet, Sir." I had to turn away so he would not see the tear in my eye. He did not have "feet," because we had amputated his right leg below the knee on the first night he came in.

I asked a Marine Lance Corporal if there was anything I could get him as I was making rounds one morning. He was an above-the-knee amputation after an IED blast, and he surprised me when he asked for a trigonometry book. "You enjoy math do you?"

He replied, "Not particularly, Sir. I was never good at it, but I need to get good at it, now."

"Are you planning on going back to school?" I asked.

"No sir, I am planning on shooting artillery. I will slow an infantry platoon down with just one good leg, but I am going to get good at math and learn how to shoot artillery."

I hope he does.

I had the sad duty of standing over a young Marine Sergeant when he recovered from anesthesia - despite our best efforts there was just no way to save his left arm, and it had to come off just below the elbow.

"Can I have my arm back, sir?" he asked.

"No, we had to cut it off, we cannot re-attach it." I said.

"But, can I have my arm?" he asked again.

"You see, we had to cut it off."

He interrupted, "I know you had to cut it off, but I want it back. It must be in a bag or something, Sir."

"Why do you want it?" I asked.

"I am going to have it stuffed and use it as a club when I get back to my unit." I must have looked shocked, because he tried to comfort me, "Don't you worry now, Colonel. You did a fine job, and I hardly hurt at all; besides I scratch and shoot with my other hand anyway."

God Bless the Marines!

HEART OF AN AMERICAN

Gunnery Sergeant Mark Francis

"America is the land of the free, _because_ of the brave!" –
Tattoo on the arm of a U.S. Marine

"I just wanted to share this email with everyone. This came from Mark tonight. What an incredible story to tell. I pray that you will share this email with others to show what kind of impact our military servicemen and women are truly having in Iraq. A special thank you to Debbie Jacks, who is Mark's brother's wife's mother! She sent over several boxes of toys & stuffed animals to Mark for the Iraqi children. This little girl was holding a bear she sent. How do we know? Mark said it was an Ohio beanie baby, and she sent over lots and lots of them. So thank you very much, your simple gift easily saved the life of my husband and many other Marines. Thank you Debbie for your heart, and for children who you may never see until you see them in heaven. Read the story and you'll see why!" - Colleen Francis, wife of GySgt Mark Francis USMC

Just wanted to write to you and tell you another story about an experience we had over here.

As you know I asked for toys for the Iraqi children, and several people (Americans that support us) sent them over by the boxful. On each patrol we take through the city, we take as many toys as will fit in our pockets and hand them out as we can. The kids take the toys and run to show them off as if they were worth a million bucks. We are as friendly as we can be to everyone we see, but especially so with the kids. Most of them don't have any idea what is going on, and are completely innocent in all of this.

On one such patrol, our lead security vehicle stopped in the middle of the street. This is not normal and is very unsafe, so the following vehicles began to inquire over the radio. The lead vehicle reported a little girl sitting in the road, and said she just would not budge. The command vehicle told the lead to simply go around her and to be kind as they did so. The street was wide enough to allow this maneuver, and so they waved to her as they drove around.

As the vehicles went around her, I soon saw her sitting there and in her arms she was clutching a little bear we had handed her a few patrols back. Feeling an immediate connection to the girl, I radioed that we were going to stop. The rest of the convoy paused, and I got out the make sure she was OK. The little girl looked scared and concerned, but there was a warmth in her eyes toward me. As I knelt down to talk to her, she moved over and pointed to a mine in the road.

Immediately a cordon was set as the Marine convoy assumed a defensive posture around the site. The mine was destroyed in place.

It was the heart of an American that sent that toy. It was the heart of an American that gave that toy to that little girl. It was the heart of an American that protected that convoy from that mine. Sure she was a little Iraqi girl, and she had no knowledge of purple mountain's majesty or fruited plains. It was a heart of acceptance, of tolerance, and of peace and grace, even through the inconveniences of conflict, that saved that convoy from hitting that mine. Those attributes are what keep American hearts beating. She may have no affiliation at all with the United States, but she knows what it is to be brave, and if we can continue to support her and her new government, she will know what it is to be free. Isn't that what Americans are, the free and the brave?

If you sent over a toy or a Marine (or any U.S. service member) you took part in this. You are a reason that Iraq has to believe in a better future. Thank you so much for supporting us, and for supporting our cause over here.

Semper Fi,
GySgt Mark J. Francis

THANK *YOU*

Tom Hayden

"For those who fight for it, freedom has a flavor the protected never know." - Written on a C-ration box lid at Khe Sanh, South Vietnam, 1968

This is part of a letter from my son, Kurt, who is helping run the port in Kuwait where these young heroes arrive in the war zone and depart from months later. If this doesn't bring a tear to your eye nothing will. Where do we get such men?

I was going to the gym tonight (really just a huge tent with weights and treadmills) when I heard that one of the MEUs (Marine Expeditionary Units) that had come out of service in the "triangle" was redeploying (leaving country). We saw their convoy roll into the Kuwait Naval Base as the desert sun was setting. I have never seen anything like this. Trucks and humvees that looked like they had just come through a shredder. Their equipment was full of shrapnel blast holes, and missing entire major pieces that you could tell had been blasted by IEDs.

These kids looked bad, too! I mean sunken eyes, thin as rails, and that thousand yard stare they talk about after direct combat. Made me pretty damn embarrassed to be a "rear area warrior." All people could do was stop in their tracks and stare... and feel like me... like I wanted to bow my head in reverence.

A Marine Captain stationed with me was standing to my left, also headed to the gym. He said, "Part of 1st Brigade Combat Team, 8th Marines, sir. Took the heaviest losses of any single unit up north as part of Task Force Danger."

As the convoy rolled up, all of us who were watching just slowly crept toward these kids as they dismounted the hummers and five- tons. Of course, we were all shiny and clean compared to these warriors. These kids looked like they had just *crawled* from Iraq. I had my security badge and ID around my neck, and started to help them unload some of their duffle bags. A crusty Gunny came up to me and said "Sir, you don't have to do that..."

"Gunny... yes I do..."

They all looked like they were in high school, or younger! All held themselves sharply and with confidence, despite the extreme fatigue you could tell they had endured. "You guys out of the triangle?" I asked.

"Yes, sir. Fourteen months, and twice into the grinder, sir." (both fights for Fallujah). All I could do was throw my arm around their shoulders and say "Thanks Marine, for taking the fight to the bad guys... we love you man." I looked at these young kids, not one of them complaining or showing signs of anything but focus, and good humor.

"Sir, they got ice cream at the DFAC sir?"

"I haven't had real ice cream since we got here..."

They continued to unload... and after I had done my handshakes and shoulder hugs, the Captain and I looked at each other... they want ice cream, we'll *get* them ice cream. You see, a squid O-5 and a focused Marine O-3 can get just about anything - even if the mess is closed. Needless to say we raided the closed DFAC (mess tent), much to the chagrin of one very pissed off Mess Sergeant, and grabbed boxes of ice cream sandwiches (as many as we could carry) and hustled back to the convoy.

I felt like Santa Claus.

"Thank you sir..." again and again from each troop as we tossed up the bars to the guys in the trucks.

"Son, what the hell are you thanking *me* for...? I can't thank *you* enough..."

They are so damn young... and I will sleep well knowing they are watching my back tonight.

A SEA STORY

Ruth L. Moseley

"Sergeants think their only flaw is their excessive modesty." - An unidentified Private

Dear Andy,

My Dad was a Chief Quartermaster in the U.S. Navy. He served from 1906 to1922, and then was recalled from 1940 to 1944. This is a story we heard growing up...

Dad served on the *USS Machias*, and at some point was stationed at or served in Haiti, Nicaragua, and several other locations. I believe that this incident occurred in Haiti.

On the same ship was legendary Marine Dan Daly. He and Dad became friends, and on one occasion went on liberty together. Dan was not a drinker, but evidently Dad made up for *both* of them. That night they were late getting back to the ship, and were ordered by the Officer of the Deck to appear before the ship's Captain the next morning. Dad was terrified that this would be the end of his Navy career and that he would be a family disgrace, but Dan assured him that he would take care of the situation.

The following morning they got ready to face the Captain. Dad was shaking in his boots - and Dan was proudly wearing his TWO Medals of Honor! They faced the Captain, who lectured them on setting a good example for the younger sailors and then dismissed them. As they exited the Captain said loudly, *"That* only works *one time*, Daly!!"

OVER THERE

Kevin C. Jones

"I didn't know the Marines who died, but I miss them just the same." - Kevin C. Jones

On this Memorial Day, more than two years after the invasion of Iraq, American troops are still fighting and dying. Their deaths have become a staple of the evening news, a permanent column on the front page. Most of the time, we don't even notice anymore. Until death touches someone we know, or someone we used to be.

On the morning of January 26, while I rushed my daughters through their bowls of cereal, brushed their hair and got them ready for school, I learned that a CH-53E Super Stallion helicopter had crashed in western Iraq, killing thirty-one men. Twenty-six of them were part of my old unit: Company C, First Battalion, Third Marine Regiment, stationed at Marine Corps Base Hawaii, Kaneohe Bay.

Later, at work, I struggled to explain how surreal it was to learn that Marines from the infantry company I served with in the Persian Gulf War had been killed in this one. I sat at my desk, processing insurance claims, surrounded by gray cubicle walls instead of sandbags and dirt, behind a computer instead of a machine gun, thinking about the business card from the recruiter tucked in my wallet. He said there's a slot for me in a reserve unit if I want it, and that I'd get a chance to go overseas again, to be part of something larger and greater than myself. To go to the war. I think about what my daughters would say if I told them that I'm leaving, and that I might not come back. I also wonder how to justify it to myself if I *don't* go.

My co-worker looked over at me from his desk and said, "Did you know any of them?"

No, I didn't know them.

What I know is the base where they lived. The way they ran up "KT," Kansas Tower, this giant hill in the middle of the base, gasping all the way to the top. I know the view from the apex, overlooking the vivid blue of Kaneohe Bay, a rainbow in the background. I know how good a cool breeze felt when they reached the top, after running past the flight line, beyond the beach where their leg muscles burned and their feet sank into soft, warm sand. I know what drives a Marine, at the end of his endurance, choking back vomit as the battalion runs in a huge formation, to suddenly break ranks and run to the man carrying the Colors, the battalion flag, and take it from him, sprinting around eight hundred Marines in a giant circle before returning it and dropping back in line. I know what they smelled like when they were sweating out the beer they drank the night before.

But I didn't know them.

I know what they felt like when they were released on liberty at 1600 on a Friday afternoon. How much time it took to iron their clothes and clean up for a night out. I know how many guys can be squeezed into a subcompact car, piling on top of each other for a ride down to Waikiki Beach and Kalakaua Avenue. I know what it's like to spend an entire paycheck in forty-eight hours, buying drinks for impossibly beautiful women from all over the world who all seem to be in the same bar on the same night.

I know the feeling of being thousands of miles from home, afraid because war is coming soon, but then a girl smiles and, for a moment, everything is O.K. I know how a woman like that can make the toughest Marine feel sixteen again, kissing a girl for the first time. I know how to get all the way across the island and back to the base from Waikiki, or Honolulu, with no money and only the other guys in my platoon to help me. I know what it is to become brothers with men you never would have met in the civilian world, and to remember them for years after they're gone.

But I didn't know them.

I know what it feels like to patrol for days without sleep in Molokai, and at Schofield Barracks, and Camp Pendleton; in Okinawa, and the Philippines, and Saudi Arabia. I know the industrial claustrophobia of being on a ship, packed in with forty other Marines in a space the size of a studio apartment. The smells, the jokes, the way the surface of the helicopter flight deck cuts into your palms when you do push-ups. I know what it's like to comfort Marines when their wives or girlfriends leave them with only a note and a bogus explanation and they want answers, but there aren't any.

But I didn't know them.

I know what it's like to ride in a CH-53 helicopter. The way it shimmies as it thunders over the terrain below, a crouched panther waiting to strike, Marines in the back, heads bowed, trying to catch some sleep, never knowing when they might get another chance to rest. Marines dreaming of their families, of home.

No, I didn't know the Marines who died, but I miss them just the same. So I go to work each day, safe in my cubicle, checking the news for word of the war dead, looking for friends - and thinking about that recruiter's card in my wallet.

Kevin C. Jones served as a Marine from 1990 to 1994. This essay originally appeared in *The New York Times* on May 30, 2005.

I'M CIVILIZED NOW

MSgt Andy Bufalo USMC (Ret)

"People sleep peaceably in their beds at night only because rough men stand ready to do violence on their behalf." - George Orwell

A terrible thing happened. I woke up this morning and came to the realization that I have become civilized. It has been a slow evolution to be sure, but a steady one nonetheless. During the twenty-five years I wore the uniform of a United States Marine I learned to accept hardship and discomfort as the norm, and in a perverse way even came to *relish* it. But that is no longer the case. How do I know? Well, just consider the evidence.

"Back in the day" I drank that nasty, brownish paste which passes for coffee on the "mid-watch" aboard dozens of Navy ships, and occasionally brewed a cup of "C-Rat" coffee in my canteen cup while out in the boonies – and was *glad* for it. Now I find myself sipping lattes at Starbucks, or drinking home-brewed Columbian coffee lightened with Coffee Mate vanilla half & half. Nothing else will do!

And speaking of ships... I once sailed the Atlantic, Pacific, Mediterranean and Caribbean aboard a succession of big, gray Navy "amphib" ships while crammed into a living space the size of a coffin, and spent hours standing in the chow line just to get a hot dog or a peanut butter and jelly sandwich. To this day I can hear the sound of boatswain's whistles and "Sweepers, sweepers, man your brooms..." echoing in the back of my mind whenever I think about the experience. Now, I sail on the big *white* ships of the cruise

142

lines, where I live in a comfortable stateroom and dine on gourmet meals twenty-four hours a day (while becoming a "fat body" in the process...).

In the Corps the "head" was often a communal one where you could hold a conversation with the man sitting next to you while doing nature's business, and we all used government-issued "John Wayne" toilet paper (it's rough, it's tough, and it doesn't take crap off of anyone!) when we were finished to, well, you get the picture. Now, I use "Charmin Ultra with Aloe" in the privacy of a bathroom that's bigger than my old berthing area, and the only conversations I have while I'm in there are on the cordless phone.

And then there's the air conditioning. I live in Florida now, and the notion of a summer without it is just *unthinkable*. We all scurry from the comfort of a climate controlled home, to an air conditioned car, to a cool and comfortable office - and back again. It's hard to believe I once lay on my rack in a condemned barracks on Onslow Beach (it once housed POWs, and has since been demolished) and hoped for just *one* cool breeze to blow in through the open window, or that I spent weeks operating in the Mojave Desert during the dog days of August without giving the heat much thought.

Now I live in a comfortable house instead of an open squadbay, have a walk-in-closet instead of a wall locker, pack a set of matched suitcases instead of a seabag, and drink bottles of *cold* Corona beer (with a lime) instead of those cans of warm, rationed (two to a man!) "near beers" we once yearned for.

Instead of reveille at zero-dark-thirty, I now sleep-in until seven AM on most days. I wear 100% cotton Dockers, tailored suits and silk ties instead of camouflage and combat boots. I mindlessly surf through hundreds of cable TV channels, instead of tuning in to the Armed Forces Network. And, worst of all, I am surrounded day in and day out by a horde of civilian whiners who don't know how good they have it, when once I kept company with the finest men this nation has to offer. You know, now that I think of it, the conditions we endured were *far* worse than anything the detainees at Gitmo have been subjected to – so I don't know *what* the heck Senator Durbin has been whining about. I'm betting that if those incarcerated terrorists were transferred to Parris Island for a few days, they'd be *begging* to go back to the relative comfort of Guantanamo Bay!

As I said, I've become civilized - and I don't much like it. The good news is, I don't think it's irreversible. If I had the opportunity to trade in my suits, silk ties and 100% cotton Dockers for a set of desert cammies and an M-16, I would jump on it in a heartbeat. Deep down in the place the fictional Colonel Nathan Jessup once pointed out "we don't talk about at parties," I will always remember that I was "born on Parris Island in the land that God forgot" – and will forever be one of Gunny Highway's "life-takers and heartbreakers." That's because I believe the "hard corps" persona that my drill instructors literally pounded into me is, and will always remain, deep inside, and if my nation should call on this old jarhead to once again "strap it on," I will gladly go. Something tells me that I am far from alone in this sentiment.

I know what I have just written is true because not a day passes that I don't yearn to stuff my 782 gear into a seabag, board one of those big gray warships, and have a cup of that nasty mid-watch coffee with my brothers-in-arms as we sail into harm's way in some distant corner of the world. I just hope they have some of that vanilla half & half on board…

THROUGH MY EYES

Lance Corporal John McConnell

"And if you gaze for long into an abyss, the abyss gazes also into you." - Friedrich Nietzsche

"I attached a letter that my brother John, the one in Iraq, wrote. My brother Ben retyped it so that we wouldn't have to suffer through reading his handwriting. It makes me want to cry. It must be so hard for him day after day." - Abigail R. Jarrell

In a country marked by war, it's hard to find anything positive. Often I wake and wonder, "What do I do this for?" I mean aside from the fact that I am a United States Marine, and it's my duty. I have to do this, but what motivates me to be thousands of miles from my home? What drives me to fight for a people who are not my own? Am I really making a difference?

I have searched myself many times to find something from within; something that will re-energize my purpose.

When I joined the Marine Corps I wanted to be the best, I wanted to serve my country, and I wanted to come to Iraq. The reason I wanted to come to Iraq was because my fellow Americans were fighting, and I wanted to help. I believed in what was going on.

Some time has passed since I joined my Corps. Many changes have taken place in Iraq - plenty of them in the five months I have been here. I have seen the Iraqi National Guard begin to take more initiative in protecting their homes. I am witnessing a government evolve, and a community become much safer. The children still smile, and the old men still sneak in a thank you. The Iraqi women wave from behind their walls, and there are many other signs that Iraq is growing.

This is not always enough to keep me going. So here are some things that do keep me going; events, or thoughts that help me through each day. This is Iraq through my eyes.

A few short months ago my unit withstood the largest attack since the Battle of Fallujah. As a Marine Infantryman, otherwise known as a "grunt" or "jarhead," I was outside the walls that would usually protect the prisoners and the U.S. military men and women at Abu Ghraib Prison. It was a very insane experience. I am proud to have had a chance to fight for my country, but the story here is not the battle, but the calm after the storm.

The days after the attack were the most peaceful I have experienced. Iraq never seemed more beautiful. The camaraderie that had been formed between me and the rest of the platoon had grown stronger! Stronger in a way only battle could forge. This experience was what I had come to Iraq for. Not to shoot and be shot at, but to see peace, for I never felt so united with America as I did here in Iraq.

The single biggest reason I am here, and what keeps me going more than anything, is my family. That is what I mean when I say I fight for my country. I really mean I fight for my friends and family. I never realized how important they are to me until I came to Iraq. They have been my support, and my saints. For it is their prayers that keep me safe, and their existence that I fight for. All I do is think of them, and I feel rejuvenated. For them I fight, for them I would lay down my life.

Some ask, "What are we doing in Iraq?" For me it is the children, the children of America. So they can be assured of a world without fear. I hope the next generation doesn't have to see Iraq as I have seen it. However, this war is more about

Iraq's future than our own. Therefore we are here for the children of Iraq. I read on a wall while patrolling, "Americans, you are the reason the children are smiling. Thank you!" That one sentence could get me through my whole deployment.

If that wasn't enough, I spoke with an Iraqi child through an interpreter. The child was about eight years old, and we asked him why he wouldn't want to help the Americans find bombs? We told him that we want to make Iraq safe for him to play. He responded by saying, "That is impossible, impossible!" "For what?" we replied. The child explained that it is impossible for him to play, because Iraq is not safe enough yet.

I want that Iraqi youth, and all the other generations after him, to experience a level of peace that has been absent for over a hundred years. The children keep me going. If all this isn't enough on a hot morning in this country, I will remember this statement by an Iraqi interpreter. He said, "If America pulls out now there will be a massive civil war that will dwarf the North-South civil war of the United States." The interpreter added that he believes it is good the Americans are in his country, and he hopes we stay longer.

I am no politician, and I am no expert on war, but I love my country, and my Marine Corps. Also, my family and friends are worth sacrifice. So this is my sacrifice; I wake up in the morning, or whenever I get roused, look around and take a deep breath, because while I run around in blazing heat, my family sleeps well. That is all I care about. Sometimes I have to dig deep for motivation. Other days it comes easily. No matter what, I have to keep going - because the children of Iraq, my fellow Marines, and my family need me to push on. That is why I do what I do, because that is what I see.

FOR LOVE AND COUNTRY

Kathryn Roth-Douquet

"Marines walk up and down concrete steps that are literally stenciled with words to live by: 'honor, commitment, duty, fidelity, courage, respect.' They talk about these words, and try to live up to them." - Kathryn Roth-Douquet

My husband, a Marine, is on his second tour of duty in Iraq. This is no occasion for pity, though, which may be perplexing to some Americans. But through the eyes of a military family, this service, devotion and sacrifice makes perfect sense.

Two months ago, my husband read our children a bedtime story until the tears in his eyes blurred the page. My daughter took the book from him.

"Daddy, I'll finish it for you," seven-year-old Sophie said. When she was done, my husband, Greg, rocked her and her younger brother, Charley, and held us all for a long goodnight kiss. Then he picked up his sea bag and walked out the door - to his car, to an air base, and to a plane that carried him to Iraq.

Seventeen thousand families in southeastern North Carolina are, like mine, sending someone to Iraq this spring. The country may think of them, and especially of the ones who don't come home, as we mark another Memorial Day at wartime.

The country is divided into separate pockets, some communities shipping folks off to war, and others - like those from my pre-marriage days - witnessing the war on television, fought by strangers. For families in those other

148

ZIP codes, the military life can sound both scary and pitiable.

But there is more to our story.

True, it is wrenching for families to send the people they love to war. As Frank Schaeffer, author of *Faith of Our Sons: A Father's Wartime Diary,* says of his Marine son, "He is my heart; he is the best I have to offer."

This echoes the bumper stickers in my neighborhood that read, "Half of my heart is in Iraq." It is hard to have your heart far away, so we who stay home do welcome your support. But neither I nor the military wives with whom I regularly talk want pity, neither for what we do, nor the reasons we do it.

"What we do" is easily understood, even by those who don't live it: We are both Mommy and Daddy to little ones who may be sad or mad that a parent is gone. We keep the household together, repair washing machines and cars. We volunteer; many of us hold demanding jobs. We e-mail our husbands, assuring them all is well; we send them kids' crayon drawings and cigars, and toys for Iraqi children. Some days we're overwhelmed; other days, we pull it off.

Why we do this, however, is a little less understood. We are motivated by the same reasons for which people have put themselves at risk through history: for love and for country. The love is for our husbands, who work with skill, discipline and determination, at a real personal cost.

The love is also for their fellow Marines. To watch a unit prepare for war is to come to care about everyone in it. Stateside, I have seen the men and women in my husband's squadron live in an environment that lacks comfort and glamour, yet strive to be their best - for the sake of their lives, each other, and the success of the mission the country asks them to do.

In their home hangar, these Marines walk up and down concrete steps that are literally stenciled with words to live by: honor, commitment, duty, fidelity, courage, respect. They talk about these words, and try to live up to them. These are real people, with real flaws. But they wanted to go to Iraq and complete their missions. And they want to bring each other home.

Would I take my husband away from these men and women? No, I wouldn't. I think he and they are better off by having each other there. I am proud of them all.

The fact that we send our husbands to war for the sake of our country may confound some people, since about half of the country wouldn't send soldiers to Iraq at all. Many military wives, too, have ambivalent feelings about the current fight. But that's exactly the point. Our position on any given policy is just that - *our opinion* - and what transcends opinion and politics is our commitment to serve.

"Looking back, I would not have changed our lives one bit," says my friend Ingrid Mollahan, a twenty-six-year Marine Corps spouse beginning her eighth six-month-plus separation from her husband. "I truly believe we have made a positive contribution to the nation and the world by our service."

That's a feeling many of us share. A recent *Military Times* Media Group poll found three-quarters of those on regular active duty would re-enlist or extend their commissions tomorrow if asked. Why? Not for money, security, or even for the global war on terror. The reason for their service is the service itself. The poll called it "patriotism."

Military families make the conscious decision to be engaged in "extreme citizenship." When we are called, we will stand. We choose this life understanding that there is a constitutional role for the military. That role is not to make policy, but to respond with ability and honor when called to action by our nation's elected leaders. No one - war critic or advocate - could want the military to behave otherwise. It's called civilian control of the military, and it's a bulwark of our democracy.

I once helped to elect a president of the United States, which is admittedly a much flashier experience than being a military wife. But the sense of privilege that I felt at being part of that American pageant - from walking through the empty West Wing of the White House on inauguration day to flying on Air Force One - was no greater a feeling than the one I feel today, in a different role for my country.

In the wonderful parenting book *The Blessing of a Skinned Knee*, author Wendy Mogel argues that trying to protect our children from hurt and difficulty is a mistake. Trials, she writes, are opportunities for character development and growth. I've learned that this lesson applies to grown-ups, too. War is no skinned knee. It's hard. But for my family, I think this experience has required us to be better people.

So the odd thing is, while my family - and most military families - struggle in some ways, we gain in others for the sacrifices we make. We're hopeful that the country and the world will gain from it, too. Yes, there is a limit to how much a small group can sacrifice, and we may be close to or over that limit. But we will continue to do our best, hoping for wisdom from our leaders and fellow citizens, and waiting faithfully for our Marines to come home.

Kathryn Roth-Douquet is an attorney and former aide who served in the Clinton White House and the Department of Defense.

I LOVE THE CORPS

Colonel "Irish" Egan, USMC (Ret)

"The mere association of the word 'Marine' with a crisis is an automatic source of confidence to America, and is encouragement to all." – Colonel "Irish" Egan

The following address was given by Colonel "Irish" Egan at a Marine Corps Birthday Ball. His views are his own (although I agree with pretty much all of them!)

Ladies, gentlemen, honored guests, Marines; first of all, I must tell you that I am deeply moved and honored to have been asked to speak to the Marines and sailors of EWTGPAC tonight. It is also fitting that we celebrate with our Navy brethren; after all, we are the "boat people." The steel of the Navy-Marine Corps team has been honed in countless fights in every clime and place. In a world of unprecedented political instability, the potential for employment of the Navy and Marine Corps team is ever present. Wherever salt water can reach, in any ocean of the world - Marines and sailors are on-watch and ready. There will be no question that they are ready to do whatever needs to be done to protect our national interests, wherever they are threatened.

I also really envy this outfit working for the likes of himself: Colonel Ric West *and* Colonel Jeff Powers: two men abandoned by wolves and raised by their parents... I know that he's the type of leader who I would follow into hell itself, just to watch him make the devil dance!!!

You know, it makes no difference where we celebrate our birthday. In a grand ballroom with a close companion by our side, or in a dark, muddy fighting hole in some third-world shithole with a match stuck in an MRE chocolate death cake - the sentiment is the same. But of course, you will agree it's always a nicer event with appropriate libations.

Our gathering this evening represents that elite fraternity of citizens who has put our nation first. You have each given up your most precious commodity - your time. No one can ever give that back. By the way, there are twenty-four hours in a day, and twenty-four beers to a case - coincidence? I think not!

You each realize that our nation may perish because too few of our people know what freedom really costs. It doesn't come without sacrifice, often on the field of battle. In our history as a nation only four million Americans have earned the right to be called "Marine," and in each generation the Marines have found the few, the proud, the brave. It is this brotherhood of Marines that has stood together not only in the pride of our nation's and Corps' great victories, but also in the pain of death. The Marine Corps has been betting its honor, its mission, and the collective and individual hides of its members for more than two centuries on the premise that teenaged Marine privates who are as green as their field uniforms can be trusted absolutely to rise to the demands of their duty - at the cost, if necessary, of their lives. Think for a minute about the Iwo Jima memorial in Washington, D.C., the most famous monument of the Twentieth Century. The words inscribed in stone are 'uncommon valor was a common virtue.'" It doesn't say, "It was easy...."

As I look back, I think of how lucky we all are to be here tonight. Many of our contemporaries are not. They never got a chance to fulfill their dreams, and it is their memory, and that of countless other Marines, that we honor this evening. Despite a lot of Hollywood hoorah and hype to the contrary, the Marine Corps does not recruit in monasteries, so why are we surprised that a young Marine likes to fight, raise hell and chase members of the opposite sex?

Our secret is that we can take ordinary young Americans and teach them that if they will work together and depend upon each other totally, they can work miracles. That trust, that confidence in each other's dependability, that sure knowledge that they will come through in the crunch, is the individual Marines' sword and shield.

Marine drill instructors have always been masters of an unfailing alchemy which converts disoriented youths into proud, lean, self-reliant citizens - into whose hands our nation's most sensitive and critical affairs can be entrusted. Every one of us once shed the vestiges of civilian life and stood bewildered on the yellow footprints and wondered what the *hell* we were doing, while some maniac berated our family lineage - unless you went to boot camp in San Diego, of course, where they never raise their voices. You know, at Parris Island, when we memorized the general orders, ya had to say 'em before a match burned down, but I hear tell that in Dago they use a flashlight and wait for the batteries to run out!!!

Each generation of Marines since 1775 has faced challenges. Your generation is no exception. We Marines know when we take the oath of enlistment that the task which awaits us will not be easy.

This is indeed a difficult time for our nation and our Corps. Make no mistake; we are at war with an elusive and determined enemy. I spent my entire career fighting the evil empire, aka communism, and was very proud to do so. America won that fight against a very tough opponent. It took great effort, and many years of sustained vigilance and sacrifice by so many whose names we will never know. Your nation needs your skills now more than ever. This campaign will be long and arduous, and I know you will more than rise to the challenge. Old Osama, Saddam and their pecker-head running mates are gonna be in a world of hurt, that's for sure.

Believe it or not, you are all joined together on an extraordinary journey, the memory of which will last forever. There will be as many wonderful moments and great sea stories of who you were and what you did, the rules you broke, and the scams you pulled, as there are Marines on the morning report. Hell, let's admit it, some of us are just incident reports waiting for a date-time-group.

Do you remember telling mom and dad and family that you were enlisting, and seeing dad's eyes well up with unabashed pride, and the look of worry come over mom's face because she knows what Marines do... and where her baby will be going?

The initial silence and uneasy jokes as the bus enters the MCRD gate in the middle of the night?

The first shattering look at what used to be open squad-bays, lined up rows of locker boxes and double-deck steel cots, and side-by-side crappers because modesty is a thing of the past?

The quick flicker of time between taps and that awful sound of a metal shitcan rolling down the center of the squadbay accompanied by that awful braying of "Get up, get up and lock your body!"?

Feet aching from hours on the grinder, lickin' and stickin' and maggies drawers?

Countless pushups, and a strange new sound as real bullets pass close overhead?

The downright haunting beauty of cadence sung by unseen voices?

Corafams on liberty in a strange new town ("how didja know I was a Marine?")

Long weary hours of field days, formations, and waiting for "the word" that always changes?

The smell of the inside of a GP tent on a hot afternoon?

Lister bags and chow lines, and, "spread out, goddamnit!!"?

Long humps at night and sleeping on cold, rocky ground, foot powder, moleskin, aching blistered feet, the soft grey light of dawn mixed with cleared throats, loud farts and the wry commentary, "Come on you scroungy rat bastards, time to rise and shine and behold the beauty of another grand and glorious day in our beloved Corps!"?

Boot lieutenants who ain't even shaving yet, and company gunnies older than dirt and harder than woodpecker lips?

The whine of rotor blades and the overpowering smell of JP5. Door gunners, and .50-cals ready to rock and roll?

MREs, tabasco, and chocolate death cake?

The old slit trench, and the joys of indoor plumbing?

Understanding the pucker factor - where the more hairy the situation, the tighter your sphincter gets? The formula is: S= suction + H=hairy situation + I=interest in staying alive + T=tracers coming your way [best expressed as SHIT!].

Curious blends of monotony, tension, physical exertion and that special sort of discipline the other services can only envy.

And if all these things which we all shared, can - by some mindless logic of a witless pissant who is completely ignorant of what it's all about - be called 'just another job,' then I don't know shit from apple butter.

In all honesty, I will not tell you that every day in the Corps is great. There are certainly peaks and valleys... not being selected for a school or promotion; seeing someone else get the command that you worked so hard for; standing at attention listening to the mournful sound of taps being played at the funeral of a close friend or brother Marine; but the peaks *more* than make up for any disappointment.

Being entrusted with the mantle of command.

Knowing that what you are doing does affect the future of our nation, our Corps and your family.

Getting a Marine back on track after they step on their sword, then seeing that young Marine years later as a SNCO and knowing that you made the right call when everyone else wanted him to burn. I am not naive, and also know that wives go thru some gut wrenching feelings - mine surely has... when you dislike the Corps for what it does to us and to you... such as trips that were cancelled at the eleventh hour for what at the time seemed like such a bogus reason, missed birthdays, holidays, and late nights just waiting for us to be secured.

But that all fades into insignificance at an event such as this, when you look at the ceremony or formation and know that's your Marine out there, who represents all that is right and good with America, or the pride you feel when someone actually thanks them for being a Marine and defending our way of life, or even better when someone tells you how much your Marine has meant to their spouse!

We all know that our Corps is steeped in tradition. NCOs only need to feel the rough cloth of the "blood stripe" on their dress blue trousers, which distinguishes officers and NCOs from non-rated Marines. I must also comment that Marine officers and NCOs carry a sword for what it implies, rather than its use. You may not know that Marine NCOs are the only NCOs in any branch of the regular U.S. armed forces who still have the privilege of carrying a sword. Our shared duty is to lead, and the sword best symbolizes the warrior image.

To the NCOs here this evening, you and I share a special bond enjoyed by very few. As you can see from my bio, I once held the distinguished title of 'Sergeant of Marines.' For that and many other reasons, NCOs will always have a special place in my heart.

Tonight, then, we celebrate the "holy grail" - the birthday of our Corps... and the least I can do is fill that grail with good Irish whiskey - so come on up later and see me, lads, for a bit o' Bushmills' finest.

To the Staff NCOS, I gotta tell you that you have always been my heroes. For it was a SNCO who taught me, and everyone here, how to be a Marine. Not an easy task - but I guess it worked! We all remember the SNCO I'm talking about – he probably was our senior DI. Hell, after all these years I still remember Gunnery Sergeant R. P. Hunt, who I swear at MCRD/PISC in July-August, never broke a sweat and could make milk curdle just by looking at it. If he walked in right now, I'd just start bending and thrusting, because I owed him at least one million...

SNCOs also carry the extremely critical responsibility of serving as the vital link between the young (or old fart) officer and the enlisted Marines in their charge. It is this unspoken relationship which is the main fabric around which our Corps is woven.

To the officers, I urge you to seek command at every opportunity. There is nothing finer a man can do than to lead Marines. Never forget that a commander exists only for his Marines. Take care of them, and together there is nothing you cannot do.

Uniforms may change, nicknames change, budget and popular sentiment changes, but through it all, there is one abiding constant - the basic issue, raggedy-ass, do-or-die

Marine. He will do damn near anything asked of him, under terrible conditions, with better results and fewer complaints than any civilized non-Marine should have reason to expect. And we, who have been privileged to lead them, make plans and execute missions based more on that one abiding constant than anything else.

My God, it's a presumption so grandiose and absurd that it appears almost foolhardy, except that for 227 years it has kept the wolf away from America's door.

Let me also direct some remarks to those of you on the check-to-wife program. We each owe much of who and what we are as Marines to our biggest fan - our spouse, whose love, devotion and support is so important. Many Marines leave our Corps because of an unhappy spouse. I completely understand that spouses put up with a lot of crap, and frequently must endure uncertainty, hardships, and loneliness. You are the silent heroes, and should be honored this evening. We all laugh sometimes, and say that the only thing harder than being a Marine is being married to one - you all know it's true. As many of you know, USMC also means "Uncle Sam's Misguided Children!" We're hard to live with, and the Corps is a hard task master and fickle mistress who sooner or later will break your heart.

So to all spouses, I say - thanks for sharing your Marine with our Corps. To the rest of the beautiful ladies here this evening, I salute your good judgment in spending some time with America's finest - a United States Marine!

To my fellow retired, and Marines who are no longer on active duty, we too have an important job ahead. I have it on good authority that we have been permanently assigned to recruiting duty. Yep, we are authorized by the CMC to interact with the youth of America so that the best and brightest continue to follow our colors.

I guess that means that sea stories are authorized and, of course, they are all true! The only difference between a fairy tale and a sea story, as we all know, is one begins with "once upon a time," and the other with "this is a no-shitter!"

You know that being a Marine is serious business. We're not a social club or a fraternal organization. We don't sell cookies or magazines. We're an assemblage of "warriors" - nothing more.

We're in the ass-kicking business, and we do it the old fashioned way, up close and personal with a rifle and bayonet. The mere association of the word "Marine" with a crisis is an automatic source of confidence to America, and encouragement to all. We Marines know that we must not only be better than everyone else, but different as well... and we are! Marines walk down the street with that salty, audacious swagger that tells the world we are a roguishly handsome, cocky, conceited, self-centered, overbearing, mean, amphibious, SOB whose sole purpose in life is to perpetrate hellacious, romping, stomping, death and destruction upon the festering sores of America's enemies around the globe. We now *own* this side of the street, and just maybe we'll come over to the other side, kick your ass, and take over that one too! Are ya listening Bin Laden? And you too, Saddam insane. We are coming, and we are very pissed, and we intend to permanently close out your health record! Oooorah!

We each fought long and hard to gain the coveted title 'U.S. Marine.' On the day when we finally became Marines, in our hearts, a flame of devotion and fierce pride burned brightly. We should never do anything to extinguish that flame in our or any other Marine's heart. I urge you to keep that flame burning brightly. That flame will keep you warm when times are hard, and your motivation might falter. It will provide light on the darkest of nights. Use it, draw strength from it, keep it shining on your Marines. Keep the feeling of being a Marine alive. The feeling of your first command; the sound of a unit humping along to the eternal rhythm that only boots can make; the feeling of rebirth as the sun creeps up over the horizon and you await the order to move out. It's waiting in the darkness and solitude of night before jumping off in the attack; being packed in the throbbing belly of a helicopter or amtrac, not knowing where you are going or if it will fly or float; or gazing from the deck of a gator at night on an empty sea. It's the beauty of a crimson dawn on a lonely hilltop at the far flung reaches of the empire; the loneliness of a long deployment, and the joy of homecoming. It's the feeling you have when a Marine tells you that you have made a difference in his or her life.

I may no longer be on active duty, but by God, I still feel that way. And if *you* don't, turn in your ID card to Sergeant Major Jones and go on home.

I'd like to share some things I know, for what they're worth. They're just statements which need no explanation:

Focus on what's important, always try to do the right thing, and *do* the thing right!

Don't pole vault over mouse turds.

Trust your instincts.

If you say you will deliver... you had better be the world's best mailman.

What scares me: a major who says, "I've been thinking..."

A second lieutenant who says, "In my experience..."

A sergeant who says; "Hey sir, watch this shit..."

Learn how to listen.

Accept that some days you are the pigeon, and some days you are the statue.

Be *for* things, not *against* them.

Remember, the mind of the average lance corporal is not only crazy; it is crazier than we can imagine.

And, finally, every day we make deposits into our subordinates' memory banks. Would your check clear, or would it be returned for insufficient funds?

Through it all, I urge you - never forget how to laugh and enjoy life. I don't trust anyone who can't laugh. That's one of my basic rules. After all, being a Marine is about as much fun as you can have with your clothes on! See? Laughter is good for the soul!

While my journey through life as an active duty Marine is over - for many of you, it's just beginning. I am not sure that I could survive as a young Marine today. My page twelve certainly wouldn't support re-enlistment, *that's* for damn sure – I'd have been 6105ED and gone. Some of the stunts I have pulled and lived to tell the tale of will now get you a general court martial and a duck dinner! Guess that's why I never got a good conduct medal.

When I was young, not that I am old, all I worried about was staying alive to see one more sunrise. You have a lot tougher challenges: a smaller Marine Corps, it's tougher to stay in, slower promotions. Hell, in my day, if you could fog a mirror and hadn't murdered anyone, say, in the last week, you could re-enlist.

There ain't nothing like being on the varsity. In the parade of years, surely, adjutants call sounded only yesterday. And yet, seemingly at the double-time, an entire generation of Marines have passed in review. I, like you, once sat out in the audience and listened to an old fart colonel like myself philosophize on what being a Marine is all about (of course, now that I *are* one, colonels are a lot younger and better looking). But the message is the same: no matter where you are assigned or what MOS you carry - datadink, sparkchaser, stewburner, wiredog, buttplate, remington raider, grunt, gunbunny, rotorhead, brig rat, legal beagle, skivvie stacker, mp, boxkicker - what you do and how well you do it is important. Always remember that the destiny of our Corps depends on each of you. For each and every one of you *are* the Corps. Let us then reaffirm our commitment to those values and virtues which distinguish us as Marines.

I am very angry that there are people in this nation who feel it is inappropriate to wear a flag on their lapel because they are on the news, or in a public job or a public school, and don't want to offend foreign students. What a crock of crap. I pity the person who tries to remove the flag from *my* lapel, or that of anyone else here tonight! The Stars and Stripes are a symbol of all that we hold dear as Americans. If you have never been abroad, or in harm's way, and seen that flag flying upon your return, then you will never know the deep pride and honor one feels to see it wave.

History will judge us. Our enemies do not really understand who we are. We are the nation of Mickey Mouse, Mickey Mantle, Microsoft, Monday Night Football and the Marines. The steel of our resolve has been forged in the heat of countless battles in every clime and place. Make no mistake, we are coming... and we will destroy you and all that you stand for. Semper Fi.

NOBLE WARRIOR

Lieutenant Colonel Gregory Johnson USMC (Ret)

"When a Marine in Vietnam is wounded, surrounded, hungry, low on ammunition or water, he looks to the sky, because he knows the choppers are coming." - General Leonard F. Chapman

Glancing around at the clutter in my attic recently, I decided it was time to sort through some of the unpacked boxes associated with my military retirement and move to Pennsylvania. A fond smile crossed my face as I gingerly pulled out aging flight logbooks. As I randomly scanned the yellowing pages, I was surprised by the vivid and detailed recall the numerous sorties inscribed on those pages evoked. Aviation seems to have that effect on the mind. Locked in a trance with my memories, it was the flutter of a small newspaper clipping surrendering to gravity, as it fell from between the pages, which snapped the spell of the moment and brought me back to reality. The clipping was a one-line notice from the Navy Times announcing the death of my friend, David Cummings, during 1988. When I first cut out the obituary notice and tucked it away in my logbook, I mentally promised myself that one day I would tell the story of his heroics - in another place and time... When Dave Cummings died unexpectedly in 1988 there were the normal expressions of loss, especially for one so young. But none who first attended his lifeless body, and only a few who were present at his hometown funeral, fully realized the magnitude of his life, or the legacy he had left with the Corps.

It was December. Reconnaissance elements from a

battalion-size Viet Cong force probed the hasty defensive perimeter set up by a remote Marine observation team atop Hill 845. From afar, an OV-10 "Bronco" aircraft, responding to an urgent call from the outpost for close air support, swept in low from the south. The confines of adjacent mountain ridges, coupled with a rapidly deteriorating cloud base, made the pending interdiction strike especially hazardous. Monsoon season was well underway and, like the distant thunder, the drone of the Bronco's propellers reverberated off the trees and mountainsides, striking fear in the guerrillas (as wounded VC prisoners would later relate) while providing some semblance of comfort to the beleaguered Marines.

The Bronco pilot and his rear seat aerial observer seemed oblivious to the danger. Directed to the attack by a ground-based forward air controller (FAC), the Bronco pilot focused his attack on a shallow ravine leading into the outpost encampment. Squeezing off two Zuni rockets, he visually tracked the missiles (with a little body language) to the ravine where they exploded in a fury of smoke and fire.

The Bronco pilot immediately banked his aircraft sharply to the left to avoid flying debris. Quickly leveling his wings, he simultaneously pulled back hard on the control stick. His Bronco was now pointed straight up. Bleeding off airspeed for rapid altitude gain in an exchange of energy, the Bronco masked itself in the clouds to escape retaliatory ground fire and also to avoid collision with the mountains. In a matter of seconds, the aircraft punched through the cloud overcast. The pilot leveled off the aircraft, adjusted the throttle, and waited for a radio call to announce the results of his attack. The FAC reported that the attack was successful. Further probing by the enemy had ceased. For the time being, a second suppression attack would not be required.

During the siege on the outpost, however, the FAC reported a young Marine had tripped off an enemy booby trap and was seriously injured. Bleeding profusely, he was going into shock. The Bronco pilot was asked to relay a call for an immediate medical evacuation.

Meanwhile, at Landing Zone Baldy, Cobra pilot First Lieutenant David Cummings and his aircraft commander, Captain Roger Henry, were standing by on routine medevac escort alert in their AH-1G helicopter gunship. The rear cockpit seat of the Cobra, normally flown by the pilot in command, would today be flown by the copilot, Lieutenant Cummings, as part of his aircraft commander check ride. When the call came to escort medevac helicopters, the pilots launched with another Cobra to marry up with two CH-46 Sea Knight transport helicopters as part of a constituted medevac (medical evacuation) package. After a smooth join-up, the flight headed forty miles southwest of Da Nang into the Que Son Mountains in Quang Nam Province where they rendezvoused with the Bronco for a mission brief.

Weather at Hill 845 had deteriorated badly. Rain and lowering cloud bases made it virtually impossible for the large Sea Knights to get into the area for the pickup. Despite persistent maneuvering, the rescue flight finally retired to the edge of the weather mass where they loitered to wait for another opportunity to come in and pick up the wounded Marine.

After obtaining approval from the medevac mission commander, the agile Cobra flown by Captain Henry and Lieutenant Cummings proceeded in to scout the landing zone in order to facilitate a more expeditious evacuation. The worsening weather, however, prompted Captain Henry, positioned in the higher visibility front gunner's seat, to assume control of the aircraft's more difficult-to-use side console forward cockpit flight controls. Visibility was now practically zero.

In those days, there was a variation of a popular song theme that "only mad dogs and Englishmen ventured into noonday monsoons!" Undaunted, Captain Henry and Lieutenant Cummings pressed on despite harrowing weather conditions. The two Marines worked their Cobra up the mountainside amidst severe turbulence generated up and down gnarled mountain slopes. Scraping tree tops at airspeeds that often dipped below thirty knots, or holding in perilous zero-visibility hovers, the flyers anxiously waited for a call from the outpost giving them either a visual or sound cue that they were above the elusive, ill-defined landing zone. After three hours and five different attempts (with refueling runs interjected in-between), the aviators finally found their mark.

Sporadic radio reports confirmed to Captain Henry and Lieutenant Cummings their worst fear - the injured Marine was succumbing to his wounds. Guiding the Cobra down through tall trees, Captain Henry landed the aircraft on the edge of a bomb crater in a skillful display of airmanship. The helicopter settled to the ground amid swirling debris. The tightness of the landing zone was such that only the front half of the aircraft's skids rested on the rocky outer lip of the bomb crater. While the Cobra loitered in this precarious teeter-totter position, Lieutenant Cummings climbed out of the aircraft to investigate the situation.

Torn and bloody, the wounded Marine was drifting in and out of shock. Having served a previous tour in Vietnam as an infantry officer, Lieutenant Cummings was intimately familiar with the situation now confronting him. He had seen the haunting lurk of death in young men's eyes enough times before to know that it was time to get this Marine out immediately. Death, Lieutenant Cummings promised himself, would not visit this Marine today if he had anything to say in the matter.

With the situation assessed, Lieutenant Cummings ordered the casualty lifted into the Cobra. Strapping the semiconscious Marine into his rear cockpit seat, Lieutenant Cummings fastened the canopy shut. As "mud Marines" looked on curiously, Lieutenant Cummings climbed atop the starboard stubwing rocket pod. Straddling the pod and facing aft, Cummings banged his fist on the wing to get Captain Henry's attention before giving him a thumbs up. With a grim smile, Captain Henry nodded and took off. The cloud base, by now, was less than one hundred feet above the outpost.

As the Cobra lifted away, the radio airways snapped to life as radio operators in the vicinity broadcast descriptions of the incredible scene they were witnessing. Atop the rocket pod, Lieutenant Cummings flashed a "V" for victory to those remaining in the zone as the Cobra vanished dramatically into the blanket overcast. It was the ultimate stage exit. Marines on the ground stood and cheered. Morale soared.

Leveling off in a cloud mass at four thousand feet, Captain Henry accelerated the Cobra to one hundred knots in order to improve maneuverability. Once stabilized, he glanced over his shoulder to check on the outrider. Lieutenant Cummings flashed him back a sheepish grin. Biting rain, extreme cold at altitude, and the deafening shrill and shuffle-vibration of engines and rotors all mixed to fill his senses. He could hold on only by squeezing his thighs tightly against the rocket pod wing mount. To exacerbate matters, the wind grabbed at the back of Cummings' helmet, flexing it forward and thereby causing the chin strap to choke him. And all the while howling winds taunted him. But at their loudest, Cummings merely glanced at the wounded Marine, and howled back.

The Bronco pilot, still orbiting on patrol in his Bronco, began his return to home base as fuel began to run low. En route, he happened to catch a chance glimpse of the Cobra darting in and out of the clouds in its tenuous race against time. Zooming down for a closer look he was unprepared for the spectacle of Lieutenant Cummings, hanging outside the aircraft, and the bleeding, semiconscious Marine within. In mild disbelief, the Bronco pilot pulled up wide abeam the Cobra, gave a thumbs up and departed. "What a crazy war!" the Bronco pilot quipped to his observer while still shaking his head in disbelief. But in his heart, he knew this was the way of the warriors!

After the twenty-five minute flight through turbulent weather, the gunship descended through the clouds and broke into relatively clear sky at twelve hundred feet over a land navigation point called 'Spider Lake.' The Cobra now headed towards a medical facility. Thoroughly exhausted from the strain of the mission, Captain Henry was having trouble discerning the exact location of the medical site when he sensed a series of thumps coming from the starboard wing. Glancing to his right he saw Lieutenant Cummings, much like a prize-winning bird dog, with locked pointed finger directing his attention to their destination below.

After landing the wounded Marine was whisked into a medical triage for stabilization while Navy Corpsmen, who thought they had seen everything, helped Cummings "defrost" himself off the rocket pod. A short time later, a CH-46 Sea Knight arrived to fly the wounded Marine to Marble Mountain for emergency surgery. Sprinting along through the sky as combat escort with the Sea Knight, to the more sophisticated "in-country" medical facility, were Cummings and Henry. The two, weary from fatigue, were nevertheless vested in their interest to culminate the safe arrival of the wounded Marine. (The young Marine survived, married, and was last known to be living in Texas.)

Despite the long day and fatiguing limits they had endured, Captain Henry continued the training portion of Lieutenant Cummings' check ride on the way back to home base. Oddly enough, among senior aviators "in-country," there was talk of censure and a court-martial for the outrider affair. The act had overtones, in their opinion, of grandstanding regardless of the fact that the young Marine would have died had he not received medical attention as soon as he did. However, when Henry and Cummings were both personally invited by the Commanding General of the First Marine Division to dine as special guests in his quarters, the issue of court-martial was moot and dead on arrival. For their actions, Captain Henry and First Lieutenant Cummings were each awarded the Distinguished Flying Cross. Years later, when asked about the dining experience with the Commanding General, both pilots readily admit they *thought* they had a great time. Libations, it appears, were liberally dispensed. And it was reported to the two aviators that both had been transported horizontally into their hooches and gently tucked into their racks by the grunts!

Nineteen years later Lieutenant Colonel Dave Cummings, en route to attend a special military course in Albany, Georgia, stopped in Atlanta for the night. After a routine workout he returned to his hotel room, where he suffered an apparent heart attack and died. He was forty-two.

Although Dave Cummings' life spanned a relatively short period of time, he managed to walk a worthy journey. Among his personal military awards were four Distinguished Flying Crosses, four single-mission Air Medals, the Bronze Star with combat "V," and a Purple Heart.

In this day and age when the term 'hero' is used so loosely, it is comforting that I can say I actually have known some true ones in my lifetime. Dave Cummings was a man who set the example. He was a guy who displayed the type of courage all of us who knew him hoped we could muster if the call came. Dave Cummings was a special piece of the Corps' past, a large measure of its tradition, and maybe, more importantly, a sizeable chunk of its soul. He will not be easily forgotten. Semper Fi, Dave.

A native of Woburn, Massachusetts, Cummings enlisted in the Marine Corps during September of 1966. Upon completion of recruit training, he attended Officer Candidate School and The Basic School at Quantico, Virginia. Cummings served several months as an infantry platoon leader with the Second Battalion, First Marine Regiment in Vietnam. After being seriously wounded in a fire fight with Viet Cong forces, he was evacuated to the States. Cummings had always wanted to fly, so it was a thrill, following recuperation, when he was selected for flight training. After earning his "Wings of Gold," Dave Cummings returned to Vietnam during September 1969 to start his combat flying career.

FLYING ANGELS

Lieutenant Colonel Jacques "Jackal" Naviaux II

"We cannot pass our guardian angel's bounds; Resigned or sullen, he will hear our sighs." - Saint Augustine

Today started out like almost every other day for me since I have been in Iraq. I got up at 0400, took a cold shower, and used my headlamp to dress in the dark so as not to wake my roommates. I walked just over a mile to the squadron hangar to receive the day's flight brief. I did not have time to eat breakfast as the chow hall had not yet opened. I picked up a nutrition bar laying on my desk and a bottle of water so I could eat and drink something before I went flying, as I didn't know if I would be back before lunch or not. I grabbed my flight equipment, M-16, and my emergency assault pack and proceeded to my helicopter. We pre-flighted the aircraft, started up, and taxied for takeoff. I assumed that today's flight would be like yesterday's, and similar to the day before. Moving people and supplies from one part of Iraq to the other. We call it "Ground Hog Day," after the movie starring Bill Murray. Every day seems the same here. However, today was not like the others. Today was different. Today was real.

Our mission today was to extract Army soldiers from the field. They had been conducting operations to quell insurgent activities in their area of operations. Our Operations department had briefed us that the soldiers had been out patrolling for over two weeks. I knew the soldiers would be tired, dirty, and more than likely a little ripe! I also knew the soldiers would be very appreciative of getting a helicopter ride back to their base camp so they could get a well deserved hot meal and a shower. As a Marine, I like to give the Army a hard time. The Army seems to enjoy giving it right back at me. This is just good-natured professional rivalry. Every service likes to think they are the toughest, smartest, and best-looking troops in the world. I was looking forward to making a few pointed remarks to my fellow warriors over the intercom system and listening to their replies. However, I never got the chance.

Our mission was changed while enroute. The extract was cancelled. Instead, we were to land at their base camp and pick up five "Angels." An "Angel" is the brevity code we use to describe the deceased. Instead of picking up hungry and tired soldiers, we now were going to be flying out the same soldiers who were just recently sharing a laugh with their friends. The five Angels were carefully loaded on our aircraft one at a time. The Commanding Officer of the unit we were supporting helped load the Angels himself. He walked past the cockpit, and reached out his hand, as the senior pilot gave the Commanding Officer his hand in return. A quick squeeze of the hand, between two strangers, and two different services, over individuals we Marines never had the pleasure to meet. However, in that quick instant, the Army and the Marines Corps were one in the same. Fellow warriors had died! The simple squeeze of the hand between the two officers let the Army know we "understood" their sorrow.

After the Angels were loaded, we completed our Take-off Checklist and began our departure from the camp. The unit stood at attention, over fifty rigid soldiers, saluting their fallen comrades as we exited the landing zone. I would be lying if I told you I did not shed a tear as I transitioned to forward flight. The Army was paying its last respects to their friends and brothers in arms. I was honored to have been a witness to this magnificent display of devotion. It is this dedication, commitment, and brotherhood, which make me proud to serve in our Armed Forces. Though the five Angels on our aircraft will never know it, they were sent off with dignity and honor. However, something tells me they do know!

Lieutenant Colonel Jacques "Jackal" Naviaux II was the Commanding Officer of HMM-764 in Al Asad, Iraq at the time this was written.

CAMOUFLAGE DISCIPLINE

Bill R. Whisenaut

"Remember, God provides the best camouflage several hours out of every twenty-four." – Colonel David M. Shoup USMC

This story took place in 1969 during Operation Kentucky, which was a sweep by the 3rd Marine Division aimed at preventing the enemy from infiltrating the DMZ through central Quang Tri Province:

We were crossing a rice paddy in the LZ, up to our ankles and beyond in the 'goo' that is a paddy, when my platoon commander turned to me and said that I needed to camouflage myself when we got past the last dike. I told the lieutenant that I was six-foot-six, had a ten-foot antenna on my back, was in the middle of an open field, and asked what difference a bunch of twigs stuck in my helmet would do to keep me from being less obvious than I already was. He insisted on being a lieutenant, however, and ordered me to camouflage anyway.

When we got through the paddy I passed by a large leafed tropical plant. The leaves were as large as I was, so the idea came to me to cut one of the leafs off the plant, cut two eye-holes in it, and put the stalk of the leaf in the rubber band that most of us had on our helmets to put our cigarettes and pencils and whatever in. I did all of this as we were continuing to go through the jungle, with the lieutenant still in front of me.

I pulled out my pistol, and with it in one hand and my K-bar in the other began to act as if I were sneaking along behind the officer. I would suddenly turn to an imaginary enemy and make motions with the pistol and K-bar from behind this large leaf. I waited for the moment that the lieutenant would turn around to see me, and that moment came when the men's laughter behind me became so obvious that he had to turn to see what was so funny.

When he did turn we made eye contact, and from his view it was a pair of eyes behind a large leaf with a pistol in one hand and a K-bar in the other. I could tell by his look that he wanted very much to burst out laughing, but he did not and said, "Whiznuts," which is what he called me instead of my real name, "I thought that I told you to camouflage!"

I screamed from behind the leaf from my eye holes, "Sir, you mean you can *see* me, Sir? I *am* camouflage!" The officer never broke into the laughter that I believe would have broken most men, and turned back away from me to continue on the trail. I walked for several more yards behind him, and finally grew tired of the game I was playing and threw the leaf beside the trail and continued on that mission.

Never again during our tour of duty did the lieutenant ask me to camouflage.

A PROPER EULOGY

Tim DeWolf

"God is Irish... if not, why do so many refer to his son as 'O'Jesus.' As in... O'Jesus, what have I done now?"

A young Army Sergeant (and former Marine Corporal) died recently in a car crash. He was held in high esteem by his Army troops because of his Marine background. He was a good Marine, and proud of his father – who was a Recon Marine in Vietnam. The following was written by another Vietnam Recon Marine. Sergeant Richard Febbi was twenty-five years old.

Sergeant Richard Matthew Febbi was laid to rest July 12, 2005 less than a mile from the house he grew up in. He rests a few hundred yards from his high school, his church, the fire station he served, and where his mother now resides. Richie was a USMC veteran, and was on active duty in the U.S. Army.

The gathering included veterans of the Army, Marines, Air Force, Navy, Fire Department, Police Department and friends from all generations. Richie's high school class was there, aunts, uncles, friends and just folks who wanted to say 'thanks' or 'goodbye.' The Honor Guard at the casket included USMC, U.S. Army and Fire Department members in dress uniforms. His escort included the same services - a spirit of cooperation between the units that Richie had devoted his life to.

The funeral procession took place on a Butler fire truck and before the church services Richie had a last tour of the places where he grew up. He was escorted by nine motorcycles from the Leathernecks Motorcycle Club of New Jersey, two fire trucks, and three police cars. He also had the pleasure of seeing his mother and father walk arm-in-arm to his grave site - something not many us would have thought we would *ever* see.

The Leathernecks MC presented the father, Sergeant Matt Febbi USMC (Ret), a picture of the flag raising at Iwo Jima. The bottom of the picture had sand collected from this most solemn place in Marine Corps history. Also presented was a small flag which had been raised on the original Iwo Jima site, and a small vial of "Black Sand - Red Blood" from the beach just below Mount Suribachi. Matt accepted with dignity.

At the close of the graveside services a small Irish ceremony was held. It is the belief of the McCuskey Clan of County Tyrone that it is easier to enter heaven if:

You are Irish.

You have the smell of good Irish Whiskey upon your breath.

Your friends are smiling.

You have a joke for St. Peter, and...

This preparation takes place under the watchful eye of the "fairies and elves of the woodland, the leprechauns, the Irish of all generations, and the watchful and reverent eye of St. Patrick. I pronounced all present Irish, as I was the senior member of the McCuskey Clan present.

We opened a quart of twelve-year-old Tullamore Dew, and Corporal J. R. Morgan USMC and I passed about libation for the family and friends. We had a toast, and J.R. offered Richie his "taste" in front of the assembled friends. Jane was presented the empty bottle, and advised that should she or Matt ever come here to have a serious discussion with Riche she must bring that bottle to remind him of his Irish duty.

We then adjourned to tell stories and laugh so that when St. Patrick and St. Peter looked down they would see that Richie had done his Irish duty and left us smiling.

WHEN HILLARY TRIED TO JOIN THE CORPS

"The American people are tired of liars and people who pretend to be something they're not." - Hillary Clinton

USA Today's report on Senator Hillary Clinton's newfound appeal as a possible commander-in-chief omitted a key part of her resume which proves she's *long* been a hawk on military and defense issues: her attempt to join the Marines thirty years ago. Or at least that's what she claimed.

Seated beside her husband, the former first lady recounted her military experience during a 1994 TV interview.

"Gee, now it was probably nineteen years ago - in 1975," Mrs. Clinton recalled. "I decided that I was very interested in having some experience in serving in some capacity in the military."

"Because we all love the military so much," Mr. Clinton interjected helpfully.

Hillary resumed: "So I walked into our local recruiting office, and I think it was just my bad luck that the person who happened to be there on duty could not have been older than twenty-one. He was in perfect physical shape."

She remembered telling the recruiter, "I wanted to explore - I didn't know whether I thought active duty would be a good idea, reserve, you know, maybe National Guard, something along those lines."

But Hillary's bid to become a leatherneck soon came unraveled.

"This young man looked at me and he said, 'How old are you?'" she recalled.

"I said, 'Well, twenty-seven'... I had these really thick glasses on."

"He said, 'How bad's your eyesight?'"

"I said, 'It's pretty bad.'"

"And he said, 'How bad?'"

"So I told him."

"He said, 'That's pretty bad.'"

"And he finally said to me, 'You're too old. You can't see. And you're a woman.' And then he went on... this man, young man, was a Marine."

"He said, 'But maybe the dogs [Army] would take you.'"

"This was not a very encouraging conversation," Mrs. Clinton recalled thinking. "So maybe I'll look for another way to serve my country."

The original transcript of Hillary's "I-tried-to-join-the-Marines" interview has vanished from the *LexisNexis* archives, but excerpts from a rebroadcast of Rush Limbaugh's old TV show are still available.

IWO JIMA

If Covered By Media Today...

Senator Zell Miller

"My only regret with Timothy McVeigh is he did not go to the *New York Times* building." - Ann Coulter

The American news media is supposed to be objective and report the news as it happens, but in recent years they have taken to editorializing, embellishing, and 'spinning' coverage to fit their own political agenda. This fictionalized version illustrates the bias of today's mainstream media perfectly:

What if today's reporters had covered the Marines landing on Iwo Jima, a small island in the far away Pacific Ocean, in the same way they're covering the war in Iraq? Here's how it might have looked:

DAY 1

With the aid of satellite technology, Cutie Cudley interviews Marine PFC John Doe, who earlier came ashore with 30,000 other Marines.

Cutie: "John, we have been told by the administration that this island has great strategic importance because if you're successful, it could become a fueling stop for our bombers on the way to Japan. But, as you know, we can't be sure this is the truth. What do you think?"

PFC Doe: "Well, I've been pinned down by enemy fire almost ever since I got here, and have had a couple of buddies killed right beside me. I'm a Marine, and I go where they send me. One thing's for sure, they are putting up a fight not to give up this island."

Cutie: "Our military analysts tell us that the Japanese are holed up in caves and miles of connecting tunnels they've built over the years. How will you ever get them out?"

PFC Doe: "With flame throwers, ma'am."

Cutie (incredulously): "Flame throwers? You'll burn them alive?"

PFC Doe: "Yes ma'am, we'll fry their asses. Excuse me, I shouldn't have said that on TV."

Cutie (audible gasp): "How horrible!"

PFC Doe (obviously wanting to move on): "We're at war ma'am."

A Marine sergeant watching nearby yells, "Ask her what does she want us to do? Sing to them, 'Come out, come out, wherever you are. Pretty please!'"

Cutie: "PFC Doe, what's that mountain in the background? Is that the one they say is impregnable?"

PFC Doe: "I don't know what that word means, ma'am, but that's Mt. Suribachi, and we're going to put a flag right up on top of it just as soon as we can. I gotta go."

Cutie to camera: "No one has yet really confirmed why this particular battle in this particular place is even being waged. Already, on the first day, at least five hundred Marines have been killed and a thousand wounded. For this? (Camera pans to a map with a speck of an island in the Pacific. Then a close-up of nothing but black volcanic ash). For this?" (Cutie's sweet voice becomes more strident as it fades out.)

DAY 2

At seven AM, Cutie's morning show opens with a shot of hundreds of dead bodies bobbing in the water's edge. Others are piled on top of each other on shore. After a few seconds, one can see Marines digging graves to bury the dead.

Cutie: "There is no way the Marines could have expected this. Someone got it all wrong. No one predicted this. This has been a horrible twenty-four hours for our country. This is simply a slaughterhouse. After all this fighting, Marines control only about a mile and a half of beach, and the casualties are now over 3,500 and rising rapidly. We'd like to know what you think. Call the number on the bottom of the screen. Give us your opinions on these three questions:

1. Were the Marines properly trained?
2. Is this 'nothing of an island' worth all these lives?
3. Has the President once again misled the American people?

"After the break we'll ask our own Democratic and Republican analysts, both shouting at the same time of course, what they have to say about all this. It should make for a very shrill, provocative morning. But before we leave this horrible - some will say needless - scene, let us give you one more look at this Godforsaken place where these young Americans are dying. Volcanic ash, cold, wet miserable Marines just thankful to be alive. And still no flag on that mountain as we had been promised. Things have gone from bad to worse in this obviously misguided military operation. One thing is certain, there should be and there will be a high-partisan - make that *bi*-partisan - congressional inquiry into this."

DAY 3

Cutie: "Marines continue to be locked in a life-or-death struggle over this worthless piece of real estate in the middle of the Pacific. The word 'quagmire' is being used in the U.S.

Senate, a body very familiar with quagmires. Senator Blowhard has called it 'a colossal military blunder.' And Senator Bombast maintains it was a fraudulent scheme hatched while the President was on his sixth vacation at the Little White House in Georgia.

The recently organized Senate Squeakers Group may ask for the president to resign. They maintain that politics should not stop at the waters edge in times of war, calling that tradition an old-fashioned idea that has no place in the new century of dysfunctional government. Over forty special-interest groups concurred, and all issued identical news releases.

We now turn to our political analyst, James Crankville."

(James): "Cutie, the overnight poll numbers have hit this President right between the eyes. Nationwide, an overwhelming ninety-eight percent said that if possible, they would like to see this country fight a war without a single American casualty. That is nearly the same percentage we saw three days ago when the American public said they would be in favor of going to war if we could win without firing a shot. So, you can see there is a trend developing here that spells trouble for this administration.

That this President is going ahead with this war is just unbelievable. The witty *New York Times* columnist, Myscream Loud, wrote in her inimitable fashion that 'The President's policy is as crippled as his legs.' (giggle) Last week she said he had reached the point where no one will 'Fala' him. F-A-L-A, his dog, get it (more giggles)? Has that woman got a way with words! You go, girl!"

DAY 4

Cutie: (holds up front page of *The New York Times*): "This morning, the *New York Times* had this photo on the front page. As you can see, the Marines have finally raised a flag on Mt. Suribachi on Iwo Jima. The fighting is still going on, but it looks like this battle is over. We tried to find PFC Doe, the young Marine I interviewed that terrible first day, but he was unavailable. Here is Corporal Smith though." (With girlish enthusiasm). "Well, we see that flag flying. It's pretty much over isn't it?"

Cpl. Smith: "Oh, no ma'am, it's not over by any means. We've got weeks of fighting and dying to go yet. This place is a long ways from being secured. But we did get that flag up there, and it sure makes us all proud."

Cutie: "I can't tell much from the photo. Their faces are not even visible, making it impossible for us to descend upon any of their families. Corporal Smith, do you know any of the flag raisers? And do you know who ordered it put up there? Did the order come directly from the President for political reasons?"

Cpl. Smith: "All I know is that I heard some colonel put the word out that he wanted 'a flag put up there where every son of a bitch on this island could see it.' Excuse me, ma'am."

Cutie: "We know you've been in the heat of battle so..."

Cpl. Smith: "Still am, ma'am."

Cutie: "Yes, of course, but it's all over. (nervous giggle). Except on Capitol Hill, of course. Corporal Smith, I wonder if you know the gender, race and ethnicity of the group that put the flag up. In other words, did that group 'look like America?'"

Cpl. Smith: "Look like America? They are Americans, ma'am. United States Marines."

Cutie: "Any females?"

Cpl. Smith: "No, ma'am."

Cutie: "Any African Americans?"

Cpl. Smith: "I don't know, ma'am. But there *is* an Indian in Easy Company."

Cutie: "You mean 'Native American'?"

Cpl. Smith: "Whatever, ma'am, I've got to cut out. My outfit is moving on, and we've got a lot to do."

Cutie: "And we've got a lot to do here too. Spring training has started, and the sun is shining brightly in Florida. But first this word from our sponsors."

Historical note: In one of the bloodiest battles of World War II, when it was said "uncommon courage was a common virtue," 6,000 Marines were killed and 18,000 wounded. Some 21,000 Japanese were killed. The island itself is still barren, and only a handful of people live on it. But after it was secured by the Marines, B-29s made over 2,200 emergency landings on it, saving the lives of more than 24,000 crewmen. AP photographer Joe Rosenthal won a Pulitzer Prize for the flag-raising photo. Of the six men in the photo, three were buried in that black volcanic ash, and one came out on a stretcher. Only two walked off the island.

MIGHTIER THAN THE PEN

Matt Pottinger

"Whoever said 'the pen is mightier than the sword' obviously never encountered automatic weapons." - General Douglas MacArthur

When people ask why I recently left *The Wall Street Journal* to join the Marines, I usually have a short answer. It felt like the time had come to stop reporting events and get more directly involved. But that's not the whole answer, and how I got to this point wasn't a straight line.

It's a cliché that you appreciate your own country more when you live abroad, but it happens to be true. Living in China for the last seven years, I've seen that country take a giant leap from a struggling Third World country into a true world power. For many people it still comes as a surprise to learn that China is chasing Japan as the second-largest economy on the globe, and could soon own a trillion dollars of American debt.

But living in China also shows you what a non-democratic country can do to its citizens. I've seen protesters tackled and beaten by plainclothes police in Tiananmen Square, and I've been videotaped by government agents while I was talking to a source. I've been arrested and forced to flush my notes down a toilet to keep the police from getting them, and I've been punched in the face in a Beijing Starbucks by a government goon who was trying to keep me from investigating a Chinese company's sale of nuclear fuel to other countries.

When you live abroad long enough, you come to understand that governments that behave this way are not the exception, but the rule. They feel alien to us, but from the viewpoint of the world's population, *we* are the aliens, not them. That makes you think about protecting your country no matter who you are, or what you're doing. What impresses you most, when you don't have them day to day, are the institutions which distinguish the U.S. like the separation of powers, a free press, the right to vote, and a culture which values civic duty and service, to name but a few.

I'm not an uncritical, 'rah-rah' American. Living abroad has sharpened my view of what's wrong with my country, too. It's obvious that we need to reinvent ourselves in various ways, but we should also be allowed to do it from within, not according to someone else's dictates.

But why the Marines?

A year ago, I was at my sister's house using her husband's laptop when I came across a video of an American in Iraq being beheaded by Abu Musab al-Zarqawi. The details are beyond description here; let's just say it was obscene. At first I admit I felt a touch of the terror they wanted me to feel, but then I felt the anger they didn't. We often talk about how our policies are radicalizing young men in the Middle East to become our enemies, but rarely do we talk about how their actions are radicalizing *us*. In a brief moment of revulsion, sitting there in that living room, I became their blowback.

Of course, a single emotional moment does not justify a career change, and that's not what happened to me. The next day I went to lunch at the Council on Foreign Relations where I happened to meet a Marine Corps colonel who'd just come back from Iraq. He gave me a no-nonsense assessment of what was happening there, but what got to me most was his description of how the Marines behaved and how they looked after each other in a hostile world. That struck me as a metaphor for how America should be in the world at large, and it also appealed to me on a personal level. At one point I said half-jokingly that, being thirty-one years old, it was a shame I was too old to serve. He sat back for a second and said, "I think I've still gotcha."

The next morning I found myself roaming around the belly of the *USS Intrepid*, a World War II aircraft carrier museum moored a few blocks from Times Square, looking for a Marine recruiting station and thinking I'd probably lost my marbles. The officer-selection officer wasn't impressed with my age, my Chinese language abilities or the fact that I worked for one of the great newspapers of the world. His only question was, "How's your endurance?"

Well, I can sit at my desk for twelve hours straight. Fourteen if I have a bag of Reese's. He said if I wanted a shot at this I'd have to ace the physical fitness test, where a perfect score consisted of twenty pull-ups, one hundred crunches in two minutes, and a three-mile run in eighteen minutes. Essentially he was telling me to pack it in and go home. After assuring him I didn't have a criminal record or any tattoos, either of which would have required yet another waiver (my age already required the first), I took an application and went back to China.

Then came the Asian tsunami last December. I was scrambled to Thailand, where thousands of people had died in the wave. After days in the midst of the devastation, I pulled back to Thailand's Utapao Air Force Base, at one time a U.S. staging area for bombing runs over Hanoi, to write a story on the U.S.-led relief efforts. The abandoned base was now bustling with air traffic and military personnel, and the man in charge was a Marine.

Warfare and relief efforts, as it turns out, involve many skills in common. In both cases it's 80% preparation and logistics, and only a small percent of actual battle. What these guys were doing was the same thing they did in a war zone, except now the tip of the spear wasn't weapons, but food, water and medicine. It was a major operation to save people's lives, and it was clear that no other country in the world could do what they were doing. Once again I was bumping into the U.S. Marines, and once again I was impressed.

The day before I left Thailand I decided to do my first physical training and see what happened. I started running and was winded in five minutes. The air quality in downtown Bangkok didn't help, but the biggest problem was me. I ducked into Lumpini Park in the heart of the city where I was chased around by a three-foot monitor lizard that ran faster than I did. At one point I found a playground jungle gym and managed to do half a pull-up. That's all.

I got back to Beijing and started running several days a week. Along the way I met a Marine who was studying in Beijing on a fellowship, and started training with him. Pretty soon I filled out the application I'd taken from New York, got letters of recommendation from old professors and mentors, and received a letter from a senior Marine officer who took a leap of faith on my behalf.

I made a quick trip back to New York in April to take a preliminary physical fitness test with the recruitment officer at the *USS Intrepid*. By then I could do thirteen pull-ups, all my crunches, and a three-mile run along the West Side Highway in a little under twenty-one minutes, all in all a mediocre performance that was barely passable. When I was done, the officer told me to wipe the foam off my mouth, but I did him one better and puked all over the tarmac. He liked that a *lot*. That's when we both knew I was going for it.

Friends ask if I worry about going from a life of

independent thought and action to a life of hierarchy and teamwork. At the moment, I find that appealing because it means being part of something bigger than I am. As for how different it's going to be, that, too, has its appeal because it's the opposite of what I've been doing up to now. Why should I do something that's a "natural fit" with what I already do? Why shouldn't I try to expand myself?

In a way, I see the Marines as a microcosm of America at its best. Their focus isn't on weapons and tactics, but on leadership. That's the whole point of the Marines. They care about each other in good times and bad, they've always had to fight for their existence - even Harry Truman saw them as nothing more than the "Navy's police force" - and they have the strength of their traditions. Their future, like the country's, is worth fighting for. I hope to be part of the effort.

Mr. Pottinger, until recently a Journal correspondent in China, was eventually commissioned as a second lieutenant. His essay originally appeared in the Wall Street Journal on December 15, 2005.

HEROIC DESERTER

"True heroism isn't a matter of chance. It's a matter of choice!" – Peter Lemmon

The story of Jack Lucas stands in stark contrast to the ones being covered by the mainstream media of today. A perfect example is the case of Jeremy Hinzman, who joined the <u>all-volunteer</u> Army in 2001 and suddenly decided to become a "conscientious objector" after the 9-11 attacks made it clear we would be going to war. I guess joining the peacetime military seemed like an easy way to pick up a paycheck. I think the truth of the matter is most of the so-called 'conscientious objectors' out there like Hinzman don't so much object to the idea of killing another human being, as they do to putting themselves in a situation where they themselves could get killed. Why not just be honest and say "I'm scared," instead of pretending to have lofty ideals? He is simply a coward who should quit making excuses from his adopted home in Canada and face the music – because people like him don't belong on the same PLANET with men like Jack Lucas!

Private First Class Jack Lucas earned the Medal of Honor during the Iwo Jima campaign for unhesitatingly hurling himself over his comrades and upon one enemy grenade, and then pulling another one under himself – and absorbing the two explosions with his own body. But there is a lot more to his story.

Jacklyn Harrell Lucas was born in Plymouth, North Carolina on 14 February, 1928 and attended high school in nearby Salemburg, where he was captain of the football team. He was an all-around sportsman, also taking part in baseball, softball, basketball, boxing, wrestling, horseback riding, trap and skeet shooting, and hunting.

Although only fourteen years of age and standing just five feet, five and one half inches tall and weighing 158 pounds, he enlisted in the Marine Corps Reserve with his mother's consent on 6 August, 1942. He gave his age as seventeen, and went to Parris Island, South Carolina, for recruit training.

During rifle training Private Lucas qualified as a sharpshooter. He was next assigned to the Marine Barracks at U.S. Naval Air Station, Jacksonville, Florida. In June of 1943 he was transferred to the 21st Replacement Battalion at New River, North Carolina, and one month later he went to the 25th Replacement Battalion, where he successfully completed schooling which qualified him as a heavy machine gun crewman.

He left the United States on 4 November, 1943 and the following month joined the 6th Base Depot of the V Amphibious Corps at Pearl Harbor, Hawaii. He was advanced to private first class in January of 1944. With statements to his buddies that he was going to join a combat organization, PFC Lucas walked out of camp on 10 January 1945, wearing a khaki uniform and carrying his dungarees and field shoes in a roll under his arm. He was declared absent without leave (AWOL) when he failed to return that night, and a month later when there was still no sign of him he was declared a "deserter" - and a reward was offered for his apprehension. He was also reduced to the rank of private at that time.

Lucas then stowed away aboard the *USS Deuel,* which was transporting units of the 5th Marine Division into combat. He surrendered to the senior troop officer present on

8 February dressed in neat, clean dungarees. He was allowed to remain, and shortly afterward was transferred to Headquarters Company, 5th Marine Division. Private Lucas also reached his seventeenth birthday while at sea, six days before he earned the Medal of Honor.

On the day following the landing at Iwo Jima, he was creeping through a twisting ravine with the three other men of his rifle team when the Japanese opened a hand grenade attack on them. The men jumped into two shallow fighting holes. A grenade landed in Private Lucas' hole, and he threw his body over it. Another one came hurtling in, and he reached out and pulled it beneath himself shortly before the explosion occurred, which lifted him off the ground and blew parts of his clothing into the air.

Private First Class Jack Lucas, the youngest Marine ever to receive the nation's highest military decoration, was presented the award by President Harry S. Truman at the White House on Friday, 5 October 1945. Although left for dead, he was miraculously still alive. Severely wounded in the right arm and wrist, right leg, thigh, and chest, Private Lucas had undoubtedly saved his companions from serious injury and probable death.

Lucas was evacuated and treated at various field hospitals prior to his arrival at San Francisco, California on 28 March 1945, and the mark of desertion was removed from his record in August of that year while he was a patient at the U.S. Naval Hospital at Charleston, South Carolina. He was then discharged from the Marine Corps Reserve on 18 September, 1945 because of disability resulting from his wounds - following his reappointment to the rank of private first class. Some deserter!

Jack Lucas died of leukemia on 5 June 2008 at the age of eighty.

YOU JUST MIGHT BE...

Kolette Abell

"If forty-five years of a full life never presented a prouder moment than watching your son confidently march across the parade deck on graduation day at Parris Island or San Diego... then you are *definitely* the very proud parent of a U. S. Marine." - Kolette Abell

If you find yourself peeking around the corner before you turn down your street checking that no military vehicles are parked in your driveway, and if you have nightmares about people wearing royal blue pants with a red stripe ringing your doorbell... you just might be the parent of a Marine serving in a combat zone.

If you put out your flag every day and find yourself wanting to rip the face off anyone who disrespects that symbol of our freedom... you just might be the parent of a U. S. Marine.

If you feel guilty for wishing your son would get 'injured just a *little* bit' because that would mean he would be safe and comfortable in a hospital for a few weeks... you might be the parent of a deployed Marine.

If you get really mad at the ignorant idiots who insist that all this fighting is just not necessary, and that the world would be at peace if the U.S. would just mind its own business... you just might be the parent of a U. S. Marine whose life is on the line to protect the freedoms these thankless bums take for granted.

If you negotiate with God every night before bed and the first thing every morning that if he will just bring your son or daughter home safe, you will do absolutely anything... then you are the parent of a Marine stationed in Iraq or Afghanistan.

If you deliberately keep yourself very busy every minute of every day for the sole purpose of distracting yourself from thinking that at that very moment someone somewhere on the other side of the planet is shooting at your child... you just might have a Marine in a combat zone.

If your shopping cart contains tuna fish, beef jerky, foot powder, Chapstick, playing cards, disposable shavers, car magazines, a pre-paid phone card and small children's toys... you just might be the parent of a Marine who is spending a lot of his time patrolling the streets of Iraq.

If your son is halfway around the world fighting in 120-degree heat with fifty pounds of equipment on his back to preserve our country's freedom while your neighbor's smartass twenty-year-old mouths off about our stupid military and you find you have to restrain yourself from slapping the crap out of him... you must be the parent of a U. S. Marine.

If you feel like an extraordinarily good mother because you know that you would sell your very soul, right now, to buy just one hug from your deployed Marine... know that you are actually only the average Marine Mom.

If you get calls at 3:00 AM and barely recognize the voice of the child you raised between his satellite-delayed comments and then can't get back to sleep because you can't stop analyzing every word he said and kicking yourself for forgetting the things you tried to remember to ask... you are the parent of a U. S. Marine who is far from home.

If you have memories of a tough, but precious little boy with a dirt-smeared face who idolized He-Man, always had a 'sword' in his belt, and a plastic knife in his boot and later played hockey or football (and definitely paintball), but who now has a very pretty girlfriend... you just might have raised a U. S. Marine.

If you are someone who hasn't penned a hand-written letter since the day email was invented, but now cranks them out daily... you just might be the parent of an active duty U. S. Marine.

If your vehicle displays a yellow ribbon *and* a red, white and blue ribbon, a USMC magnet, a blue star, a "Marine Mom" license plate holder and an American flag sticker... you are a proud mother of a U. S. Marine.

If you find yourself shamelessly, repeatedly, asking your friends and family to please send cards and packages to your child... you are the parent of a deployed Marine.

If you have never felt more heavy-hearted (and somehow guilty) at a wake than you did at the one you just attended for a handsome young man whose solitary portrait sat near his flag-draped casket... then your Marine may have just lost a good buddy.

If forty-five years of a full life never presented a prouder moment than watching your son confidently march across the parade deck on graduation day at Parris Island or San Diego... then you are *definitely* the very proud parent of a U. S. Marine.

Kolette is the proud mom of Corporal Brian Abell, who was serving in Iraq with WPNS Company 3/25 when this was written.

U.S. 1ˢᵗ MARINE DIVISION

Lee Sang-don

"Do Korea's politicians and people know that the Marines who are conducting dangerous combat operations everyday in Iraq belong to the *same* Marine division which saved Korea fifty years ago?" - Lee Sang-don

On December 7, 2004 - the sixty-third anniversary of Pearl Harbor - U.S. President George W. Bush visited Camp Pendleton in the United States, which is the 1st Marine Division's hometown base. Bush had good reason to visit Camp Pendleton, as the Marines from there were engaging in heavy fighting in Fallujah, Iraq - the stronghold of radical Islamic militants. The U.S. assault on Fallujah was long overdue because of the U.S. presidential election, and probably because of such lateness the Marines endured many casualties. Bush talked to a large crowd of Marines at Camp Pendleton about the war on terror, and the valor and sacrifice of the U.S. troops.

Bush then mentioned the Changjin Lake Campaign (or the 'Chosin Reservoir Campaign' as it is commonly known in the U.S.) during the Korean War, a major battle fought by the U.S. Marines in the mountainous area near Changjin Lake in the eastern part of North Korea during the cold winter of 1950-51. Bush said that the 1st U.S. Marine Division heroically fought against ten divisions of Red China's army which had already infiltrated deep into North Korea. Bush animated the Marines at Camp Pendleton by saying that the troops in Korea at the time were in the right place to kill many enemy soldiers - since they were

199

completely surrounded by them. Most Korean news media overlooked this event, which I think has an important implication for the current Korea-U.S. relationship.

The Changjin Lake Campaign was one of the most notable battles won by the U.S. military. The 1st Marine Division, under the command of Major General Oliver Smith, fought in severe cold weather, successfully repelling the People's Republic of China's 9th Army - which had ten-to-one superiority over the U.S. Marines in manpower. If the Marines couldn't have defeated China's 9th Army, the Red Army might have well pushed the U.S. 8th Army and ROK Army to the southern end of the Korean Peninsula. One can easily imagine how the Korean peninsula's political map could have been shaped after such a major retreat of the Korean and U.S. Armies. That means those brave young Marines virtually saved Korea from falling into the bloody hands of the communist regime.

The importance of the Changjin Lake Campaign is not well understood in Korea. Although many Koreans know of, or have at least heard about, General MacArthur's brilliant landing at Inchon in September of 1950 (a scaled-downed version of the Normandy Operation during World War II) not many Koreans remember or have even heard of the Changjin Lake Campaign. The reason may be that the battle was fought between the two foreign armies, American Marines and the Red Chinese army, not between South and North Korean soldiers. Clearly, it is a shame that very few Koreans remember the U.S. Marines' heroic campaign during the Korean War.

The Changjin Lake Campaign was never forgotten in the United States, however. President Ronald Reagan mentioned it in his 1981 inaugural address, and in 1999 Martin Russ published a best-selling non-fiction novel entitled *Breakout* about the campaign. Then came President Bush's mention at Camp Pendleton.

Bush's mention made me feel mixed emotions. Korea dispatched a military unit to Iraq, but it is a non-combat duty force. While U.S. Marines are engaging in a fierce combat mission against radical militants in Fallujah and other places in Iraq, Korea's non-combat soldiers are simply digging in. Of course, I do not argue that Korean soldiers should engage in combat operations in Iraq. But, I would like to raise the following question: Do Korea's politicians and people know that the Marines who are conducting dangerous combat operations everyday in Iraq belong to the *same* Marine division which saved Korea fifty years ago?

Fortunately, there was recently an occasion which showed the American Marines that their efforts were not completely forgotten in Korea. In the spring of 2004 Martin Russ' *Breakout* was translated into Korean and published in Seoul. The publication itself was a kind of an epic story. Yim Sang-kyun, an insurance firm manager who went to college in Seoul in the 1970s and served as an army officer, had bought a copy of *Breakout* while on a business trip in the United States. Yim read the book while he was in hotels and airplanes, and was very impressed. Returning back to Seoul, he was disappointed to find the book had not been translated into Korean. He had never written a book or even an article, but decided to translate it into Korean as a kind of mission. As he was a busy man at his insurance firm, it took him four years to complete. While he was working on the translation, he visited the Korean War Memorial Hall in Yongsan. On the wall where the fallen U.S. soldiers' names are inscribed, he found those of U.S. Marines who made the ultimate sacrifice during the Changjin Lake Campaign. For Yim, it was a very powerful moment.

I would like to tell the Americans that in Korea there are still people like Yim who do not forget what American Marines did for a small poor country in Asia when it was threatened by communist aggression a half century ago. God bless the U.S 1st Marine Division!

Lee Sang-don is a professor of Law at Chung-Ang University in Seoul.

BEANS, BULLETS, BAND-AIDS...
And Beer!

MSgt Andy Bufalo USMC (Ret)

"If eighteen-year-olds... are *not* mature enough to drink, they sure as hell are not old enough to drive, vote, smoke, or die in combat." – MSgt Andy Bufalo USMC (Ret)

"Ed - Great stuff here by Top Bufalo. His point is well taken. In my (our) early days it wasn't a problem. I recall a tent on Vieques inside a fenced compound; fondly called the "JESS" – Junior Enlisted Slop Shute. Yes, it should have been <u>Chute</u>, but Marines couldn't spell worth a damn back then, and it didn't matter anyway. There was one picnic table in the center of the tent, the sides were rolled up and the OD & Sergeant of the Guard were armed as they roamed around the perimeter. The duty company had additional sentries outside the wire, and a reaction force back in the company area.

It was here that your hard-working, hard-driving Marines would enjoy their well-earned beer ration under the careful supervision of their brother Marines, and of course the duty rotated so everybody got their shot.

We did NOT have drinking problems back then. We took care of each other - same as now. Of all the basic elements of the Marine Corps, the most basic is WE TAKE CARE OF EACH OTHER!!! Get the picture America, we don't need your asinine laws from half wits, and the sniveling of non-hacking no-loads telling us when our Marines can have a beer. We can and will determine when they have beer call. We still do that, and they have damn sure earned it! -

Rip" *(Colonel John Ripley)*

It was bound to happen sooner or later, in fact I kind of *expected* it to happen someday - but even so I was dumbfounded. During a recent trip to a local restaurant I was waiting in the bar area (which doubled as the waiting area) for a table to become available when I noticed a young Marine Lance Corporal in his "Charlie" uniform doing the same. I instinctively scanned the ribbons on his chest, and immediately recognized that he was wearing a Combat Action Ribbon and Purple Heart, which as we all know is awarded for wounds received in combat (unless, of course, your name is John Kerry...).

I waved the waitress over, pointed out the young Devil Dog, and told her that I'd like to buy the wounded combat veteran a beer. She nodded, smiled at me approvingly, and headed over to find out what brand the Marine preferred. I was quite pleased to have an opportunity to show my gratitude, if only in a small way, to one of the heroes who puts his country first and his personal safety second. A minute later the waitress returned – and informed me that I could NOT buy the Leatherneck any alcoholic beverages because he was – gasp! – *under age.*

I was stunned. Of course I realize the law says you have to be twenty-one or older to drink, but I found that hard to swallow given the circumstances. How can this be? At eighteen these guys are old enough to sign on the dotted line, go through the meat-grinder of Parris Island or San Diego, and proudly pin on the Eagle, Globe and Anchor of a United States Marine (or, in the case of our sister services, some shiny emblem located between their "I made it through basic training" ribbon and the grenade throwing badge). But... they can't have a beer!

Those newly graduated members of the Armed Forces are then sent to schools to learn their Military Occupational Specialties, and when finished are assigned duties as plane captains in charge of multi-million dollar jet fighters, intelligence analysts, communications technicians - and grunts with the mission of assaulting the terrorist stronghold of Fallujah (as was the case with the Marine in the restaurant). Those young Americans are entrusted with millions of dollars worth of equipment, and their ability to do their jobs properly often determines whether their comrades live or die on the battlefield. But... they can't have a beer!

At eighteen they can enter into legal contracts. At eighteen they can get a license to drive a car. At eighteen they can get married and have children. At eighteen they can legally buy a pack of cigarettes and smoke every one of them if they want (although I've never really understood why anyone would do that). At eighteen they can even go to the ballot box and help choose our nation's leaders. But... they can't have a beer!

Every year, eighteen-year-old (and younger) college students pour across the border into Mexico during spring break to take advantage of the nonexistent drinking age laws in that country, and while they are partying their hearts out the members of our newest "greatest generation" are guarding the frontiers of our great nation. While those college kids are filming "girls gone wild" videos in Cancun, the members of our military are living in conditions which make those of the Gitmo detainees seem luxurious in comparison, and are putting their lives on the line for their families and friends. But... they still can't buy a beer!

Wisconsin State Representative and Navy veteran Mark Pettis recently proposed a bill that would drop the legal drinking age for servicemen in his state to nineteen, and while that is a small step in the right direction it is far from enough. A federal law ties millions of dollars in highway funds to states' compliance with the twenty-one year old drinking age, and so it is at the *federal* level that this issue must be addressed.

I know, I know... Mothers Against Drunk Driving and other groups are against lowering the age. They cite statistics which show there have been fewer highway fatalities since the enactment of these laws in the 1980s, but they don't take into account the possibility that the numbers are down because today's drivers are better educated, law enforcement agencies are more proactive, and cars are generally safer than they were back then. They also say "the brain is not fully developed until age twenty-one" and tell us that "It's for their own good." That strikes me as an odd thing to say. You mean to say it's okay to send these young people to a place where *bullets* are flying and mortar rounds are falling from the sky... but feel the need to "protect" them from the dangers of a *Budweiser?* At eighteen they are old enough to die for our country. But... they can't have a beer!

Here's what I think. If eighteen-year-olds are mature enough to do all of the things I have mentioned, they should be allowed to drink – and if they are *not* mature enough to drink, they sure as hell are not old enough to drive, vote, smoke, or die in combat. You just can't have it both ways.

BETTER LATE THAN NEVER

Jack Riley

On March 30, 1967, at Hill 70 west of Con Thien in the Republic of Vietnam, the Marines of the "Flaming I" (India Company 3/9) were attacked by a numerically superior force of the North Vietnamese Army (NVA). It was a battle that became known as the "Battle at Getlin's Corner" in honor of our commanding officer, Captain Mike Getlin (KIA-Navy Cross) and was the start of Operation Prairie 3. Specific details of the battle are recorded in a book written by Colonel George D. Navadel and his troops entitled *A Rifle Company's Tale*.

The CP Group and two squads from 2nd Platoon were located on Hill 70, while 1st (rein) and 3rd Platoons were ordered to ambush positions 1800 meters apart and 900 meters from the Hill. In the ensuing battle fifteen of our brothers were killed in action, while over sixty of us were wounded. Although greatly outnumbered, India Company held that hill in a battle lasting many hours. I was a Squad Leader, and lost four Marines from my squad while most of us were wounded. Our Corpsman, Doc Ken Braun, kept us patched up and able to continue the fight. In between treating our wounded, he used one of my wounded Marine's M-14 – ultimately killing five NVA soldiers. His M-14 had been damaged by a mortar round, requiring him to kick the operating rod back with each round fired.

Doc was treating wounded Marines all over that small hill. Each time "Corpsman Up" was yelled out, Doc was on the move, never hesitating even though mortars and machine gun fire were sweeping our positions. Doc Braun tightened a

207

web belt tourniquet on the almost amputated leg of Lieutenant. John P. Bobo (KIA-Medal of Honor) and then dragged Lieutenant Bobo up the hill, where they lay side by side firing into the advancing enemy. An NVA soldier stood up in the tall grass firing his AK-47 into the Lieutenant, killing him, and also hit Doc Braun three times in the chest and shoulder - tearing out muscle and exposing his spine. When Doc regained consciousness he managed to crawl into our final-stand position. He instructed me how to treat his wound, and made sure all of our wounded were receiving treatment. He never moaned, cried, or complained; in fact, when it looked like one more attack by the NVA would overrun our position due to lack of ammo, Doc never made a sound to give away our position in the dark. I characterize Doc Ken Braun as the epitome of the Navy Corpsman!

India Company killed so many enemy soldiers that evening that the NVA could be heard dragging their dead from the field all night long. They left over sixty of their dead, plus we captured others. All of our officers on the hill had been killed, which meant recommendations for decorations would have to come from the enlisted. Getlin's Corner produced one Medal of Honor, three Navy Crosses, and several Silver and Bronze Stars. Upon my release from the hospital at Marble Mountain, I returned to Camp Carroll with my third Purple Heart. No, not all three-Heart Marines left Vietnam - in fact many chose to stay with their brothers. I gave a statement upon my return that Doc, and the others previously mentioned, should be decorated.

I did not know if Doc lived or died from his terrible wounds. When the names of all Vietnam KIAs were eventually made known, I was grateful his was not on the list. Doc was alive, but I was unable to locate him. Then, thirty-five years later, I received a phone call late one night, and it was Doc Braun calling from Missoula, Montana! After an hour or so I finally asked him what medal he received for Getlin's Corner. His response was, "Another Purple Heart, just like you." I immediately decided something had to be done to recognize this hero! Doc had been previously decorated in 1966 with a Bronze Star while we were down south in Antennae Valley. He had gone out into a rice paddy under enemy machine gun fire to save a Marine from 2/9 who was shot in the leg. This tells you something about his courage! A Marine not from our company was wounded, and Doc didn't hesitate to save him. Had he been in something besides the Marines (after all, an FMF Corpsman is, for all intents and purposes, a Marine) his Bronze Star would have been a Distinguished Service Cross. As we know, most decorated Marines and Corpsmen received posthumous awards! In 2000 I resubmitted my eyewitness account along with two other Marines from my squad, and hoped time had not prevented our Corps from recognizing this hero.

It took thirty-eight years, but on Flag Day in 2005 - in front of the Iwo Jima Monument in Arlington, Virginia - Doc Kenneth Braun was presented his long overdue Navy Cross by General Richard I. Neal, USMC (Ret). It just so happens that General Neal, then Lieutenant Neal, had lead our 1st Platoon as they fought their way to rescue us at Getlin's Corner.

Doc Braun, you are a true American Hero. Your Marine brothers will never forget your courage and devotion to duty!

The Medal of Honor was awarded to Lieutenant John Bobo, and the Navy Cross to Captain Michael Getlin (KIA), Corporal John Loweranitis (KIA), and Master Sergeant Raymond Rogers (WIA).

HAVE YOU FORGOTTEN?

Sergeant Sam Kille, USMCR

"Have you forgotten how it felt that day? To see your homeland under fire, and her people blown away. Have you forgotten, when those towers fell? We had neighbors still inside, going thru a living hell. And you say we shouldn't worry 'bout bin Laden. Have you forgotten?"
- Darryl Worley in his song *'Have You Forgotten?'*

It's a sad state of affairs when someone like Darryl Worley has to write a song to REMIND some people in this country (i.e. the "blame America first" crowd) about what happened on September 11, 2001 only a few short years after it happened – but it is safe to say no one will ever have to remind the U.S. Marine Corps!

Deeply embedded in every Marine's heart is a strong sense of devotion to duty, and a love of tradition. Whether still in uniform or not, Marines - who believe that "Once a Marine, Always a Marine" is more than a mere saying - gather each year to celebrate the Corps' birth on November 10.

In the wake of the recent terrorist attacks in New York, this year's 226th birthday celebration has taken on new meaning for many, especially for those most affected by the tragedy. Keeping this in mind, the NYPD Marine Corps Association's annual celebration, held at One Police Plaza in Manhattan on November 9, was a ceremony ripe with tradition and solemn remembrance.

"I am deeply humbled to be here celebrating our Corps' birthday with those who fought the first battle in the global war on terrorism," said guest speaker Brigadier General Gordon Nash, the director of the Operations Division for Plans, Policies and Operations, at Headquarters Marine Corps. "I want you to know that we will win this war."

The NYPD Marine Corps Association, formed in 1993, is comprised of New York City police officers who have served in the Corps. In addition to the traditional cake cutting ceremony and the playing of the Commandant's Birthday Message, the group recognized those who had made the ultimate sacrifice during rescue efforts at the World Trade Center. Twenty-three of the law enforcement, firefighters and rescue personnel who died on September 11 had served as Marines. Of those, Firefighter Matthew Garvey and Firefighter Sean Tallon were drilling reservists with 6th Communications Battalion, and 2nd Battalion, 25th Marines.

A highlight of the ceremony for many were the remarks made by guest speaker and author, James Bradley - the son of John "Doc" Bradley - one of the six flag raisers immortalized in Joe Rosenthal's famed photograph of the flag raising during the battle for Iwo Jima. Bradley spoke of how "the valor witnessed at Iwo Jima was due to a common virtue in all Marines, which is still evident today."

Bradley's emotional comparison to the Marines of past and present drew a standing ovation from the audience of nearly one thousand.

"Those we lost may not be here in body," said Tom Sullivan, a retired NYPD detective and the event's master of ceremonies. "But I guarantee they are looking down on us with pride."

"And if the Army and the Navy ever look on Heaven's scenes," Sullivan added while paraphrasing a verse from the Marine's Hymn, "They will find the streets are guarded by THESE United States Marines."

The twenty-three Fallen Marines of the World Trade Center Attack:

NYPD
Sgt. Michael Curtin
Sgt. John Coughlin
PO Vincent Danz

Port Authority PD
PO Paul Jurgens
PO James Parham

FDNY
Bn. Chief Raymond Downey
Bn. Chief Joseph Grezlak
Capt. Patrick Brown
Lt. Michael Esposito
FF Calixto Anaya
FF Ruben Correa
FF John Chipura
FF Matthew Garvey
FF Gary Geidel
FF Ronnie Henderson
FF William Krukowski
FF Manual Mojica
FF Christian Regenhard
FF Gregory Sikorsky
FF Kevin Smith
FF Sean Tallon
FF Allan Tarasiewicz

FBI
Special Agent Leonard Hatton

PET PEEVES

MSgt Andy Bufalo USMC (Ret)

"Certain individuals now insist on referring to our sacred symbol, the Eagle, Globe and Anchor, as an 'EGA.' Is that term concise? Sure. Is it economical? Obviously. Does it show proper respect for the device which symbolizes our beloved Corps? Absolutely not!" – MSgt Andy Bufalo, USMC (Ret)

When this essay first circulated on the internet I received a LOT of emailed responses both thanking me for making a valid point, and chiding me for omitting THEIR own personal pet peeve – and believe me, there were a lot of them!

Remember the scene in the movie *Bull Durham* where the team is riding on the bus, and Tim Robbins breaks out his guitar and starts singing what he thinks are the lyrics to the old *Three Dog Night* song *Try a Little Tenderness*? "They get wooly, young girls do get wooly, etc..." Suddenly Kevin Costner comes flying over the seat, grabs the guitar, and yells, "They get *weary*, not wooly! Nobody gets wooly! I HATE it when people get the words wrong!"

I know exactly how he felt. Throughout my career, and even now in retirement, there are a few terms people seem to get wrong more often than they get right – so listen up!

First and foremost, there is *no such thing* as the CONGRESSIONAL Medal of Honor. If you read the citation, it says "the President of the United States takes pleasure in awarding the Medal of Honor to..." Nowhere to be seen are the words Congress, or Congressional. Let's face it, the 535 members of that august body are *way* too busy bickering amongst themselves and voting each other pay raises to find time to recognize anyone for valor. People even screw this one up when they abbreviate it, calling the medal the CMH instead of the MOH. It even happened in the movie *Heartbreak Ridge,* when Stitch Jones says, "I didn't know Gunny Highway had the CMH..." Geez!

The second one on the list is butchered in nine out of ten cases, and it's just *got* to stop. Repeat after me: There is *no such thing* as the Marine Corps Hymn! It's called the Marines' Hymn. And while we are on the subject, the fourth line in the first stanza reads, "In the air, on land and sea." I don't know why, but people always seem to mumble when they get to that part. It's not that hard, guys. Square yourselves away! (You know who you are).

Next is the location of Marine Barracks, Washington, D.C., which can be found at the intersection of 8th and I Streets – hence the term, "8th & I." For some reason I keep seeing people writing "8th and Eye" on the calendar when they are making plans to attend the Evening Parade. When they do that I invariable picture a squared away Cyclops in dress blues spinning an M-1 rifle and popping his heels. And by the way, the Evening Parade is a *separate* event from the Sunset Parade - but you can research that one on your own.

Finally comes a term which evolved near the end of my time on active duty. Certain individuals now insist on referring to our sacred symbol, the Eagle, Globe and Anchor, as an "EGA." Is that term concise? Sure. Is it economical? Obviously. Does it show proper respect for the device which symbolizes our beloved Corps? Absolutely not! Let's start policing ourselves, and put an end to this unsat practice of the fast food eating, video game playing MTV generation.

At this point you are probably saying to yourselves,

"What a crotchety old SOB!" You bet I am. If we don't nip this stuff in the bud, the next thing you know we'll be calling all of our NCOs and SNCOs "Sarge" like they do in a certain other service. Then we'll *definitely* be in a world of discharged fecal matter!

THE MARINES HAVE LANDED
Again!

David H. Hackworth

"The law of nature is simple: survival of the fittest. And in the 21st century, heartbreaking as it is for me to admit, the forward-based and highly deployable U.S. Marine Corps is the fittest." – Colonel David H. Hackworth, U. S. Army (Ret)

Colonel David Haskell Hackworth U.S. Army (Ret), who was a true warrior and great admirer of the Marine Corps, lost his battle with cancer and passed away in May of 2005. "Hack," as he was widely known, won a battlefield commission in Korea, and was a leading advocate for the enlisted men of all services. The stories about him are legion, but a couple immediately come to mind. In the aftermath of the Battle of Dak To, Hack marched his entire battalion back to base camp (the other units had returned by helicopter) and, somehow, managed to scrounge up an Army band to lead the procession back through the gate. Then in March of 1969, while Hack was in command of the 4/39th Infantry Battalion in Vietnam, a small group of his soldiers were pinned down by a much larger Viet Cong force. He flew to the scene, and tried everything to free them from the enemy's grip - close air support, field artillery, naval gunfire and smoke screens – but nothing worked. Finally Hack ordered his helicopter to land in the middle of the inferno. The bird was still five feet from the ground when he leaped out and sprinted into a torrent of enemy tracers, and he quickly returned with a wounded soldier. He repeated this over and over until the chopper was full of wounded – so full

216

that when it lifted off, Hack was forced to stand outside on one of its landing skids, grasping the door frame while a soldier inside held onto his belt. The Army is still considering awarding him the Medal of Honor for that night's rescue of his troops. He certainly earned it. He certainly <u>deserves</u> it. The Marine Corps has lost a great friend, and the nation a great hero.

The first non-Special Ops unit deployed to Afghanistan is the United States Marines Corps - no big surprise to this old Army doggie.

In World War II's South Pacific, Marines were "the firstus with the mostus" into the Solomons, and they led the way into Vietnam. In Korea, they landed second, but unlike the Army units initially deployed there, General Edward Craig's Marine brigade hit the beach ready to fight. And without their skill, sacrifice and courage, the beleaguered Eighth Army would've been pushed into the sea during the early months of the conflict. A similar scenario occurred during the early stages of Desert Storm, in which Marine units came in ready to fight while the first Army troops - the 82nd Airborne Division, with its insufficient anti-tank capability - were a potential speed bump waiting to be flattened.

The Corps, which has never lost sight that its primary mission is to fight, remains superbly trained and disciplined - true to its time-honored slogan, "We don't promise you a rose garden." When, under Clinton, the Army lowered its standards to Boy Scout summer-camp level in order to increase enlistment, the Corps responded by making boot training *longer* and *tougher*. Now under USMC Commandant James Jones, that training has gotten even meaner for the young Marine wannabes waiting in line to join up, as well as for Leathernecks already serving in regular and reserve units. Unlike U.S. Army conventional units - their new slogan, "An Army of One," says it all - the U.S. Marine Corps remains a highly mobile, fierce fighting team that has never forgotten: "The more we sweat on the training field, the less we bleed on the battlefield."

The Marines are flexible, agile, ready and deadly, while the Army remains configured to fight the Soviets - who disappeared off the Order of Battle charts a decade ago. For example, right after September 11, the two Army heavy divisions in Germany - with their 68-ton tanks that can crush almost every bridge they cross - deployed to Poland for war games.

Hello, is there a brain at the top somewhere beneath that snazzy Black Beret being modeled at most U.S. airports by too many overweight Army National Guard troops?

The Army has eight other regular divisions, all designed to fight 20th-century wars. Three are heavy - Tank and Mech Infantry - and two are light, the storied 82nd Airborne and the elite 101st Airborne (now helicopter), and then there's the light/heavy 10,000-man 2nd Division that's in Korea backing up a million-man, superbly fit South Korean Army.

Less the light divisions, our Army's not versatile, deployable, swift or sustainable. The heavy units require fleets of ships and planes to move them, and it takes months to get them there - it took Stormin' Norman six months to ready a force for Desert Storm. The 101st - while deadly, as Desert Storm proved - is also a slow mover requiring a huge amount of strategic-lift ships and giant planes - to get to the battlefield, not to mention the massive tax-dollar load to outfit and maintain it. Sadly, today's Army is like a street fighter with brass knuckles too heavy to lift.

After the Rangers' disaster in Somalia - where there were no tanks to break through to relieve them - and the embarrassment of not being able to fight in the war in Serbia,

Army Chief of Staff Eric Shinseki started forming light brigades strikingly similar to USMC units. When I asked, "Why the copycatting?" an Army officer said: "It was either copy, or go out of business. We'd become redundant because of long-term lack of boldness and imagination at the top."

The Army costs about eighty billion dollars a year to run. It's time for Congress to do its duty and stop enjoying the benefits of all the pork this obsolescence and redundancy provides. If the Army can't change with the times - as the powerful horse cavalry generals couldn't just prior to World War II - then it should fold up its tents and turn the ground-fighting mission over to the Marines.

The law of nature is simple: survival of the fittest. And in the 21st century, heartbreaking as it is for me to admit, the forward-based and highly deployable U.S. Marine Corps is the fittest.

Colonel David H. Hackworth joined the Merchant Marine when he was 14 and the U.S. Army when he was 15. He was battlefield commissioned in Korea and became the youngest Captain and later the youngest Colonel in the Army. Colonel Hackworth was awarded 10 Silver Stars, 7 Bronze Stars for Valor, 8 Purple Hearts, 35 Air Medals, and 48 additional personal and unit awards.

ULTIMATE COMPLIMENT

This, and the next anecdote, are taken from messages on the 'Compuserve' Military Forum, and were part of a thread on enemy perceptions of Marines:

From a Marine fighter pilot:

In Japan, we had several of our officers/attack pilots execute an exchange visit with a Japan Air Self Defense Squadron who flew F-4s. They even had call signs... "Gunner" who was the top-scoring pilot in shooting the banner, "Doc," and "Sleepy." These guys didn't know about Snow White, and that their callsigns made us think of that. They were all consumate gentlemen, better behaved than my fellow squadron pilots, but they were awed by us. I asked "Gunner," who was the most mature and stately of the Japanese pilots, about this degree of respect he was showing us.

His reply was that we (the U.S. Marine Corps) had defeated Japan. I told him that there were many forces arrayed against Japan: the Army, Navy, and Air Force. He said, "No... *Marines* defeated Japan."

They were awed by our fighting ability. It is an interesting anecdote, especially since he had not even been *born* at the end of WWII!

From an Ambulatory Care Coordinator:

Last year I was assessing a new patient for a vascular problem. The patient was male, early 70's, of oriental persuasion. I'll call him 'Nguyen X.' In listening to his accent, and by the spelling of his name, it became obvious

220

that he was Vietnamese.

During the examination he cautiously raised the right sleeve of my scrub top, just enough to expose my USMC tattoo. I raised the sleeve up further to satisfy his curiosity, and allowed him to see the Bulldog with the WWI style helmet.

He stated, "Marines, huh?"

I answered, "Yes sir, a long time ago."

He asked, "Did you have to be sent to Vietnam?"

I replied in the affirmative, and told him when and where I had served or seen action.

He smiled up at me and said, "Very strange that we meet like this... I was a Medical Officer in the North Vietnam Army." He went on to tell me about his outfit, and how he happened to be here now, etc.

He made it a point to tell me how 'bothered' the NVA soldiers would get when they had to move out against Marines. "We were told many things about you Marines, about your history, and especially how stubbornly you would fight. We weren't so worried about the Army soldiers. But we were very respectful of you Marines."

I really didn't know what to say, and then he continued, "We knew we could win our war against America by just wearing the soldiers down, but sometimes made jokes about maybe not being able to hold out too long if only Marines were in Vietnam. This was a very unhappy thing to think of. We did not like to have to fight Marines... Marines don't run, and America is very honored to have them."

I thanked him and continued with his assessment. At the end he shook my hand and said, "I'm very sorry Marines had to die for Vietnam, but all Marines are good and honorable. All Marines are heroes... Marines made my job *very* difficult..."

221

THE OLD BREED

This was the genesis of the First Marine Division at the onset of WWII:

These are "The Old Breed," as described by Lieutenant Colonel Samuel B. Griffith, who was one of their own, as the 1st Marine Division formed up for Guadalcanal: "...first sergeants yanked off 'planks' in navy yards, sergeants from recruiting duty, gunnery sergeants who had fought in France, perennial privates with disciplinary records a yard long. These were the professionals, the 'Old Breed' of the United States Marines. Many had fought 'Cacos' in Haiti, 'bandidos' in Nicaragua, and French, English, Italian, and American soldiers and sailors in every bar in Shanghai, Manila, Tsingtao, Tientsin, and Peking.

They were inveterate gamblers, and accomplished scroungers, who drank hair tonic in preference to Post Exchange beer ('horse piss'), cursed with wonderful fluency, and never went to chapel ('the Godbox') unless forced to. Many dipped snuff, smoked rank cigars, or chewed tobacco (cigarettes were for women and children). They had little use for libraries or organized athletics... they could live on jerked goat, the strong black coffee they called 'boiler compound,' and hash cooked in a tin hat.

Many wore expert badges with bars for proficiency in rifle, pistol, machine gun, hand grenade, auto-rifle, mortar and bayonet. They knew their weapons, and they knew their tactics. They knew they were tough, and they knew they were good. There were enough of them to leaven the Division, and to impart to the thousands of younger men a share of both the unique spirit which animated them and the skills they possessed. They were like a drop of dye in a gallon of water - they gave the whole division an unmistakable hue, and they stamped a nickname on the division: 'the Old Breed.'"

From *Guadalcanal, The Definitive Account* by Richard B. Frank.

REPARATIONS
From the British

"We are not moved by the gloomy smile of a worthless king, but by the ardent glow of generous patriotism. We fight not to enslave, but to set a country free, and to make room upon the earth for honest men to live in." - Thomas Paine

Every year on the 4th of July a cookout is held on the ramparts of Marine Barracks, Washington with senior Royal Marines in attendance – and the Crown is put on trial for their "high crimes" during the War of 1812:

"Order! Order!" shouts the Honorable General Robert Magnus to the gentlemen of the Marine Barracks Center House Officer's Mess. Looking sternly over his spectacles, he directs his words to the defendant, one Colonel Timothy Chicken, senior officer of the British Embassy Royal Marines. "Sir, you and your party have been charged with the following transgressions on or about the 24th and 25th days of August in the year 1814. You did willfully and negligently destroy, by fire, public and private property within the District of Columbia. You did willfully loot and pillage certain public and private antiquities from the U.S. Capitol Building and the President's White House. And you did, through the commission of incorrigible public acts, incite a riot within the District of Columbia."

Here, the general is abruptly cut off by "boos" and gasps from the assembly. Thus begins the evening's reparations trial for the British hazing of the national capitol region... again.

By Marine Barracks order, the senior officer of the British Embassy Royal Marines (who is also a member of the Center House Mess) is required to repair to the Marine Barracks every year to stand his fellow messmates to a drink. A trial is conducted to determine the amount of reparations owed for British damages to the capitol during the War of 1812.

According to the order, "This responsibility shall remain in force until such a time as the full membership of the mess agrees that indemnities for the loss and damage suffered to our capitol at the hands of the British forces have been satisfied." Judging by this crowd, it's not going to be *tonight*.

Reparations Night, a tradition begun in 1982 by then Marine Barracks commanding officer, Colonel Orlo K. Steele, and the senior British Embassy Royal Marine, Colonel Michael J. Reece, has found the defendant guilty on all charges every year thus far.

"There are generations yet to be born who will continue to observe this tradition," said Colonel Terry M. Lockard, MBW commanding officer. "We're brothers in arms. We work together. We fight together. We socialize together. Marine Barracks is the ideal place to do that because of the history that surrounds us."

Staging a trial for events that took place nearly two hundred years ago certainly puts a new spin on the word "socialize," but according to Lockard, it's just the thing to introduce younger officers of both countries to the history and traditions of the British Royal Marines and the United States Marine Corps' "Oldest Post."

"Our countries are the greatest of allies," said Lockard. "This is something that educates the officers about those ties and creates new relationships."

Dressed in an orange D.C. Jail jumpsuit, Chicken replied audaciously to the charges, "Not guilty! We might have burned one or two federal buildings in Washington, but we employed strict orders against damaging civilian buildings and looting or terrorizing civilian populations - unlike the U.S. forces in Toronto, by the way."

His defense continued with increasingly elaborate arguments as the night wore on.

"You call that a riot?" Chicken retorted at one point to accusations that the British incited a massive public riot in August of 1814. "What you saw in Washington D.C. was some young British servicemen playing Rugby – one of the four great games we have given the world (football, rugby, hockey and cricket). More people play these games in the rest of the world than watch your versions in the U.S.A.! Sadly, years of mind-altering narcotics and steroid abuse have skewed your interpretation. What are you people smoking?" Chicken continued to take jabs at U.S. sports, and any other American pop-culture reference he could think of throughout the evening.

Chicken said he and his Marines look forward to the opportunity to defend themselves at Reparations Night every year, and despite consistently unfavorable verdicts, they would be saddened if the trials were ever to cease.

"It is an opportunity, in a convivial atmosphere, to remind ourselves that, whilst once there were some differences between our nations, and indeed, our armed forces, those are now buried," he said. "We can remind ourselves of the great bond that has been forged between us whilst enjoying an excellent annual opportunity for some light-hearted verbal sparring. The U.S. Marine Corps pits its most innovative thinkers against a redoubtable Royal who is desperate not to have to pay reparations!"

Leading those innovated thinkers in the prosecution was Captain Jason M. Pelt, Marine Barracks Washington legal officer.

"Your honor, through the advances of modern technology I have been able to obtain photographic evidence of the event in question," Pelt stated towards the end of his case. "I would like to present before this court actual pictures of British forces in our nation's capitol on the 25th of August, 1814."

Sure enough, photos of British troops bearing signs with anti-American slogans such as "Down With Madison" were exhibited. The officers bore a striking resemblance to current members of the Center House Officer's Mess. Things were looking grim for Chicken and his mates. It's a good thing he had a backup plan – a keg of their finest ale.

"The bond between our two Corps is founded on one word - Marine," said Chicken. "We share the same ethos, the same values and the same aims and desires - if not always the same language! Our relationship has developed over many years on operations, exercises, training, social and sporting exchanges."

Lockard echoed the sentiment. "The camaraderie between U.S. Marines and British Royal Marines is something special and very important to us," he said. "As long as there's an officers' mess, we will continue to hold the senior Royal Marine responsible for reparations every year."

And what exactly is that responsibility?

"Sir, the current running total of damages still owed to the Center House Mess stands at 150 trillion, 600 billion, 998 million, 876 thousand, 875 dollars and 63 cents," announces Pelt after a guilty verdict is pronounced.

Chicken offered the keg.

"Very well," General Magnus pronounced. "In lieu of cash or check, this court will accept a barrel of your finest ale as a down payment. This Supreme Court of the Center

House Mess stands adjourned!

The Commandant's House at MBW is the oldest operating public building in Washington, D.C. Legend has it that the British did not burn it and the Marine Barracks during the War of 1812 out of respect for the United States Marine Corps.

SCHOOL'S OUT

"Freedom is not free, but the U.S. Marine Corps will pay most of your share." - Ned Dolan

Marine Corps Sergeant Zach Richardson survived Iraq, but not Carson Middle School in Greensboro, Georgia. When Richardson walked into the Greene County school, he expected to meet some of the sixth-graders who had written to him during his seven-month deployment. Instead he was shown the door, coming under the scrutiny of a principal enforcing a policy which required prior approval for visiting speakers. Principal Ulrica Corbett told teacher Matthew Lund, the Marine's host, to escort Richardson from the campus.

Matthew Lund and Zach Richardson had been college roommates. After college Richardson joined the Marines, and Lund started teaching. Richardson went to Iraq, and Lund to Carson Middle School - where he taught a 6th grade language arts class. As a class assignment he gave his students the opportunity to write a letter to Sergeant Richardson in Iraq. Richardson wrote back, and gave the class the names of five other Marines who would like to receive letters. Soon other middle school classes were also sending letters to the Marines.

When Sergeant Richardson returned to the United States he told Matthew Lund that he wanted to come to the Carson Middle School to personally thank the students for their support and letters. Lund filled out and submitted a "Resource Visitor or Guest Speaker Form," and submitted it to Principal Corbett. He never got the form back, and when he asked her about it was told she was not going to look at it.

229

Lund realized his request to have Richardson visit the school was going to be ignored by Principal Corbett, and made the decision to proceed with plans for the visit on May 23rd, one week before Memorial Day.

When Sergeant Richardson showed up at Carson Middle School Lund took him to the school's media center to prepare to meet the students. At that point, Principal Corbett called him into the hall and said the Marine was not approved to be at the school. Lund told Corbett the proper form had been submitted, and had been ignored. Corbett's response was "that's your problem, not mine." She also told Lund the students had not earned the visit from the Marine, and closed the discussion with the phrase "what part of what we just discussed do you not understand?" She then ordered Lund to escort Sergeant Richardson off the school campus.

When this story hit the local newspaper Ulrica Corbett thought it best to do a little CYA (Cover Your Ass) work. She submitted a written statement to the *Herald-Journal* in which she stated "My decision not to allow Zach Richardson to speak with the students on Monday came out of my regard for the safety and welfare of our children." Apparently Ulrica Corbett felt that this U.S. Marine, who had just spent a year putting his life on the line for his country, presented some sort of threat to the children of Carson Middle School.

It became obvious that this self-important middle school principal harbored a dislike, if not an outright hatred, for the American armed forces, and was steadfastly opposed to our actions in Iraq and quite possibly in Afghanistan. She had decided to let her petty prejudices stand in the way of what would have been a memorable and rewarding experience for both Zach Richardson and the children of Matthew Lund's 6th grade class.

Corbett claimed the teacher didn't follow protocol, but the

newspaper had signed and dated copies of the documentation submitted by Lund. Someone wasn't telling the truth, but one thing is for sure - if she had wanted to, Ulrica Corbett could have found a way to allow this Marine to speak to the students who had befriended him. She didn't.

This treatment, coming a few days before the Memorial Day holiday, led to front-page coverage in the local weekly, the *Herald-Journal*. The story, written by editor Carey Williams and capped with a triple-decker headline, attracted the attention of talk radio, and then the nation. By the following Wednesday people from Kansas and Louisiana were calling Greensboro, about midway between Atlanta and Augusta, and asking the editor to fax his story. Most were sympathetic veterans, he said. "The people here, they just can't believe it happened," Williams said. "They respect the Marine."

In his written apology, Superintendent John Jackson said the situation could have been handled differently. The principal, he said, could have allowed the Marine sergeant to speak with students, and then dealt with the teacher who purportedly did not secure written permission for the visit.

But that's not what happened.

FIVE MONTHS IN THE BOX

James H. Warner

"Conservatives saw the savagery of 9/11 attacks and prepared for war. Liberals saw the savagery of the 9/11 attacks and wanted to prepare indictments, and offer therapy and understanding for our attackers... Al Jazeera now broadcasts the words of Senator Durbin to the Mideast, certainly putting our troops in greater danger." - Karl Rove

Senator Dick Durbin (D-IL) had the following to say on the floor of the Senate: "...a detainee chained hand and foot in a fetal position to the floor, with no chair, food or water. Most times they urinated or defecated on themselves, and had been left there for 18-24 hours or more. On one occasion, the air conditioning had been turned down so far and the temperature was so cold in the room, that the barefooted detainee was shaking with cold... On another occasion, the [air conditioner] had been turned off, making the temperature in the unventilated room well over 100 degrees. The detainee was almost unconscious on the floor, with a pile of hair next to him. He had apparently been literally pulling his hair out throughout the night. On another occasion, not only was the temperature unbearably hot, but extremely loud rap music was being played in the room, and had been since the day before, with the detainee chained hand and foot in the fetal position on the tile floor... you would most certainly believe this must have been done by Nazis, Soviets in their gulags, or some mad regime - Pol Pot or others - that had no concern for human beings. Sadly, that is not the case. This was the action of Americans in the treatment of their prisoners."

As a Marine Corps officer, I spent five years and five months in a prisoner of war camp in North Vietnam. I believe this gives me a benchmark against which to measure the treatment which Senator Richard Durbin, Illinois Democrat, complained of at the Camp of Detention for Islamo-fascists at Guantanamo Bay, Cuba.

The senator's argument is silly. If he believes what he has said his judgment is so poor that his countrymen, assuming, of course, that he *considers* us his countrymen, have no reason not to dismiss him as a witless boob. On the other hand, if he does not believe what he said, the other members of the Senate may wish to consider censure.

Consider nutrition. I have severe peripheral neuropathy in both legs as a residual of beriberi. I am fortunate. Some of my comrades suffer partial blindness or ischemic heart disease as a result of beriberi, a degenerate disease of peripheral nerves caused by a lack of thiamin, vitamin B-1. It is easily treated, but is extremely painful.

Did Mr. Durbin say that some of the Islamo-fascist prisoners are suffering from beriberi? Actually, the diet enjoyed by the prisoners seems to be healthy. I saw the menu that Representative Duncan Hunter presented a few days ago. It looks as though the food given the detainees at Guantanamo is wholesome, nutritious and appealing. I would be curious to hear Mr. Durbin explain how 'orange glazed chicken and rice pilaf' can be compared to the moldy bread laced with rat droppings *I* was served while in captivity.

In May of 1969, I was taken out for interrogation on suspicion of planning an escape. I was forced to remain awake for long periods of time - three weeks on one occasion. On the first of June, I was put in a cement box with a steel door, which sat out in the tropical summer sun. There, I was put in leg irons which were then wired to a small stool. In this position I could neither sit nor stand comfortably. Within ten days, every muscle in my body was in pain (here began a shoulder injury which is now inoperable). The heat was almost beyond bearing. My feet had swollen, literally, to the size of footballs. I cannot describe the pain. When they took the leg irons off, they had to actually dig them out of the swollen flesh. It was five days before I could walk, because the weight of the leg irons on my Achilles tendons had paralyzed them and hamstrung me. I stayed in the box from June 1 until November 10, 1969. While in the box, I lost at least thirty pounds. I would be curious to hear Mr. Durbin explain how this compares with having a female invade my private space, and whether a box in which the heat nearly killed me is the same as turning up the air conditioning.

The detainees at Guantanamo receive new Korans and prayer rugs, and the guards are instructed not to disturb the inmates' prayers. Compare this with my experience in February 1971, when I watched as armed men dragged from our cell, successively, four of my cell mates after they had led us in the Lord's Prayer. Their prayers were in defiance of a January 1971 regulation in which the Communists forbade any religious observances in our cells. Does Mr. Durbin somehow argue that our behavior is the equivalent of the behavior of the Communists?

Actually, I was one of the lucky ones. At another camp, during the time I was being interrogated in the summer of 1969, one man was tortured to death and several others were severely beaten. In fact, according to Headquarters Marine Corps, twenty percent of my fellow Marines failed to survive captivity. Have twenty percent of the Islamo-fascists failed to survive Guantanamo?

The argument that detainees at Guantanamo are being treated badly is specious and silly. In the eyes of normal Americans, Democrats believe this argument because, as Jeanne Kirkpatrick said twenty years ago, they "always blame America first."

Mr. Warner's letter originally appeared in *The Washington Times*.

Note: T. "Bubba" Bechtol, part time City Councilman from Pensacola, Florida, was asked on a local live radio talk show what he thought of the allegations of torture of the Iraqi prisoners. His reply prompted his ejection from the studio, but to thunderous applause from the audience. "If hooking up an Iraqi prisoner's scrotum to a car's battery cables will save one American GI's life, then I have just two things to say: "Red is positive. Black is negative."

THE NAVY'S POLICE FORCE

"The Marine Corps is the Navy's police force, and as long as I am President that is what it will remain. They have a propaganda machine that is almost equal to Stalin's..." – President Harry S. Truman

This letter was written by President Harry S. Truman while the 1st Provisional Marine Brigade was engaged in saving the Pusan perimeter, and just prior to the 1st Marine Division landing at Inchon and liberating Seoul. Bad timing, Harry!

My Dear Congressman McDonough,

I read with a lot of interest your letter in regard to the Marine Corps... and your idea of placing a Marine general on the Joint Chiefs of Staff. For your information, the Marine Corps is the Navy's police force, and as long as I am President that is what it will remain. They have a propaganda machine that is almost equal to Stalin's...

Nobody desires to belittle the efforts of the Marine Corps, but when the Marine Corps goes into the Army it will work with and for the Army, and that is the way it should be...

I am more than happy to have your expression of interest in this naval military organization... the Chief of Naval Operations is the Chief of Staff of the Navy, of which the Marines are a part.

Sincerely yours,

Harry S. Truman

Congressman McDonough forwarded the letter to the Commandant of the Marine Corps, General Clifton B. Cates, and the General wasted no time in making his displeasure known to the President. Mr. Truman then wrote this second letter in an attempt to make peace with the Corps.

Dear General Cates,

I sincerely regret the unfortunate choice of language which I used in my letter of August 29 to Congressman McDonough concerning the Marine Corps.

What I had in mind at the time this letter was written was the specific question raised by Mr. McDonough, namely the representation of the Marine Corps on the Joint Chiefs of Staff. I have been disturbed by the number of communications which have been brought to my attention proposing that the Marine Corps have such representation. I feel that, inasmuch as the Marine Corps is by law an integral part of the Navy, it is already represented on the Joint Chiefs of Staff by the Chief of Naval Operations. The Congress concurs in this point of view, as evidenced by the fact that, in passing the National Security Act of 1947, and again in amending that Act in 1949, the Congress considered the question of Marine Corps representation on the Joint Chiefs of Staff and did not provide for it. It is my feeling that many of the new pleas for such representation are the results of propaganda inspired by individuals who may not be aware of the best interests of our defense establishment as a whole, and it was this feeling which I was expressing to Mr. McDonough. I am certain that the Marine Corps itself does not indulge in such propaganda.

I am profoundly aware of the magnificent history of the United States Marine Corps, and of the many heroic deeds of the Marines since the Corps was established in 1775. I personally learned of the splendid combat spirit of the Marines when the Fourth Marine Brigade of the Second Infantry Division fought in France in 1918.

On numerous occasions since I assumed office I have stated my conviction that the Marine Corps has a vital role in our organization for national security, and I will continue to support and maintain its identity. I regard the Marine Corps as a force available for use in any emergency, wherever or whenever necessary. When I spoke of the Marines as the "Navy's police force," I had in mind its immediate readiness, and the provision of the National Security Act which states that "the Marine Corps shall be organized, trained, and equipped to provide Fleet Marine Forces of combined arms, together with supporting air components, for service with the fleet in the seizure of defense of advanced naval bases and for the conduct of such land operations as may seem essential to the prosecution of a naval campaign."

The Corps' ability to carry out whatever task may be assigned to it has been splendidly demonstrated many times in our history. It has again been shown by the immediate response of the Marine Corps to a call for duty in Korea. Since Marine ground and air forces have arrived in Korea I have received a daily report of their actions. The country may feel sure that the record of the Marines now fighting there will add new laurels to the already illustrious record of the Marine Corps.

Sincerely yours,

Harry S. Truman

THE MARINES HAVE...
Arrived!

Harry Levins

"The bended knee is not a tradition of our Corps." - General A. A. Vandegrift, testifying before Congress regarding the possible dissolution of the Marine Corps

In the book "First To Fight" by General Victor H. 'Brute' Krulak, the general detailed to activities of the "Marching and Chowder Society," which was an ad hoc group of Marines with the mission of saving the Corps from being disbanded. Over the years there have been many attempts by our "sister" services to get rid of the Marine Corps in one way or another, all (obviously) unsuccessful - and as a result the appointment of General Pace is all the sweeter.

The next chairman of the Joint Chiefs of Staff is a four-star surprise - a Marine, the first ever to hold the job. President George W. Bush took Defense Secretary Donald Rumsfeld's advice that the job go to Marine General Peter Pace, who is now the vice chairman.

Some see the pick as a salute to the Marines. "It's a final indication that the Marine Corps is fully accepted as a separate service," says retired Marine Colonel Mackubin T. Owens, who teaches strategy at the Naval War College.

From the University of North Carolina, military historian Richard H. Kohn agrees. "What it says is that the Marines are full players at the table - that they're no longer considered officers of limited perspective and parochial concerns."

Owens and Kohn are backed by military writer Ralph Peters, a retired Army officer but an active Marine Corps admirer. Peters calls the selection of Pace "a recognition of the Marine Corps' success and values - of its leading role in rethinking military affairs."

It could also be a reward, says Jerry Cooper, professor emeritus of military history at the University of Missouri at St. Louis. "The Marines have carried a far heavier proportional load in Iraq than the other services," says Cooper. He adds, "The Marine Corps seems to suit Rumsfeld well as 'a lean, mean fighting machine.'"

Peters sees the Marines as "expeditionary knife-fighters. And they've never lost the tradition of being warriors, not just technocrats."

Whatever, the Marines have come a long way. Only in the Korean War era did the Marines get a seat at the Joint Chiefs' table. And not until 1976 did the Marine Commandant become a full-time voting member.

Since the Goldwater-Nichols Act of 1986, power has drained from the service chiefs and flowed to the chairman and the chiefs of the nine "combatant commands" - the U.S. Central Command and the rest.

Although people in Air Force blue outnumber people in Marine Corps green, the Marines outnumber the Air Force in generals running those nine commands. Both the U.S. European Command and the U.S. Strategic Command answer to Marine generals. The Air Force runs only one - the U.S. Transportation Command.

Cooper says that although all services take pride in themselves, the Marines do it best. "I've never seen a socialization system like the one the Marines have for instilling institutional loyalty," Cooper says. "They're better than Notre Dame!"

I'M AN FMF CORPSMAN

HM2 Maria Gilmore

"Marines do not want to go into harm's way without their corpsmen, and corpsmen do not want their Marines to go into harm's way without *them*."

Yes, I'm a Corpsman. I know the Marines sure like us, but I'm just another Navy person this tour (aside from when I went to Iraq with the Marines). Marines are awesome to serve with – it's a different world when you're with them, more work, but most of all more fun, and their devotion to each other is just amazing - it used to crack me up to see a couple of them who can't stand each other on a normal day, then as soon as an Airmen would start something with them, they'd all be backing each other up.

They treat us very, very well as long as we aren't "dirtbag" corpsmen. You always knew who the bad ones were, because instead of calling them "Doc" they'd call them "Petty Officer." It took some getting used to when I went to a Navy command, and we were *all* just Petty Officers.

Those of us who are FMF corpsman love our Marines. I would take a year in the dirt with them over an hour on a ship any day. Military funerals still make me weepy - when we would send someone home from over there we would walk their flag-draped casket to the C-130 in formation and it was so hard seeing all of the Marines trying so hard to be tough and keep their composure, though few of them really held it together in the end. I can't describe the feeling.

The bottom line is, I'm so lucky to have had the opportunity to serve with America's finest!

TRUE ACTION HEROES

"It's great to be here with the greatest of the great, and the strongest of the strong... I only *play* an action hero, but you people are the *true* action heroes." – Governor Arnold Schwarzenegger

For some, he's the action hero that killed the alien in "Predator." To others, he's the "Terminator." To California residents he's Governor Schwarzenegger. But to Arnold Schwarzenegger, the men of the U.S. Marine Corps are the true action stars.

Schwarzenegger expressed that sentiment Friday night at the New Sanno Hotel in Tokyo, where he was the surprise special guest at the Marine Security Guard Detachment's Marine Corps Ball. The Governor, who has been in Japan on a trade mission, was invited to the celebration by Howard Baker, the U.S. ambassador to Japan, and the U.S. Embassy Marine Security Guard detachment.

"When I heard you had this celebration here today, I told the ambassador that there is no way I would miss it," Schwarzenegger told the crowd. "It's great to be here with the greatest of the great, and the strongest of the strong. I am honored to join you tonight, to celebrate the 229th anniversary of the birth of the Marine Corps."

During his speech to the more than one hundred Marine Corps Ball guests, the governor spoke reverently about the Marine Corps' past. "You have always been there on the front lines fighting to protect America, and I know you have a great history of kicking some serious butt. The only reason why people become so successful in America, and the only reason why this country is so successful, is because of you brave men and women right here, you are the ones who protect the liberty," he said. "You are protecting this great country of America and defending the American dream. I want to thank all of you for the great work you are doing. You are doing a fantastic job of protecting our nation and safeguarding the stability of the Western Pacific." Schwarzenegger closed by saying, "I only *play* an action hero, but you people are the *true* action heroes."

TO OUR BRITISH FRIENDS

MSgt Andy Bufalo, USMC (Ret)

"This was the first time that the Marines of the two nations had fought side by side since the defense of the Peking Legations in 1900. Let it be said that the admiration of all ranks of 41 Commando (of the Royal Marines) for their brothers in arms was, and is, unbounded. They fought like tigers, and their morale and esprit de corps is second to none." - Lieutenant Colonel D.B. Drysdale, Commanding 41 Commando, Chosen Reservoir, speaking about the 1st Marine Division

When I heard about the London subway bombings which took place in July of 2005 I felt compelled to write something about the close bond between our two nations. This was emailed to some of my British friends the next day, and ended up in many more mailboxes than I had expected:

Many times during my Marine Corps career I had the good fortune and distinct pleasure of socializing with and serving alongside soldiers, sailors, Marines and citizens of the British Empire. As a recon team leader I called in air strikes on (opposing force) elements of the Royal Marines' 45 Commando, while serving as MSG Detachment Commander in Canberra, Australia I invited the Defense Attaché' of the British High Commission to be our guest of honor at a Mess Night celebrating Independence Day (no small bit of irony there), and I have consumed more than a bit of English ale in the pubs of Portsmouth and Plymouth. On every occasion I was impressed by the stoic nature of the Brits, and by the incredibly civilized society they have built. It is because of the latter that I join all decent people in condemning the cowardly and barbaric attacks on London and mourn the losses suffered by our British friends - and because of the former I know our friends across the Big Pond will display their famed "stiff upper lip" and prevail against the terrorists. This is the worst attack against the Crown since the Nazis launched the Blitz, and it calls to mind the words of Sir Winston Churchill - words which are as true now as when he first spoke them:

"I have, myself, full confidence that if all do their duty, if nothing is neglected, and if the best arrangements are made, as they are being made, we shall prove ourselves once again able to defend our Island home, to ride out the storm of war, and to outlive the menace of tyranny, if necessary for years, if necessary alone... We shall go on to the end, we shall fight in France, we shall fight on the seas and oceans, we shall fight with growing confidence and growing strength in the air, we shall defend our Island, whatever the cost may be, we shall fight on the beaches, we shall fight on the landing grounds, we shall fight in the fields and in the streets, we shall fight in the hills; we shall never surrender, and even if, which I do not for a moment believe, this Island or a large part of it were subjugated and starving, then our Empire beyond the seas, armed and guarded by the British Fleet, would carry on the struggle, until, in God's good time, the New World, with all its power and might, steps forth to the rescue and the liberation of the old."

The words "United We Stand" do not apply only to Americans - they apply to all who love freedom. We stand with our British friends on this day, and will do so until the world is safe for our children and our children's children.

OUR TOUGHEST FIGHT
Discipline Problems of the 1970's

Lieutenant General William K. Jones USMC (Ret)

"Almighty Father... if I am inclined to doubt, steady my faith. If I am tempted, make me strong to resist. If I should miss the mark, give me courage to try again..."
– From '*The Marines' Prayer*'

This piece really struck a chord with me. I was part of the Corps back then, and in fact participated in the very Solid Shield, Northern Wedding, and Bold Guard exercises cited by the general. Drug use was so widespread back then that my recruiter wanted me to request a waiver for "experimental marijuana use" in order to cover his butt, but when I <u>insisted</u> I had never tried the stuff (after a fifteen minute grilling) he reluctantly processed my paperwork without one!

Many returning American veterans of the Vietnam War believed that they were not honored as they had been in previous wars. Some felt they had risked their lives in vain, and were embittered by the memory of the approximately 55,000 of their buddies who had been killed. They were angry over an amnesty for draft-dodgers who had fled to Canada, Sweden, and other countries to avoid the war.

As anti-war sentiment developed in the country, drug usage also was making progress in all classes of society and in various age groups. There was a growing drug problem among the troops both at home and abroad. As it grew, morale and discipline declined. As troops were rotated from abroad, they brought the problem with them. Other factors

246

strongly influencing military affairs in the early 1970's were the ending of the draft and the advent of the all-volunteer force in 1973.

The Armed Forces were experiencing many difficulties. Pressure was strong to keep up the level of manpower. Yet during the last phases of the American presence in Vietnam, the anti-war movement had gained great influence. There were numerous racial incidents. Some troops refused to carry out their orders if there was danger involved. Fragging (directing a fragmentation grenade at an unpopular officer or NCO) resulted in some deaths. It also took other forms such as booby trapping a jeep and even shooting some men in the back. Through fear of retaliation and the dislike of informing against another man, it often was extremely difficult to locate the culprit.

Back in the United States, racial incidents grew at the various camps. Gangs of black Marines would roam Camp Lejeune or other posts and stations, and beat up white Marines found to be alone. Soon there was a backlash, continuing the violence.

Traditionally high morale was sadly shaken. A true crisis was threatening the 200-year-old Corps. Many of the problems could be traced to the end of the draft and the pressure of keeping up the size of the Marine Corps. In the process, a number of society's misfits had been recruited.

A commanding officer of the 6th Marines from those challenging days, Colonel Paul B. Haigwood, recalls that the regiment spent approximately fifty percent of its time in the field with every regimental unit available participating. Although the training was extreme and repetitive, it was necessary because of the high personnel turnover and the requirement to meet the many commitments referred to earlier. Further, it served to lessen the racial tensions as the

Category IV (less intelligent) Marines seemed to forget their problems and concentrated on being Marines. Maybe they were too tired to do anything else.

In any event, over time the regimental incident rate, desertions, and other indicators of discipline improved to the point where the 6th Marines could truthfully be called the most combat-ready unit in the division.

The regiment won almost every divisional contest such as football, basketball, boxing, and marksmanship. Nevertheless, there still were unfortunate incidents. Following a movie at the Camp Lejeune post theater, there was a gang fight among some twenty-five to thirty black and white Marines from the 1st Battalion, 6th Marines. It ended with one Marine being killed. This, of course, was labeled a riot by the press, and caused unfavorable publicity for the Corps.

It was not easy being a commanding officer in those days, but as usual in Marine Corps life, there were many responsibilities to be met, and there was always a belief in a better future.

Further, amusing incidents occurred to lighten the load. During a Headquarters Marine Corps Inspector General's inspection, Colonel Haigwood was showing the Inspector General around his area. When they visited the 2nd Battalion armory, they found everything to be outstanding - weapons, records, cleanliness - everything. The Inspector General announced to everyone present that this was "the best" armory he had seen in a long time, and that he would personally like to shake the hand of the NCO in charge. A young Marine stepped forward immediately, and said, "General sir, I am Corporal 'Smith,' MFICC of the Armory." The general congratulated the corporal, praised him for what he had accomplished, and the inspection party moved on.

Approximately two blocks down the street the Inspector General stopped, turned to Haigwood and said, "What in the *hell* does MFICC mean?" Taking a deep breath, the regimental commander answered, "It stands for Mother F*&%er In Complete Charge." The general laughed until he almost popped a button from his blouse.

In spite of the many problems encountered, training continued during the 1970s. Not only were deployments made to the Caribbean and Mediterranean, but training was also held with the 82nd Airborne Division, both at Fort Bragg and in the Camp Lejeune area. In 1973, during DesEx Alkali Canyon, USMCR units from the 4th Marine Division were successfully integrated into a major exercise. This was valuable to all the participants. Also, planning was started for Alpine Warrior 74, to be held at Camp Drum, New York. In 1974, training with U.S. Army units at Camp Pickett, Virginia, took place during Exercise Solid Punch, involving Army armor and armored infantry units. Cold-weather training at Camp Drum took place, as did other types of routine training.

Finally, the Twenty-sixth Commandant, General Lewis H. Wilson, took office. He had earned the Medal of Honor on Guam during World War II, and was a strict disciplinarian. This occurred on 1 July 1975, after his predecessor requested an early retirement.

Wilson immediately started to clean out the true misfits from the Marine Corps. The 6th Marines themselves offered a typical example. An article by Walter V. Robinson of the *Boston Globe* staff, dated 6 June 1976, set forth the situation. It was written from Camp Lejeune. Mr. Robinson was writing about an amphibious operation conducted by the 6th Marines. Commenting on the high seas encountered, and the fact that five Marines were injured by lightning, he still felt that the operation was more satisfactory than a similar one the year before.

He said, "Last year the same could not be said. Although 2,500 men of the 3,000-man 6th Regiment were slated to participate, only 1200 of them waded ashore in Operation Solid Shield 1975. Of the remaining 1,300 men, 800 were back in their barracks awaiting undesirable discharges. More than 200 others were over the hill - AWOL. Still others were on the regimental rolls; they had been classified as deserters. And 267 of the 6th Regiment's Marines had been administratively reassigned to the brig where they were imprisoned for a variety of offenses."

The career officers and NCOs previously had been disgusted. The reforms instituted by General Wilson, however, got rid of more than 6,000 problem Marines out of a total strength of 196,000. Enlistment standards were raised. Physical training and discipline were improved. The percentage of high school graduates in the 2nd Division had dropped to 38 percent.

Their commanding general had estimated perhaps eighty percent of the Marines had tried marijuana. One rifle company commander recalled he had only seventeen of 189 men available for training because of personnel problems. The 2nd Division discharged as undesirable 2,400 men in 1975. Of those, 1,027 belonged to the 3,000-man 6th Marines. Since December of 1975 another 600 2nd Division Marines had left early under an "expeditious discharge program" initiated by the Commandant.

When Colonel (later Major General) Harold G. Glasgow took command of the 6th Marines in May 1975, he found 294 of his Marines were carried in an unauthorized leave status and 231 more were either confined or under restraint. He told a reporter later that at the time he was lucky if one in every five Marines saluted him. Between ten percent and fifteen percent were intentionally trying to fail their physical fitness tests.

The problems encountered by the commanders in training and administering their units were complex and challenging. Their strength of character was tested many times in a variety of ways. In fact, company commanders were so involved in Office Hours, Request Masts, and writing up administrative discharges it was difficult to maintain any semblance of a training program.

Nevertheless, operational and training exercises were held, including a Mediterranean deployment of the 1st Battalion; Solid Shield 75 locally; two battalion-size exercises at Fort Pickett; two special exercises (reinforced rifle companies) to Guantanamo Bay, Cuba; a combined-arms exercise at Twenty-nine Palms, California; a cold-weather exercise at Fort Drum; and a Division CPX. A full schedule indeed, one that cut down on the time Marines had to be drawn into unwanted incidents.

During August 1976, the 36th Marine Amphibious Unit (MAU) was formed around the 6th Marines. The 2nd Battalion became the ground element, a composite squadron from MAGs 26 and 29 became the aviation combat element, while the MAU Service Support Group (MSSG) was formed from the 2nd Force Service Support Group (FSSG). After the very detailed planning required and appropriate training, the 36th MAU deployed to Europe for participation in Operation Straffe Zugel and Operation Triple Jubilee.

Operation Straffe Zugel was part of Reforger Exercise 75 and was conducted in the central plains of West Germany near the city of Hanover. The 36th MAU's participation represented the first Marine Corps maneuver elements in Germany since World War I. This exercise further paved the way for subsequent Marine participation in larger training exercises in Germany - Teamwork/ Bonded Item and Northern Wedding/Bold Guard. The Marine Corps was again becoming involved in the defense of western Europe, as it was in World War I.

Operation Triple Jubilee was conducted in three separate locations in the United Kingdom. According to the account of then Colonel Glasgow, the first phase was near Plymouth. This exercise concentrated on small-unit training with the Royal Marines. A memorable occurrence was the celebration of the 200th Marine Corps Birthday at the Royal Marines' Stonehouse Barracks. The Royal Marines were hosts, then-Assistant Commandant of the Marine Corps General Samuel Jaskilka was the guest of honor, and the other guests included both General Peter Whitely, Commandant General of the Royal Marines, and General A. C. Lammers, Commandant of the Royal Netherlands Marine Corps.

The second phase of Triple Jubilee was conducted on Salisbury Plain near Portsmouth and Southhampton. The 3rd Brigade of the Royal Marines both controlled the exercise and acted as aggressors. It was a rewarding, excellent exercise.

The third phase of Triple Jubilee consisted of an amphibious landing across the beach at Barry Buddon, Scotland, near Arbroath. The North Sea was rough, and the weather cold, but the 6th Marines looked like real professionals. After liberty at Dundee, the regiment returned to Camp Lejeune exhilarated by the many interesting and satisfying times it had experienced.

Between the two main operations, 36th MAU made port visits to Amsterdam and Rotterdam in the Netherlands and Brest and Le Havre, in France. The stiffer enlistment standards paid off. The 2nd Division's high-school-completion rate jumped to sixty percent within a year, and the greater emphasis on physical fitness soon made a leaner, stronger, and more confident Marine Corps.

Already a marked change could be seen. The quality of the Marines had improved, morale was high, the disciplinary rate was falling - the Marine Corps had won its fight. As the *Boston Globe* article of 6 June 1976 had labeled it – *"The Marines' Toughest Fight: Long Battle for Respectability."*

This article was excerpted from *"A Brief History of the 6th Marines,"* by Lieutenant General William K. Jones USMC (Ret) and published in 1987 by the History and Museum Division, Headquarters U.S. Marine Corps Washington, D.C.

I AM "THEY"

General Carl Mundy

"Let's be damn sure that no man's ghost will ever say: 'If your training program had only done its job.'" - DI Motto

I was a no-rank fuzz-butt in the Marine Corps when General Wilson took the helm, and the sweeping changes he made were felt right down to the last private in the rearmost rank. General Jones was not exaggerating when he said he is the man who 'saved' the Corps. The following eulogy was given by the 30th Commandant, General Carl Mundy, Jr., in remembrance of General Louis Wilson, Jr., 26th Commandant of the Marine Corps.

Three years after I graduated from the Basic School at Quantico, I was ordered back to become an instructor. I reported to the Adjutant, who informed me that the Commanding Officer was absent for a few days, but would return the following week. He advised, further, that it was the colonel's policy to address all newly forming companies of lieutenants on the first day of training, which would occur, coincidentally, on the day of his return - and that I should be there.

At 0700 on the prescribed day, I mustered with a half-dozen instructors and couple of hundred new lieutenants in the outdoor classroom just in front of the headquarters building. Precisely at 0715 the front door opened and a tall, rangy, all-business-looking colonel walked out. We were called to attention, then put at ease and given our seats.

The colonel spoke for probably no more than eight to ten minutes, citing what was to be accomplished and what was

254

expected of the lieutenants in the next six months. He concluded by saying: "While you're here, you'll find many things that are wrong... that are not to your liking... not the way you would do them - and you'll find yourselves talking about how 'they' ought to change this or that... and how 'they' just don't understand the problem. When you have those thoughts or discussions" he went on, "I want you to remember this: I... *am* they!"

He stood looking at us for probably no more than five seconds, which seemed like minutes. Not a head turned; not an eye blinked, and I'm sure two hundred second-lieutenant minds were working in unison to figure out how they could go through twenty-six weeks of training without ever once uttering the word, "they"!

This was my first association with then-Colonel Louis Wilson. Like a few others, the "I am they" assertion became pure "Wilsonian" over the years, and like me, I suspect that many here this morning have heard it on more than one occasion. It contained a little humor, but it also characterized the man as the leader he was: "I am 'they'; I'm in command; I'm responsible; I give the orders."

Even beyond his years in the Corps, these characteristics continued. His good friend, Bill Schreyer – the Chairman of the Board of Merrill-Lynch when General Wilson served, after retirement, as a Director of that company, tells the story of a board meeting at which a particularly difficult issue was being deliberated. After considerable discussion, during which a number of thoughts and ideas emerged, but without definitive resolution of the issue, Director Wilson said, "Mr. Chairman, if Moses had been a member of this Board, instead of 'The Ten Commandments,' we would have wound up with 'The Ten Suggestions!'"

Louis Hugh Wilson, Jr., was born and grew up in

Brandon, Mississippi. His father died when he was five, and those family members who knew him then characterized him - even as a small boy - as exhibiting a clear feeling of responsibility for his mother and sister. He worked at a variety of jobs throughout his school years to help with their support. After graduation from high school, he enrolled at nearby Millsaps College, majored in economics, ran track, played football and joined the "Pikes" – the Pi Kappa Alpha Fraternity.

In the summer after his freshman year he and a buddy took a job laying asphalt over the dirt and gravel roads of Mississippi, and while working one day a car passed carrying an attractive local high school graduate named Jane Clark. "I sure would like to get to know that girl," Louis remarked to his buddy. "No chance, Lou, she's taken," his friend answered.

Wrong answer! Within a short time, Lou and Jane were dating, and by the time she followed him a year or so later to Millsaps, they were courting. When he graduated in 1941 and went off to officer candidate training in the Marines, and then into the war in the Pacific, they "had an understanding," and she waited. They became 'Captain and Mrs. Wilson' three years later, when he returned from hospitalization after the battle for Guam.

Captain Wilson got a bride, but the Corps got one of its most gracious future First Ladies - one beloved by all who have had the privilege of knowing her - but none more-so than the Wilson aides-de-camp over the years to whom she became known as "President of the Aides' Protective Society" with an occasional early morning call just after the General departed quarters for the office, wishing them – in her soft, Southern manner – "a wonderful day - even though it may not start that way!"

Throughout their career, and to the present, Jane has been an inspiring role-model to all of us in both the good, and the hard times. Indeed, a legion of Marines are glad that Lou's friend on the hot asphalt road in Mississippi in 1938 was wrong when he predicted: "No chance, Lou."

Captain Wilson's action on Guam was the beginning of the many highlights in his career. I was privileged to be on the island with him in 1994 for the 50th Anniversary of its liberation, and while there, walked the battleground on Fonte Hill with him where he remembered and described every move as he assembled and maneuvered the remnants of his company and those of the other companies of his battalion to secure the heights. Only then... having been wounded three times... did he allow treatment of his wounds and medical evacuation.

The following day, I hosted a sad ceremony at Asan Point - near the beach where, fifty-years earlier, he had landed. Because of mandated personnel reductions in the Corps, the 9th Marines - the regiment with which he had served on Guam - was being deactivated. As its proud battle color was furled, General Wilson placed the casement over it.

There is, however, a humorous sequel to this event. Enroute back from Guam, we stopped in Hawaii to attend the change of command of Marine Forces, Pacific. The day allowed time for a round of golf before the ceremonies that evening. As General Wilson and I were having breakfast before teeing-off, a retired Marine - red baseball cap and all - came over to our table to warmly greet the General. It turned out they had been in the 9th Marines together, and the conversation turned quickly to something like this: "Lou, who's this new Commandant that's doing away with the 9th Marines? What does he think he's doing? You need to get hold of him and straighten him out!"

The breakfast would have undoubtedly been more entertaining for those around us had he done so, but without introducing me, General Wilson graciously responded that he knew it was a tough decision, but that were he still Commandant, he probably would have had to make the same one. He wished his retired friend a good game, and sat back down to breakfast with a wink and big grin for me. I was grateful to have "They" on my team *that* morning!

Throughout the decades of service that marked his career, Louis Wilson established the reputation of a firm, but fair leader who was devoted to the welfare and readiness of Marines and would lay his career on the line for them; who asked straight questions and expected no "off the record" answers or hidden agendas; and who, while he could show understanding, did not easily suffer fools.

During his tenure as Commanding General of Fleet Marine Force, Pacific, as North Vietnamese forces closed in, the evacuation of the U.S. Embassy in Saigon was ordered, using ships of the U.S. Seventh Fleet and embarked Marines from Okinawa, including then-Colonel Al Gray's 4th Marines.

As the day wore on far longer than had been planned due to the panicky influx of hundreds more evacuees than the Embassy had planned for, the operation continued through the night and into the wee hours of the following morning. About three AM, word came into the command center in Hawaii that the Seventh Fleet Commander had signaled that the helicopter crews which had been flying since early that day had reached their administrative maximum allowed flying hours and that he intended to suspend flight operations to allow crew rest, even though a hundred or more Marines still remained in the besieged Embassy.

Although he was not in the direct chain of command for

the operation, an infuriated General Wilson immediately sent back a message stating that under no circumstances would such an order be given, that Marine helicopters would continue to fly so long as Marines remained in Saigon, and that if the Seventh Fleet Commander issued such an order, he, Wilson, would personally prefer court martial charges against him. The order was never issued, the helicopter crews kept flying, and the remaining Marines were evacuated.

A year later found the Secretary of Defense looking for a new Commandant, and 'Wilson' was a name high on the list. While many important people are involved in the naming of any new Commandant, there are a couple who merit special note in this case.

The Wilsons had become very happy in Hawaii, and since he was nearing the point at which his career might come to an end, he had been extended a lucrative job offer; his daughter Janet was a senior in high school; and Jane had found a 'Dream House' on the slopes overlooking Waialae Golf Course and the blue Pacific. As the likelihood of his being nominated to become Commandant took shape, the Wilsons sat down for a family conference to discuss the choices.

After a brief discussion, Janet brought a decisive end to their deliberations when she said, "Dad, you've talked for a long time about all the things that are wrong in the Marine Corps. This is your chance to *fix* them." He thought for a moment, and then responded, "O.K., we'll do it." And so, perhaps history should record that it was Miss Janet Wilson who, as much as anyone, brought us the 26th Commandant!

But there was another player who should not go without note. When the selection was made, Secretary of Defense Jim Schlesinger directed an assistant to "Get General Wilson in Hawaii on the phone." Moments later, the assistant reported, "Sir, he's on the line." Schlesinger picked up the phone and said, "Lou, I'm delighted to inform you that the President has selected you to be the next Commandant of the Marine Corps."

There was a pause, and the voice at the other end of the line responded, "Sir, I'm deeply honored by your call. I've always had great admiration for the Marines, but do you really think I'm qualified to become Commandant?"

Schlesinger's assistant had dialed the Commander of Pacific Air Forces in Hawaii - also a Lieutenant General named Lou Wilson!

A few minutes later, when the *right* Wilson was reached, Schlesinger repeated the same congratulatory message, but ended by saying: "However, Lou, you should know that my first call turned me down!" So perhaps - in the spirit of jointness - we also owe the U.S. Air Force a debt of gratitude!

Lou Wilson became Commandant at a time when the Corps needed him. Fewer than fifty percent of those who filled our ranks were high school graduates. Illegal drug use was rampant. Lingering Vietnam-era recruiting had brought a fair number of criminals into the Corps. Riots and gang intimidation were common. His comment when he assumed command set the stage for his attack on these problems: "I call on all Marines to get in step, and do so smartly!"

His tenure as Commandant would be marked by firm initiatives to "get the Corps in step" again. Overweight Marines, "high-water" trousers, shaggy haircuts, and moustaches became early points of focus. The word went out: "If I see a fat Marine, he's in trouble - and so is his commanding officer!"

More than a few commanders got early morning calls

from the Commandant that began: "Who's minding the store down there? Seems like you might be looking for a different line of work!" Prompt administrative discharges from the Corps for "those who can't, or don't want to, measure up to our standards" were authorized. The Air-Ground Combat Center at Twentynine Palms came into being to cause Marines to prepare for the next war, instead of the last one - and it might be recalled that the "next big one" after Vietnam was in the desert sands of Kuwait, and the Combined Arms Exercises at Twentynine Palms were the training grounds.

The Wilson years, and those that followed, would re-hone the Marine Corps into what it remains today - the finest military organization in the history of the world. But if Fonte Hill on Guam, and the Medal of Honor, was the *early* signature of Lou Wilson, it may be that his *enduring* mark on the Corps - and our entire joint military establishment - is that which he achieved in his final "Hill" battle near the end of his tenure as Commandant.

A quarter-century earlier, after a period of intense debate as to the role of the Marine Corps in the national defense establishment, the National Security Act had made the Commandant of the Marine Corps a "part time" member of the Joint Chiefs of Staff only when matters of Marine Corps interest were at issue. This denigration of the Corps to second-class citizenship had long been an insult and irritation. Within the organization of the Joint Chiefs, a policy existed that when the Chairman was absent from Washington, the next ranking Chief would assume authority as "Acting Chairman."

In early 1978 the Chairman and all other chiefs of service, except General Wilson, were absent from Washington. A memorandum from the Director of the Joint Staff indicated that in the absence of the Chairman, and the Chiefs of the

Army, Navy, and Air Force, the Vice Chief of Staff of the Army was appointed "Acting Chairman." An irritated inquiry from the Marine Corps gained a response from the Director that "the Commandant cannot be appointed Acting Chairman because he is only a part-time member of the Joint Chiefs."

Like when Miss Jane Clark drove by four decades earlier - already with a "steady" and "no chance" - or when the Seventh Fleet Commander was about to suspend flight operations: Wrong answer!

General Wilson quietly and without fanfare took the issue to Capitol Hill, and when the 1979 Defense Authorization Bill came out, it contained a provision which made the Commandant of the Marine Corps a full-fledged member of the Joint Chiefs of Staff.

Indeed, the legacy achieved by its 26th Commandant for the Corps sits before us today. Without Lou Wilson's personal perseverance and victory, it is not likely that General Pete Pace, the Chairman Designate, or General Jim Jones, the Supreme Allied Commander in Europe, or General Jim Cartwright, the Commander, U. S. Strategic Command, would be in their positions today.

Lou Wilson elevated his Corps from a bureaucratic, second-class category to co-equal status with every other branch of the armed services... and his country - and the profession of those who bear arms in its defense - will be forever the beneficiaries.

And so, as we assemble today to bid farewell to one of the true giants of our Corps and our Nation, let us do so with gratitude that America produces men the likes of Louis Wilson - and that "They" choose to become Marines.

PROFILE OF A MARINE

"You are not forgotten." – Words on the POW/MIA Flag

Prisoners of War, soldiers captured by enemy soldiers during times of war, are casualties that can all too often be easy to forget. You can't ignore the image of crosses lined in neat rows at Arlington, and other National cemeteries, which remind us of the high cost of freedom. In any gathering of veterans, the scars of war wounds and evidence of missing limbs quickly reminds us of the sacrifice of those who have fought for freedom. It is impossible to forget those who have been killed in or wounded in action, because the evidence of their sacrifice is ever before us.

Sadly, the same cannot be said for those who are missing in action, or who may have been taken prisoner by the enemy and never repatriated. Since World War I more than 200,000 Americans have been listed as Prisoners of War or Missing in Action. Less than half of them were returned at the end of hostilities, leaving more than 125,000 American servicemen missing since the beginning of World War I.

Because of that issue, only one flag besides the Stars and Stripes representing the United States has ever flown over the White House in Washington, DC. Only one flag is ever displayed in the U.S. Capitol Rotunda. That flag does not represent an individual state, branch of service, or other select group. It is the POW/MIA (Prisoners of War/Missing In Action) Flag which calls to mind the sacrifice and plight of those Americans who have sacrificed their own freedom in order to preserve liberty for all of us. Its presence serves to remind us that, while we enjoy the privileges of freedom, somewhere there are soldiers, sailors, Marines and airmen who have not been accounted for and that some may, in fact, still be held against their will by the enemies of freedom.

While most people are familiar with the flag, few know the story behind its creation. It started when Mrs. Michael Hoff of Jacksonville, Florida, an MIA wife and member of the National League of Families, wrote to Annin & Co., the world's largest flag company, and said, "We'd like to have a banner for our organization." That letter came to the attention of Norman Rivikies, vice president of Annin, and he in turn passed along the request to the graphics design company which employed a fellow by the name of Newt Heisley.

Newt had himself been a pilot during World War II, a dangerous role which has accounted for many wartime POWs and MIAs. Years after the war he had come to New York looking for work. "It took me four days to find a bad job at low pay," he later said of his introduction to "Big Apple" advertising agencies. But, by working hard, he gradually moved upward in the industry, eventually working for an agency with many national accounts.

As a veteran, the call for a flag designed to raise awareness of our Nation's POW/MIAs was a personal challenge. It was even more challenging when he considered that his oldest son Jeffrey was, during those Vietnam War years, training for combat with the United States Marine Corps at Quantico, Virginia. As he pondered this new challenge a series of events set in motion the ideas that would create a flag unlike anything since the days of Betsy Ross. First, Jeffery became very ill while training for combat. The illness, diagnosed as hepatitis, ravaged his body, emaciating his face and structure. When he returned home, medically discharged and unable to continue further, his father looked in horror at what had once been a strong young man. Then, as Newt Heisley looked closer at his son's gaunt features, he began to imagine what life must be like for those behind barbed wire fences on foreign shores. Slowly he began to sketch the profile of his son, working in pencil to create a black and white silhouette, as the new flag's design was created in his mind. Barbed wire, a tower, and most prominently the visage of a gaunt young man became the initial proposal.

Newt Heisley's black and white pencil sketch was one of several designs considered for the new POW/MIA flag. Newt planned, should his design be accepted, to add color at a later date... perhaps a deep purple and white. "In the advertising industry, you do everything in black and white first, then add the color later," he said. Mr. Heisley's proposal for the new flag was unique. Rarely does a flag prominently display the likeness of a person. Nevertheless, it was the design featuring the gaunt silhouette of his son Jeffrey which was accepted and, before Mr. Heisly could return to refine his proposal and add the colors he had planned, the black and white flags were already being printed in quantity by Annon & Company. (Though the POW/MIA flag has been produced in other colors, often in red and white, the black and white design became the most commonly used version.)

The design for the MIA/POW flag was never copyrighted. It became a flag which belongs to everyone, a design that hauntingly reminds us of those we dare not ever forget. And, by a turn of fate, it was the profile of a Marine which came to represent all who failed to return home. Behind the black and white silhouette is a face we can't see... the face of a husband, a father, or a son who has paid with their freedom, for our freedom. Beneath the image are the words.... "You Are Not Forgotten."

On August 10, 1990, the 101st Congress passed Public Law 101-355, designating the POW/MIA flag "the symbol of our nation's concern and commitment to resolving as fully as possible the fates of Americans still prisoner, missing and unaccounted for in Southeast Asia, thus ending the uncertainty for their families and the nation"

HISTORY OF THE HYMN

"...The band broke out into the Marines' Hymn as Bull stood at attention, the flow of history seizing him. Lillian... felt the tears come as they always did when she saw strong men march and heard this song that lived in the center of her... it was the Hymn that made this night a holy night for all time." – From Pat Conroy's 'The Great Santini'

The Colors of the Corps were inscribed with the word "to the shores of Tripoli" based upon incidents which began prior to 1805, but were not resolved for several years thereafter. These incidents revolved around demands made by the Barbary States which, if not complied with, led to piracy on ships moving through their area - including American ships. The American Consul to Tunis, William Eaton, wrote to the U.S. Secretary of State describing the character of the local Muslim population in 1799: "Taught by revelation that war with the Christians will guarantee the salvation of their souls, and finding so great secular advantages in the observance of this religious duty [i.e. keeping captured cargoes] their inducements to desperate fighting are very powerful."

In 1805 Lieutenant Presley O'Bannon & his small force of Marines famously captured a fortress of the Old World for the first time at Derne in an attempt to deal with the piracy of the Barbary States. During the next decade, with Napoleon on the offensive, America at war with Britain and other issues, the problem of the Barbary pirates was set aside. However, after the war of 1812 the United States once more found their ships coming under attack while voyaging in the Mediterranean. To deal with this resurgence of the Barbary pirate problem two naval squadrons were sent under the joint command of Commodores Decatur and Bainbridge. Under threat of annihilation by heavy bombardment, "...the Bey of Algiers agreed to a new treaty which protected the United States from future predation by Barbary corsairs." In the end, freedom from piracy and the threat of piracy had been paid for with the volatile currency of the lives of American men.

Returning to the United States, Commodore Stephen Decatur made his famous toast: "Our country! In her intercourse with foreign nations, may she always be in the right; but our country, right or wrong!"

Some years later, after the Marines captured and occupied Mexico City and the Castle of Chapultepec (The Halls of Montezuma) during the Mexican-American War, the Colors were changed to read "From the Shores of Tripoli to the Halls of Montezuma." According to tradition, an unknown Marine penned the words to the first two verses of the Marines' Hymn at the close of the Mexican War, and with each new campaign a new verse was added - although there is an official version.

The music itself seems to have been derived from a Spanish folk melody which was incorporated into an aria by the French composer Offenbach for a very popular French comic opera, *Genevieve de Brabant*, which had opened in Paris in 1859.

From the Halls of Montezuma to the Shores of Tripoli, indeed. Semper Fidelis!

Copyright ownership of the Marines' Hymn is now in the public domain – as it should be.

I'M SORRY

Attributed to Lieutenant General Chuck Pittman USMC (Ret)

"I am *sorry* that the last seven times we Americans took up arms and sacrificed the blood of our youth, it was in the defense of Muslims." – Lieutenant General Chuck Pittman USMC (Ret)

For good and ill, the Abu Ghraib prisoner abuse mess will remain an issue. On the one hand, right thinking Americans will harbor the stupidity of the actions, while on the other hand political glee will take control and fashion this minor event into some modern day massacre. The latter group thinks an apology is in order, so I humbly offer one here:

I am *sorry* that the last seven times we Americans took up arms and sacrificed the blood of our youth, it was in the defense of Muslims (Bosnia, Kosovo, Gulf War 1, Kuwait, etc.).

I am *sorry* that no such call for an apology upon the extremists came after 9/11.

I am *sorry* that all of the murderers on 9/11 were Islamic Arabs.

I am *sorry* that most Arabs and Muslims have to live in squalor under savage dictatorships.

I am *sorry* that their leaders squander their wealth.

I am *sorry* that their governments breed hate for the U.S. in their religious schools, mosques, and government-controlled media.

I am *sorry* that Yassar Arafat was kicked out of every Arab country and high-jacked the Palestinian "cause."

I am *sorry* that no other Arab country will take in or offer more than a token amount of financial help to those same

Palestinians.

I am *sorry* that the USA has to step in and be the biggest financial supporter of poverty stricken Arabs while the insanely wealthy Arabs blame *us* for all their problems.

I am *sorry* that our own left wing, our media, and our own brainwashed masses do not understand any of this (due to misleading vocal elements of our society like radical professors, CNN and the *New York Times*).

I am *sorry* the United Nations scammed the poor people of Iraq out of the "food for oil" money so they could get rich while the common folk suffered.

I am *sorry* that some Arab governments pay the families of homicide bombers upon their death.

I am *sorry* that those same bombers are brainwashed into thinking they will receive 72 virgins in "paradise."

I am *sorry* that the homicide bombers think pregnant women, babies, children, the elderly and other noncombatant civilians are legitimate targets.

I am *sorry* that our troops die to free more Arabs from the gang rape rooms and the filling of mass graves of dissidents of their own making.

I am *sorry* that Muslim extremists have killed more Arabs than any other group.

I am *sorry* that foreign trained terrorists are trying to seize control of Iraq and return it to a terrorist state.

I am *sorry* we didn't drop a few dozen Daisy Cutters on Fallujah.

I am *sorry* that every time terrorists hide, they find a convenient "Holy Site" to do it in.

I am *sorry* they didn't apologize for driving a jet into the World Trade Center, which then collapsed and severely damaged Saint Nicholas Greek Orthodox Church - one of *our* Holy Sites.

I am *sorry* they didn't apologize for flights 93 and 175, the *USS Cole*, the embassy bombings, the murder and beheading of Nick Berg and Daniel Pearl, etc... etc!

We hang out our dirty laundry for the entire world to see. We move on. That's one of the reasons we are hated so much. We don't hide this stuff like all those Arab countries that are now demanding an apology.

Deep down inside, when most Americans saw this reported in the news, we were like - so what? We lost hundreds, and made fun of a few prisoners. Sure, it was wrong, and sure, it dramatically hurt our cause, but until they were captured we were trying to *kill* those very same prisoners. Now we're supposed to wring our hands because a few were humiliated?

Our compassion is tempered with the vivid memories of our own people who were killed, mutilated and burnt amongst a joyous crowd of celebrating Fallujahans.

If you want an apology from *this* American, you're going to have a long wait. In fact, you have a *much* better chance of finding those seventy-two virgins!

Chuck Pitman
Lieutenant General
U.S. Marine Corps (Retired)

The preceding was *not* actually written by General Pittman, but it still makes an excellent point!

THE LEECH

Billy R. Whisenant

We were on patrol east of Camp Carroll in Vietnam some rainy month in 1968. I was a forward observer radio operator for artillery. I don't remember the month, but I do remember a leech that got on the inside of my leg when we crossed a small stream.

I could feel the leech crawling up my leg, and was about to pull down my trousers and remove it when we made contact and came under small arms fire. As we were rushing up the side of a hill my attention was torn between getting shot at - and the leech which was steadily crawling up my leg. The higher that leech climbed up the inside of my leg, the less I thought about getting shot. And he was pretty high up my leg when we reached the top of the hill.

We spotted a handful of the enemy who had been shooting at us running over the top of another hill, and I radioed the coordinates of the fire mission to the artillery at Camp Carroll as I was dropping my trousers. I then bent over, with my backside facing the Marines still charging up the hill behind us. I had a lit cigarette by this time, and was in the process of burning that leech off.

By this time the leech had gotten too close to where I didn't want him to be, but he and the enemy were now no longer a threat to me. Our guys were shooting at the retreating enemy, so the men rushing up behind us didn't know what was going on as they came into view of me bending over.

In true Marine spirit, under fire and fear, the first man to see this sight said "Tex, it's bad enough that I'm getting shot at, but do you have to *moon* me too?" The leech removed, I pulled up my trousers and adjusted the artillery onto the hills beyond.

That Marine never broke stride as he moved up on past me to the line.

The author served with 2nd Battalion, 9th Marines in Vietnam from 10/67 to 10/68.

THEIR BLOOD
Our Freedom

Simone Ledeen

"Of all that is written, I love only what a person has written with his own blood." – Friedrich Nietzsche

When I returned from Iraq earlier this year, I discovered my family had been doing volunteer work at Walter Reed Army Medical Center, where many of our wounded troops go for treatment and rehabilitation. I was so moved that they had begun doing this, and that they didn't tell anyone about it - didn't brag - they just went and did their part. A little-reported fact is that many Americans have been doing exactly that.

Every month, patients newly well enough to travel are loaded, along with their families, into buses that take them from Walter Reed to the Pentagon. They are treated like VIPs - given police escorts through the city and across the bridge to their disembarkation point. They are met by carefully chosen escorts from whichever office is sponsoring that month's visit, and brought up to one of the entrances where there is a band waiting for them along with several thousand Pentagon employees. The troops walk, hobble or wheel down several long corridors stacked two and three people deep - people who cheer and cry and say thank you. Last month was particularly poignant as all the wounded visitors were amputees. The guys took their time, shaking hundreds of hands, thanking those who turned out to support them. I saw one soldier with his arm blown off who cried down three corridors with his sister walking next to him, tears streaming down her face.

The West Point Pep Band turned out, complete with cheerleaders, which our wounded absolutely loved. After the pep band the troops did the Pentagon tour, visited the 9/11 memorial, and then went up to the Executive Dining Room. There all the guys and their families had lunch, and the VIPs showed up. Secretary Rumsfeld came, as did Mrs. Rumsfeld (who frequently goes to Walter Reed unannounced, with boxes of freshly baked cookies). Also in attendance were various undersecretaries who sat with the troops for over an hour, writing down names and phone numbers and giving business cards with cell and home phone numbers scrawled on the back, saying "Call me if you need anything."

General Nyland, the Assistant Commandant of the Marine Corps, was there too. He talked to all the Marines and their families to find out what they needed and how he could help. He spent a particularly long time with a young enlisted man who had lost both of his legs and was there with his mother.

Another little-mentioned event was the holiday party at Walter Reed held by the 'Helping Our Heroes Foundation.' The party room, in the old Red Cross building, was filled to capacity with both wounded and volunteers. There was live country music, a choir, and even a Santa Claus. Several high-ranking government officials also came - someone from Vice President Cheney's office as well as Doug Feith and Secretary Mineta, both with their wives.

I spent some time there with soldiers and their families. I met one kid whose head (the top of it) had gotten blown off last month. It's amazing that he's able to walk and talk - he even makes sense. He really wants to get his Purple Heart from President Bush, and was meeting with the Command Sergeant Major of the Army the next day to talk about it. His dad was there too, in a wheelchair - a Vietnam vet. I could barely control my emotions in front of them. But if *they* can handle it, what right do I have to be overwhelmed?

This past weekend I got up early and went with some friends to Walter Reed to meet two soldiers we had promised to visit. One is named Rob - he is here for a cochlear implant to get his hearing back. He was wounded in Afghanistan early this year and is completely deaf. On September 11, 2001 Rob was a normal college student at Florida State University. He and several of his friends were so affected by the events of that day they dropped out of school and joined the Army. Rob is now a Ranger and hopes to go back to active duty, assuming the surgery is successful. Right now we have to communicate with him by writing everything out on notepads. He has droopy puppy-dog eyes and a shy smile. He also has a huge tattoo on his right arm with the two towers and the date of his injury.

Adam is the other soldier we visited - he is twenty-one and was in Iraq as a member of a special-operations group. He was hit three times within an hour and has problems with excess spinal fluid and blood in his brain. He also can't feel his legs. His favorite restaurant in the area is Steamer's in Bethesda, Maryland. He recounted how he and some of his fellow wounded went over there recently (by taxi) and racked up a bill for almost $400, which someone paid. When they argued, the woman said: "I'm old, what am I going to spend my money on?" Whenever they go to Steamer's, the cook and several waiters carry the guys and their wheelchairs up and down a dozen stairs.

He also told us they went to see Chris Isaak last weekend at a legendary D.C. nightspot. They were treated like kings, and offered VIP tickets to any show they wanted.

Another evening the same friends of mine took two young

Marines out for dinner and a movie. Both Marines were walking with canes; they were amputees (one had lost a leg, the other a foot, in Iraq) and they were still mastering their prosthetic limbs. With their haircuts it was pretty easy to tell who they were. When they asked for the bill at the end of the night they were told (again) it had been taken care of. This time the tab had been paid by the father of the hostess, himself a Vietnam vet. When pressed, he came over to the table. The two Marines stood up straight, shook his hand, and said, "Thank you, sir." The man responded, "Welcome home," and thanked them right back. When he left, one of the guys turned and said that every single time he went out someone paid for his dinner.

For me, spending time with our troops at Walter Reed is very personal. I think about all the convoys I rode in all those months to and from the Iraqi Ministry of Finance. All those hours our escorts sat out in front of the ministry, waiting for us to finish our work. I frequently wondered, "Why is my life worth more than theirs? Why do I get to be protected by these young, beautiful men who have their whole lives in front of them? What makes me so special?" I came to see it was the *work* I was doing that was important, so *every single time* I went their presence motivated me to get more done, to push the Iraqis to work harder, because if someone was going to die that day I wanted it to have some meaning.

Spending time with these wounded heroes is my way of thanking the guys who did that for me - who guarded my life every day. And even though most of America hasn't been to Iraq, we know that our troops are overseas protecting all of us, just as they protected me. I am proud and happy to see how America thanks these brave men and women.

Simone Ledeen is a former adviser to the Iraqi Ministry of Finance in Baghdad and originally wrote this essay for *National Review*.

LAST GOODBYE

Lynne Duke

"A man's dying is more the survivors' affair than his own." - Thomas Mann

They lay in a pile on the red clay of Vietnam. Four dead men. One was already smoldering. The elephant grass was on fire. Three other Marines were still alive for now, but if the North Vietnamese Army didn't get them, the fires surely would.

It was late morning, May 10, 1967 on Hill 665 northwest of Khe Sanh. A Marine reconnaissance patrol named 'Breaker' was in trouble, and was being picked off or blasted apart for twelve hours by NVA snipers and grenades.

U.S. forces threw hellfire onto that hill. Jets cratered the area. Gunships rocketed enemy bunkers; Gatling guns fired 6,000 rounds per minute, pulverizing flesh and bone. And the napalm fires burned. But the NVA were relentless. They turned chopper after chopper into Swiss cheese. One took 182 hits, wounding the whole crew; in another, a pilot died.

Suddenly a Huey flew in fast and low, just dropped from the sky, and slipped in under a blanket of ferocious cover fire. The chopper slid onto the hilltop, within feet of the Marines. Ron Zaczek, the Marine crew chief, jumped out with a crewmate to haul the survivors aboard. It took only seconds.

The young Marines were sprawled on the deck. Clarence R. Carlson and Steven D. Lopez were bloodied and dazed. Carl Friery was clinging to life. Zaczek tried in vain to stuff Friery's intestines back into his gaping abdomen. Then he just rocked him gently, whispering helplessly, "There, there. There, there."

The chopper struggled for lift. It skidded and bounced, nearly crushing the four dead men on the ground. Zaczek remembered one face. Oddly clean and calm, facing the sky. The man's blond eyelashes fluttered as the Huey's rotor whipped the air and finally lifted the bird. The dead remained where they lay. It was the last time any Marine would see the bodies of Heinz Ahlmeyer Jr., James N. Tycz, Samuel A. Sharp Jr. and Malcolm T. Miller.

They receded into the distance, into the past, already a haunting memory. Vietnam's red earth had claimed them. Some say if they have had no proper burial, the spirits of the dead wander. That is what Buddhists believe. To bring them home, to put them to rest, the spirits must be guided - with prayer, with incense. So a villager from Huong Hoa district in South Vietnam placed burning incense around the mesa of Hill 665 on an April day in 2003 when the red earth started disgorging its buried secrets.

Ahlmeyer. Tycz. Sharp. Miller. Thirty-eight years later their families finally marked their return. For all that time their families waited for some physical remnant: a bone, a tooth perhaps, even just a dog tag. Something to bring them closure. They finally got their wish, with full military honors for the fallen Marines, at an Arlington National Cemetery ceremony which ended their uncertainty and closed a bitter chapter of the Vietnam War.

Lost in the infamous hill battles of Khe Sanh, the missing men of Breaker patrol were among the many abiding mysteries of a war from which there are still more than 1,800 listed as missing in action. The job of finding them was left to anthropologist Sam Connell, who specializes in the ancient civilizations of the Maya and Inca. He'd signed on with the Pentagon's Joint POW/MIA Accounting Command (JPAC) in 2002 to lead excavation teams. The work is a blending of archaeology and forensics, not unlike a criminal investigation.

The search for remains is never simple, especially with the passage of time. Remains of almost 750 U.S. MIAs have been found since the Vietnam War's end. The cases that linger are the most challenging.

Hill 665 was indeed complex - a troubled place, its terrain disturbed. Near the old demilitarized zone and the Laotian border, 665 had been bombed and cratered repeatedly. It had been picked over by scavengers searching for scrap metal, and by bone traders looking for human remains to sell or barter. The secrets of Hill 665 had eluded investigators for years. There had been but a few random clues, and no dots to connect them.

U.S. officials in the capital, Hanoi, met with a steady flow of local people trying to sell information or human remains, although U.S. policy prohibits investigators from buying. Often, the clues offered little beyond the obvious: Someone died. But who? Where? In which battle?

And those questions weren't easy to answer, because the location of the Breaker incident was in dispute for several years. In 1993 a search was mounted, but it turned out the coordinates were wrong and investigators found nothing. The case was shelved until 1998, when a villager scavenging for metal found boots atop Hill 665. But a backlog of hundreds of other Vietnam cases delayed the Breaker investigation. (Not to mention the 78,000 MIA cases from World War II or the 8,000 from the Korean War that JPAC is also investigating.)

Delays were as simple, sometimes, as the weather: Investigative trips are limited to those few months each year that aren't in monsoon season. Finally, in 2002, a test excavation was conducted atop Hill 665. It turned up a few boots.

After launching a more extensive dig, the team immediately found three or four other boots. Then they began excavating, and found eleven boots, which is more than the four men had. The team also found C-ration containers, combs, toothbrushes, toothpaste tubes, bits of socks, artillery casings, sandbags. The discoveries, at first, made no sense. Obviously, other battles had been fought there. Other U.S. troops had occupied that hill, and the team soon would learn that the 101st Airborne Division had set up a firebase on Hill 665, unknowingly atop the Breaker patrol's remains. In warfare things are messy like that.

Connell's team hired about fifty villagers to sift the dirt through mesh screens which would tease out even the smallest fragment. They found snaps, a 1964 penny, cartridge casings, wing nuts, a battery, a ballpoint pen case, belt buckles, and fragments of a plastic insect-repellent container. And by the end of the two-week mission, the searchers also had found thirty-one individual teeth or tooth fragments, plus fragments of bone.

Connell could tell right away that the incisors did not have the shovel shape of Asian incisors. And dental fillings, which some of these teeth had, are not commonly found in the less developed world. In Hanoi, a review panel of U.S. and Vietnamese experts agreed the teeth were American. The tooth fragments were stored inside evidence bags, placed in a flag-draped casket, and flown to JPAC headquarters at Hickam Air Force Base in Hawaii. There, the JPAC laboratory would try to identify them.

"Dear Mom, Dad and Sis: Well, I'm just fine. They took Hill

861 and 881 and things are beginning to quiet down. We can sit on our chairs out in the back of the tent and watch the jets and B-52s make the runs on 811."

Lance Corporal Samuel A. Sharp Jr.'s last letter home to San Jose, California sounded like a Vietnam picnic - watching the bombing runs. It was dated May 7, 1967, as the infamous hill battles of Khe Sanh were ending. He was twenty years old and tall, the son of a Navy man, and a worshiper of John Wayne. He had joined the Marines to be with Ed, his best friend. From Vietnam, he sent his little sister a fiver for her eighteenth birthday. Janet Caldera has kept it all these years. Love, frozen in time.

"Dear Mom and Pop... Our company has been hit pretty hard, too, with casualties; 100 percent casualties in one of our eight-man patrols hit by mortars while waiting for helicopters to pick them up... Mom and Dad, I have had opportunities to write sooner than tonight, but I hope you will understand that writing about an unpopular war like this one is not easy... I had an interruption just now. Our lieutenant passed me the word that we go in at 7:30 a.m. tomorrow. None of us want to go, but that's our job and I pray I will never fail to do it. Your Marine Son, Neil"

Sergeant James Neil Tycz was a Marine's Marine. The men trusted him. He knew the jungle, and had been on several patrols. Back home in Milwaukee, he ran cross-country, and played some tennis. He'd thought of becoming a priest. In Vietnam, he sometimes led the men in prayer before they departed on patrols. Tycz's last letter arrived home in Milwaukee on May 9, 1967. He died the next day, at age twenty-two.

They all have their stories, these families. They are

wonderful in their ordinariness, precious with each recollection. How Navy Petty Officer 3rd Class Malcolm T. Miller, the hospital corpsman, didn't have to be there in Vietnam, could have avoided it by taking advantage of the sibling rule since he had an older brother already stationed at Tan Son Nhut, according to their sister, Sandra (his brother, Air Force Sergeant Wes Miller, returned home alive.)

Second Lieutenant Heinz Ahlmeyer Jr., a graduate of the State University of New York at New Paltz, had just completed Officer Candidate School when he was shipped to Vietnam. Hill 665 was his first patrol. Guts and devotion were his defining traits, according to his big sister, Irene. Since his death, SUNY New Paltz has given out an award each year in his name to a student with just those attributes.

The families received their telegrams long ago, confirming the deaths and the Marines' inability to recover their remains. The families held their memorial services. They gathered up their memories and assembled them in photo albums, on walls, in keepsake chests. They carried their heartache. The years did not erode their longing, their unspoken wish that it was a mistake.

"In the early days, after the war ended, anytime prisoners of war were brought home you'd always hope," said Tycz's older brother, Phillip. "You're told it's a definite 'killed in action,' but until you have remains, you never know."

The Vietnam War mushroomed into a broad social and political force. But for these families, it remained deeply personal. They received briefings over the years from JPAC or its predecessor agencies. They knew the contours of the search, its ups and downs. Life went on. And yet they remained emotionally tethered to Hill 665, Khe Sanh, 1967.

For Miller's sister, when the phone call came with word that the remains had been positively identified, it was as if her brother had died all over again.

"I had to leave work. I couldn't deal with it," she said. "I thought after all these years it would be easy. But it's like knowing that someone you love is dying and even when the time comes it's still hard to take. That's how it was. I just started crying, and I had to go home."

On the day it happened, the Marines had rolled themselves into their ponchos and slept in a circle in the tall grass. One man kept watch. Technically, they had accomplished their mission: Put down on Hill 665 by chopper at 5 p.m. on May 9 to check for enemy movement into the area. Breaker patrol had radioed back to the Khe Sanh base that it had found a series of empty but recently used NVA bunkers and spider holes, perhaps for a company-size contingent. That's well over one hundred men. And they were only seven.

They could have left the area and hunkered down elsewhere. But they didn't. And around 10 p.m., the NVA returned. They walked right up to Breaker patrol's position. PFC Lopez saw them.

"They walked up to the side of the circle that I was facing, and the first one or two people that came in, I shot them," recalled Lopez, uncomfortably recalling events he's rarely spoken about in thirty-eight years.

Hill 665 lit up, and stayed that way for twelve hours. Ahlmeyer and Tycz got hit in the first volleys. Tycz was the patrol leader, showing the higher-ranking Ahlmeyer the ropes on his first patrol.

"Ahlmeyer was hit harder than Tycz and started moaning, and they threw grenades at the sounds," said Friery, who now lives on military disability after a long struggle with post-traumatic stress disorder.

The recollections of Friery and Lopez complement the account of the battle written by Lawrence C. Vetter Jr. in his

1996 book, *Never Without Heroes*, about Marine recon units in Vietnam.

"Grenades were flying around and rolling right around the position," said Lopez, a radio man on the patrol who today is a public school behavioral specialist.

Tycz, like them all, was throwing back grenades. One exploded near his head. Soon he was dead. Lance Corporal Clarence R. Carlson took shrapnel from the blast. Both radios were hit. Carlson mixed and matched parts, and rigged up a working unit. He then started calling for artillery support. He handed the radio off to Lopez, who was shot in the chest but stayed on the air anyway. Sharp took a round to the chest, too. PFC Friery crawled over to him. His best friend in Vietnam was beyond help. A grenade landed next to Friery. He threw it back, and was hit with gunfire in the gut. Then Miller, the corpsman, took a round, gushing blood from a femoral artery. Carlson tried to stanch the flow from Miller's leg, and another grenade blast wounded them both. Miller asked to be propped up with a gun, which Carlson did. And Miller slumped over. Dead.

All ears in the region were on the Hill 665 radio traffic. Marines back at the Khe Sanh base were virtually *begging* to be sent in to help the men of Breaker. So many U.S. rockets and gunships were shooting at NVA positions on 665 that huge globs of damp jungle soil rained down on the patrol, recalled Friery, the other radioman. He passed out when he was hit again by another grenade.

Carlson and Lopez scrounged among the fallen for more ammunition. They piled the dead - their own and the enemy's - as a barricade around their position. They killed many NVA, but they were outmanned.

Carlson tried to throw a grenade, was shot in the arm, and then dropped the grenade and took shrapnel in the back when he tried to dive away from it. He injected himself with morphine. Then he was shot in the leg.

The NVA troops were so close that Lopez heard them talking, and could hear them dragging their dead through the tall grass. He was calling in air support all the while.

"Drop it closer! Drop it closer," he was quoted as saying in a wire dispatch in *The Washington Post* on May 11, 1967.

Though he didn't remember all the details, Lopez said, "I know that I asked for napalm. I was asking for anything I could get. And then I asked for more and more."

By daybreak, the fires were menacing.

"Scarface, this is Breaker," Lopez radioed at one point, according to Ron Zaczek's 1994 book, *Farewell, Darkness.* Lopez's pleading transmission would haunt Zaczek for decades:

"We're burning. You gotta get us out. Scarface, you gotta get us out. We're burning up."

Lopez explained: "We were all pretty much engulfed in flame, but it wasn't a roaring inferno. It was spots of fire and you could negotiate it, if you were on your toes." A very big "if."

By the time Zaczek's Huey flew in, Lopez has chest, leg, head and abdomen wounds. Carlson was equally shot up and blasted. Friery was effectively disemboweled, and would be hospitalized for nine months.

After the rescue, the Khe Sanh Marine command ordered the all-out bombing of Hill 665. The men received Purple Hearts, including the dead. Carlson was awarded the Silver Star; Lopez and Tycz got the Navy Cross.

The four flag-draped caskets finally arrived on a Sunday at Dulles International Airport on a United Airlines flight from Hawaii. Four hearses awaited them. Military escorts saluted.

The caskets of Ahlmeyer, Tycz and Miller each contained a folded green blanket. Wrapped inside were a few teeth, positively linked to each man by the JPAC. Atop the blanket lay a dress-blue uniform, pressed and laid out with all their ribbons and decorations. Sharp's remains would later put to rest beside his father's in San Jose.

The fourth casket at Dulles represented the group, and held teeth and bone fragments found on Hill 665 that were circumstantially linked to the four men. The hearses left Dulles in a convoy, carrying the dead from a long-ago war, to be interred at Arlington National Cemetery.

Friery was there. Lopez was, too. Other men of Alpha Company, 3rd Reconnaissance Battalion, 3rd Marine Division, had looked forward to the event for weeks, and so did Zaczek and the men who manned the gunships during the Breaker rescue. *"Mission accomplished,"* they wanted to say: *"Breaker patrol is home."* And they wanted to put to rest their private demons from Hill 665, too.

From each family, scores of relatives and friends came. They received the folded flags, and heard the volleys of rifle fire, and the sounding of taps.

They had waited so long. So long to say goodbye. Again.

This article originally appeared in the *Washington Post.*

WELCOME STOP
For Warriors

Tony Perry

Most of us have seen that great Budweiser TV commercial, but many think it was based on fantasy rather than fact. Not the case. This is the true story behind the ad. Locals in Bangor, Maine were on a mission to greet every military plane, at any time, in any weather. As of this writing they had greeted almost 200,000 troops. You know, come to think of it, "Maine" becomes "Marine" if you simply add an "R!"

Tired and bleary-eyed, the Marines of the 1st Battalion, 7th Marine Regiment were finally back on U.S. soil after seven months on the front lines in Iraq. But they were still many miles and hours from their families, and the homecoming they longed for. Their officers told them they would be on the ground for sixty to ninety minutes while their chartered plane was refueled. So they disembarked and began walking through the airport terminal corridor to a small waiting room. That's when they heard the applause.

Lining the hall and clapping were dozens of Bangor residents who have set a daunting task for themselves: They want every Marine, soldier, sailor and airman returning through the tiny international airport there to get a hero's welcome. Even if the planes arrived in the middle of the night or a blizzard, they were there.

Composed mostly from the generation that served in World War II and Korea, they called themselves the 'Maine Troop Greeters.' They met every flight bringing troops home

288

from Iraq for nearly two years – more than 1,000 flights and nearly 200,000 troops.

"Here they come. Everybody get ready," said seventy-one year old Joyce Goodwin, her voice full of excitement, undiminished by the hundreds of times she has shown up to embrace returning troops.

As dozens more Marines came down the corridor, the applause grew louder and was accompanied by handshakes, hugs, and a stream of well wishes:

"Welcome home."

"Thank you for your service."

"God bless you."

"Thank you for everything."

Faces brightened. Grouchiness disappeared. Greeters and Marines alike began taking photographs. The Marines were directed down a corridor decorated with American flags and red, white and blue posters to cellphones for free calls to family members. They found a table with cookies and candies. Plates of homemade fudge circulated.

"Welcome home, Gunny," said seventy-four year old Al Dall, who had served in the Marines during the Korean War, as he thrust his hand at startled Gunnery Sergeant Edward Parsons.

"This is incredible," Parsons said. "Now I know I'm really back in the world."

The greeters lined the corridor both as the troops arrived and then, minutes later, as they returned to their planes to continue their journey to Twentynine Palms.

The airport gift store opened early. T-shirts saying "I Love Maine" were popular. So were adult magazines. The store even took military scrip from troops low on cash, even though there was no way for the store to get reimbursed.

The airport bar did a brisk business, selling Budweiser at

three dollars a bottle. Even though some officers have rules against their troops consuming alcohol before a flight, the Commanding Officer of this battalion had no such restriction, and the bar was full of Marines laughing, singing, and joking.

"We appreciate everything you've done for us," said Bud Tower, an Air Force veteran who, at fifty-eight, considered himself "a kid" among the other greeters.

Eighty-nine year old Kay Lebowitz had such severe arthritis that she could not shake hands - so she hugged every Marine she could. Some of the larger, more exuberant troops then lifted her off the ground.

"Many of the Marines told me they can't wait to see their grandmothers," she said. "That's what I am: a substitute grandma."

The core of the Maine Troop Greeters was a dedicated group of about thirty residents who developed "telephone tree" to get the word out about impending arrivals. Their numbers swelled on weekends when particular brigades were due back, such as local National Guard units. Families with young children even joined in.

Most of the greeters supported the U.S. mission in Iraq, but their goal was historic, not political. Discussion of politics was banned. The greeters didn't want America to repeat what they considered a shameful episode in history: the indifference, even hostility, the public displayed to troops returning from Vietnam.

"I think there's a lot of collective guilt about the '60s," said greeter Dusty Fisher, a retired high school history teacher now serving in the State Legislature.

Once the troops found seats, the greeters fanned out. Phillip Eckert, a bantam-sized former Marine with an outsized personality, liked to talk about the "Old Corps" and tell stories of the tough-as-nails sergeants and crazy-brave officers he knew from Korea. Naturally, he wore a red sweatshirt that said, "Not As Lean, Not as Mean, But Still A Marine."

Eckert led the Marines in raspy versions of the Marines' Hymn. He also did his drill-instructor imitation: "Move it, Move It, MOVE IT!" he said in a mock-urgent voice.

"I whooped and hollered at the troops, and they seemed to like it, I guess," he said.

Jerry Mundy, also a former Marine, liked to dispense mildly salty jokes.

"My lady friend just bought us one of those king-size beds," he said. "Trouble is at my age, after I finally found her, I forgot what it was for."

Others tried a quieter approach. Dall made himself available if the troops wanted to talk about the traumas of combat.

"I've been there, so I know what they've gone through," he said. "I said, 'Forget me, this is your time.' I'm here if you need me."

On one window of the greeters' office at the end of the corridor were hundreds of photographs of Marines and soldiers killed in Iraq taken from newspaper stories. Inevitably, troops drifted toward the window and searched for their buddies. Sometimes they scribbled small notes of remembrance next to the photos.

The 1st Battalion of the 7th Marine Regiment suffered fifteen dead and eighty-six wounded. The Marines were left alone to search for their buddies' photos. "There's Wilt," said a Marine pointing to one of Lance Corporal Nicholas Wilt.

"There's Rowe," said another, a reference to Captain Alan Rowe.

After several long and silent minutes, Staff Sergeant Larry

Long finally found the photo he was searching for of PFC Ryan Cox.

"He was a good Marine, a hard-charger," Long said with a catch in his voice. "He would have been a good squad leader."

Marine Lieutenant David Tumanjan said the Bangor greeting is both humbling and gratifying. "It shows us that what we did wasn't in vain," he said.

The greeters said their payoff was seeing the surprise and smiles on the faces of the troops. "Every flight coming home makes it like Christmas Eve," Tower said.

Don Guptill, who served in Korea, listened as an enlisted Marine, his eyes fixed on the carpet, talked quietly about being wounded three times.

When the call came over the loudspeaker to return to the plane, the young Marine reluctantly pulled something from his back pocket. It was his Purple Heart.

"He said he was embarrassed to wear it," Guptill said. "I told him: 'You wear it. You earned it. You wear it for all the guys who didn't make it home.'"

This article originally appeared in the Los Angeles Times on April 20, 2005

DEAR MOM

"When I was growing up, it was the 'Communists.' Now it's 'Terrorists.' So you always have to have somebody to fight and be afraid of, so the war machine can build more bombs, guns, and bullets and everything." - Cindy Sheehan

We have all heard of 'peace mom' Cindy Sheehan and her demand to meet with President Bush (again) at his ranch in Crawford, Texas. I initially felt sorry for her, until I learned she believes 9/11 was "made up" by the government and came to realize she is little more than a political pawn. I took particular exception to the mock 'Cemetery' she constructed in Crawford, using the names of fallen Marines and other service members without their families' consent. I became so disgusted I ended up helping some of the families contact the local Sheriff to have him remove the names of their loved ones. It's amazing what some people will do for their fifteen minutes of fame. This is what I think her son, Specialist Casey Sheehan, might say to his mother if he were able – and I made a point of emailing it to Ms. Sheehan so she could read it. Of course I can't say he'd feel this way for certain, but I do know one thing for sure - it's what I would say to MY mother if I were in his place:

Dear Mom,

I, along with the rest of my buddies, have been following what has been going on in Texas - and I want you to know a few things before you go any further. First of all, please remember that I joined the Army of my own free will. I was not drafted. I also knew that the purpose of the Army is to fight our nation's wars, and that it could be dangerous. Even so, I *reenlisted* when my time was up - because I felt it was the right thing to do. I know you are hurting right now, but would it have been any less painful for you if I had died fighting for our independence in the American Revolution, freeing the slaves during the Civil War, or saving the world from the Nazis during World War II?

I know that you love me very much, as I love you, but you shouldn't allow your emotions to cloud your judgment. I saw the recent terrorist attacks in London, and it reminded me of why it was I joined the military in the first place. I did it to protect you, and Dad, and Andy, and Carly, and Jane, and every free person who wants to walk the streets of London, New York and even Vacaville without having to worry about a terrorist attack. I didn't want to die, but if I didn't stand up for freedom, then who would?

Thousands and thousands of good people have died protecting our way of life over the past 230 years, and without our sacrifices you would not be free today. I was only in Iraq for two weeks before I was killed, but I saw a lot in that time. If only you could have seen the gratitude on the faces of the Iraqis, you would know that I did not die in vain.

Mom, the people we are fighting are the very same ones who attacked the *USS Cole*, bombed our embassies, cut off Nick Berg's head, knocked down the twin towers, and perpetrated numerous additional acts of terrorism. I am now among the people who perished in those attacks, and every single one of them has thanked me for my role in fighting the terrorists. Every one of them has a mother just like I do, but none of them are there with you in Crawford. The reason should be obvious. Please go home and deal with your grief, and let the President do what he must. To pull out of Iraq now would make my death pointless, and more importantly, it would make the world less safe for our family and friends.

Love,
Your Son Casey

P.S. - Stop hanging around with people like Michael Moore. He doesn't have your best interests at heart, only his political agenda. Remember, I can see *everything* from up here.

THE LAST FULL MEASURE

Colonel Brett Wyrick, USAF

"The first rule of war is that young men and women die. The second rule of war is that surgeons cannot change the first rule." – Colonel Brett Wyrick

We had already done around a dozen surgical cases in the morning and the early afternoon. The entire medical staff then had a professional meeting to discuss the business of the hospital and the care and treatment of burns.

It is not boastful or arrogant when I tell you that some of the best surgeons in the world were present - I have been to many institutions, and I have been all around the world, and at this point in time, with this level of experience, the best in the world are assembled here at Balad.

Lieutenant Colonel Dave "S," the Trauma Czar, and a real American hero, was present. He has saved more people out here than anyone can imagine. The cast of characters includes two Air Force Academy graduates, Colonel (select) Joe "W" and Major Max "L." When you watch 'ER' on television, the guys on the show are trying to be like Max - cool, methodical and professional. Max never misses anything on a trauma case because he sees everything on a patient, and notes it the same way the great NFL running backs see the entire playing field when they are carrying the ball.

Joe is an ENT surgeon who is tenacious, bright, and technically correct every single time – and I mean *every* single time. The guy has a lower tolerance for variance than NASA. Lieutenant Colonel (select) Chris "C." was the

Surgeon of the Day (SOD), and I was the back-up SOD. Everyone else was there and available - as I said, the best in the world.

As the meeting was breaking up, the call came in. An American Marine had been injured in an IED blast, and he was in a bad way with head trauma. The specifics were fuzzy, but after three months here what would need to be done was perfectly clear - the 332nd Expeditionary Medical Group readied for "battle." All the surgeons started to gravitate toward the PLX, which is the surgeons' ready room and centrally located midway to the ER, OR and radiology.

The lab personnel checked precious units of blood, and the pharmacy made ready all the medications and drugs we would need for the upcoming fight. An operating room was cleared, surgical instruments were laid out, the anesthesia circuits were switched over, and the gasses were checked and rechecked. An anesthesiologist and two nurse anesthetists went over the plan of action as the OR supervisor made the personnel assignments.

In the ER, bags of IV fluids were carefully hung, battery packs were checked, and the ER nursing supervisor looked over the equipment to make sure all was in working order and the back-ups were ready just in case the primaries failed. The radiology techs moved forward in their lead gowns bringing their portable machines like artillery men of old wheeling their cannon into place. Respiratory therapy set the mechanical ventilator, and double-checked the oxygen. Gowns, gloves, boots, and masks were donned by those who would be directly in the battle.

All of the resources - medical, mechanical and technological that America can bring to a war - were in place and ready along with the best skill and talent from techs to surgeons. The two neurosurgeons gathered by themselves to plan.

Lieutenant Colonel "A" is a neurosurgeon who still wears his pilot wings proudly. He used to be a T-38 instructor pilot, and some of the guys he trained to fly are now flying F-16s right here at Balad. He is good with his hands, and calm under pressure. The other neurosurgeon is Major "W," a gem of a surgeon who could play the guitar professionally if he was not dedicated to saving lives. A long time ago, at a place on the other side of the world called Oklahoma, I had operated on his little brother after a car accident and helped to save his life.

The two neurosurgeons, Chris, and I joined for the briefing. Although I was the ranking officer of the group, Chris was the SOD and would be the flight lead. If this had been a fighter sweep, all three of those guys would be Weapons School Patch wearers.

The plan was for me and the ER folks to assess, treat and stabilize the patient as rapidly as possible to get him into the hands of the neurosurgeons. The intel was that this was an IED blast, and those rarely come with a single, isolated injury. It makes no sense to save the guy's brain if you have not saved the heart pump that brings the oxygenated blood to the brain. With this kind of trauma, you must be deliberate and methodical, and you must be deliberate and methodical in a pretty damn big *hurry*.

All was ready, and we did not have to wait very long. The approaching rotors of a Blackhawk were heard, and Chris and I moved forward to the ER followed by several sets of surgeons' eyes as we went. We have also learned not to clog up the ER with surgeons giving orders. One guy runs the code, and the rest follow his instructions or stay out the way until they are needed.

They wheeled the Marine into the ER on a NATO gurney

shortly after the chopper touched down. One look at the PJs' faces told me that the situation was grim. Their young faces were drawn and tight, and they moved with a sense of directed urgency. They did not even need to speak because the look in their eyes was pleading with us - hurry. And hurry we did.

In a flurry of activity that would seem like chaos to the uninitiated, many things happened simultaneously. Max and I received the patient as Chris watched over the shoulder to pick out anything that might be missed. An initial survey indicated a young man with a wound to the head, and several other obvious lacerations on the extremities.

Max called out the injuries as they were found, and one of the techs wrote them down. The C-collar was checked, and the chest was auscultated as the ET tube was switched to the ventilator. Chris took the history from the PJs because the patient was not conscious. All the wounds were examined, and the dressings were removed except for the one on the head.

The patient was rolled on to his side while his neck was stabilized by my hands, and Max examined the backside from the toes to the head. When we rolled the patient back over, it was onto an X-ray plate that would allow us to take the chest X-Ray immediately. The first set of vitals revealed a low blood pressure; fluid would need to be given, and it appeared as though the peripheral vascular system was on the verge of collapse.

I called the move as experienced hands rolled him again for the final survey of the back and flanks and the X-Ray plate was removed and sent for development. As we positioned him for the next part of the trauma examination, I noted that the hands that were laid on this young man were Black, White, Hispanic, Asian, American Indian, Australian,

Army, Navy, Air Force, Marine, Man, Woman, Young and Old(er): a true cross-section of our effort here in Iraq, but there was not much time to reflect.

The patient needed fluid resuscitation fast, and there were other things yet to be done. Chris watched the initial survey and the secondary survey with a situational awareness that comes from competence and experience. Chris is never flustered, never out of ideas, and his pulse is never above fifty.

With a steady, calm, and re-assuring voice, he directed the next steps to be taken. I moved down to the chest to start a central line, and Max began an ultrasonic evaluation of the abdomen and pelvis. The X-rays and ultrasound examination were reviewed as I sewed the line in place, and it was clear to Chris that the young Marine's head was the only apparent life-threatening injury.

The two neurosurgeons came forward, removed the gauze covering the wounded head, and everyone's heart sank as we saw the blossom of red blood spreading out from shredded white and grey matter of the brain. Experience told all the surgeons present there was no way to survive the injury, and that this was one battle the Medical Group was going to lose. But he was an American, and it was not time to quit, not yet.

Gentle pressure was applied over the wound, and the patient went directly to the CT scanner as drugs and fluids were pumped into the line to keep his heart and lungs functioning in a fading hope to restore the brain. The time elapsed from his arrival in the ER to the time he was in the CT scanner was five minutes.

The CT scan confirmed what we had feared. The wounds to the brain were horrific and mortal, and there was no way on earth to replace the volume of tissue that had been blasted away by the explosion. The neurosurgeons looked at the scan, they looked at the scan a second time, and then they re-examined the patient to confirm once again.

The OR crew waited anxiously outside the doors of radiology in the hope they would be utilized, but we all agreed - there was no brain activity whatsoever. The chaplain came to pray, and reluctantly, the vent was turned from full mechanical ventilation to flow by. He had no hint of respiratory activity, and the heart that had beat so strongly earlier in the day ceased to beat forever. He was pronounced dead.

The pumps were turned off; the machines were stopped, and the IVs were discontinued. Respectful quiet remained, and it was time to get ready for the next round of casualties. The techs and nurses gently moved the body over to the back of the ER to await mortuary services. And everyone agreed there was nothing more we could have done.

When it was quiet, there was time to really look at the young Marine and see him as he was. He was young, probably in his late teens, with not an ounce of fat anywhere. His muscles were powerful and well defined, and in death, his face was pleasant and calm.

I am always surprised that anyone still has tears to shed here at Balad, but thank God they still do. The nurses and techs continued to care for him and do what they could. Not all the tubes and catheters can be removed because there is always a forensic investigation to be done at Dover AFB, but the nurses took out the lines they could. Fresh bandages were placed over the wounds, and the blood clots were washed from his hair as his wound was covered once more. His hands and feet were washed with care. A broken toenail was trimmed, and he was silently placed in the body bag when mortuary services arrived as gently as if they were tucking him into bed.

301

Later that night was 'Patriot Detail' - our last goodbye for an American hero. All the volunteers gathered at Base Ops after midnight under a three-quarter moon that was partially hidden by high, thin clouds. There was only silence as the chief master sergeant gave the detail its instructions. Soldiers, Airmen, and Marines, colonels, privates and sergeants, pilots, gunners, mechanics, surgeons and clerks all marched out side-by-side to the back of the waiting transport, and presently, the flag-draped coffin was carried through the cordon as military salutes were rendered.

The detail marched back from the flight line, and slowly the doors of the big transport were secured. The chaplain offered prayers for anyone who wanted to participate, and then the group broke up as the people started to move away into the darkness. The big engines on the transport fired up, and the ground rumbled for miles as they took the runway. His duty was done - he had given the last full measure, and he was on his way home.

The first rule of war is that young men and women die. The second rule of war is that surgeons cannot change the first rule. I think the third rule of war should be that those who have given their all for our freedom are never forgotten, and that they will always be honored.

I wish there was not a war, and I wish our young people did not have to fight and die. But I cannot wish away evil men like Bin Laden and al-Zarqawi. These men are not wayward children who have gone astray; they are not great men who are simply misunderstood. These are cold-blooded killers and they will kill you, me, and everyone we love and hold dear if we do not kill them first. You cannot reason with these people, you cannot negotiate with these people, and this war will not be over until they are dead. That is the ugly, awful, and brutal truth. I wish the situation was different, but it is not.

Americans have two choices. We can run from the threat, deny it exists, candy-coat it, debate it, and hope it goes away. And then, Americans will become fair game around the world and be slaughtered by the thousands for the sheep they have become.

Our second choice is to crush these evil men where they live, and for us to have the political will and courage to finish what we came over here to do. The last thing we need here in Iraq is an exit strategy or some damn timetable for withdrawal. Thank God there was no timetable for withdrawal after the Battle of the Bulge or Iwo Jima. Thank God there was no exit strategy at Valley Forge. Freedom is not easy, and it comes with a terrible price – I know, because I saw someone pay the bill here just yesterday.

The third rule of war should be that we never forget the sacrifices made by our young men and women, and that we always honor them. We honor them by finishing what they came to accomplish. We remember them by never quitting, and having the backbone and the guts never to bend to the yoke of oppression.

We honor them and remember them by having the courage to live free.

At the time this letter was written Colonel Brett Wyrick was commander of the 154th Medical Group, Hawaii Air National Guard, and was serving as a surgeon in Balad with the 332nd Expeditionary Medical Group.

COMING HOME

Greg Moore

"In war it is necessary that commanders be able to delay their emotions until they can afford them." - General Tommy Franks

There are no longer generators running, or armored vehicles rumbling, or mortars exploding, and the roar of the silence is deafening to me. What I hear at night now is the gentle breaths released from the perfect lips of my sons. The same lips that I cannot kiss enough. The lips that make my eyes fill with tears every time they touch my cheeks.

My release from the base came earlier than expected, so when I pulled into my driveway at noon the house was empty. I dropped my bags inside and walked alone through the rooms, soaking in the images and smells that had been only a memory during ten months in Iraq.

My older son's first-grade teacher had been wonderful to me while I was away. She sent school updates and pictures via e-mail almost weekly. So when I popped my head into her classroom she came running and gave me a "welcome home" hug.

"Easton is practicing a song. Why don't you surprise him?"

My heart was racing. I followed the sound of the piano and the little voices singing, then stood and watched. Trickles of love and pride started involuntarily down my cheeks as I listened to my son. He has gotten so big. The anticipation built as I waited for him to see me.

The little girl next to him was the first to notice the uniformed man standing in the doorway. The image she saw and the facts she had been told were doing battle in her brain. Then her eyes grew wide and her mouth fell open.

"Easton! Easton...your Daddy's here!" she said in an electrified whisper.

My son's head snapped around. The excitement and disbelief on his face is something I will never forget. I motioned him to me, and he ran into my open arms. There was no hiding my tears, and I didn't care to. This was the day I had waited for.

I choked out my words of love, and hung on to this boy who had cried so many nights, who said he didn't care if he got any other presents for Christmas, he only wanted his Daddy to come home. This boy who had used up all his wishes on me. He kept pulling his head back from my shoulder to look at my face. Cheers rose from the other kids and teachers.

Hand-in-hand, Easton and I stepped outside and drove to the other side of town. I had another little boy to catch up with. When I went inside he was napping. "Marshal, wake up. I have a surprise for you," I heard his day-care provider say.

She came out with his head on her shoulder. When he looked up his eyes grew wide and all signs of sleepiness disappeared. "Daddy!" he exclaimed in pure excitement as he fell forward into my arms. My heart ached with love, and pure joy soaked my cheeks.

I was complete again. I had my boys. And there have never been more perfect words spoken to me than "I love you, Dad."

It may take my wife and children a long time to realize that while I look the same, I am not the same person who said goodbye to them many months ago. I will never be the same again - and thankfully so.

Each day now I am acutely aware of what makes me happy, and what it is I do that makes other people happy. Walking point through the volatile streets in Iraq helped me see this much more clearly, and I will make every effort to preserve that awareness for the rest of my days.

When I look through my photo album I think about the men I served with, and learned to count on, who are no longer by my side. The men who had their bodies pierced by the hatred of terrorists, men who left their last breaths in a place far away. Great men doing a job that allows this noble country the freedoms it deserves.

I have seen the dark side of humanity, and it has forever changed me. As I sit here in my house, with the sun streaming through the windows, I look out and see the boughs of the evergreens blowing in the breeze.

There are no armed guards on the roof. No sandbags. I don't call in grid coordinates of my whereabouts any more.

Mission briefs have been replaced by wonderful communication between two parents. As I drive through town, I am alone; with no turret and no gunner above me. I don't have to scrutinize every pile of dirt, every plastic bag to check whether it may explode.

Amazingly, I am safe.

SELF-INFLICTED WOUND

Bob Neener

"A letter of reprimand is better than no mail at all."
- Spray-painted on the side of a tent in Vietnam

It was early June 1966. Lima Company 3/3 had been sent back to the rear area for some working R&R (Rest & Relaxation) - but for us Grunts it was always a *working* R&R. This was almost always some form of guard duty in a relaxed environment where no one was shooting at us, and the enemy threat was very minimal.

In early June 1966, Lima 3/3's 3rd Platoon was assigned to perimeter security for NSAH, a MASH Type Naval Hospital on Highway 1 near Marble Mountain. Our duty consisted of manning a handful of perimeter bunkers, and sentry duty at the main gate.

The duty at the Navy Hospital was cushy - this was a 24-on, 24-off duty assignment. During our off time we squared away USMC style during the day, and spent most of the evening hours at the "E" Club on base.

This was a "Number 1" E Club, with air conditioning, ice cubes, mixed drinks, very cold beer, slot machines and cute round-eyed, Vietnamese waitresses. For most of that month I was second-guessing my enlistment choice.

This was a very secure base, as you would expect of a rear area hospital. It was located on Route 1, on a large hill about two klicks or so south of DaNang Air Base and about a klick or two north of Marble Mountain, across the road from the south end of MAG-16.

The first line of defense was our perimeter of bunkers. Immediately below us was Thon My Thi Village, a small village which housed the civilian base laborers. Below the village there were tanks, and a battery of 155 Artillery. Below them there was a grunt battalion, either 2/9 or 2/7.

Our bunkers were probably built by the SeaBees, since they were very elaborate in contrast to what we were used to in the field. Each bunker was approximately twelve feet long, six feet wide and eight feet deep from the roof to the dirt floor, and there was a "fighting ledge" about four feet from the top front edge. The roof was made from corrugated steel with four layers of sand bags, and hung out over the fighting ledge so that even a direct hit from a rocket attack would be deflected.

My boots were made for walking, and these bunkers were made for fighting! I was nearing the end of my tour, with less than a month left, and I had never felt safer. Our day on duty consisted of 24 hours in one of these bunkers, with three the men in each bunker taking turns sleeping and talking about home, cars and girls most of the time.

The main bunker was located at the right, rear portion of the base next to the back gate which led to the village and artillery area. When assigned to the main bunker, one of our duties was to check the civilians for base IDs, and generally observe anyone coming and going through this rear point. The civilians came and went twice daily, and many of the tankers and cannon cockers came through to enjoy the E-Club, so this post had some intermittent activity - which helped to eliminate any boredom.

Early one evening while on duty at the main bunker we spotted a Tanker PFC who had apparently spent the entire day at the E-Club and was stumbling back to his unit. When he got to our post, he loaded his M-14 and began mumbling about how he was going to "kill him a gook."

Inebriation notwithstanding, this was a normal frustration

many of us had suffered from early in our tours. With the "can't shoot until shot at" rule in play, and the constant ever present threat of danger, we all experienced frustrations. Add a little alcohol, and it can become a very combustible situation. (If I had only known this then!).

We talked to him for probably half an hour trying to mellow him out. It was getting dark, and after we got him to unload his rifle we thought he was okay - and since we didn't want him to get into any trouble let him continue on to his unit.

We sat on top of our bunker and watched him as he went through the gate and down the hill towards the village. Only a few minutes had passed when it started - tracer rounds began flying over our heads in long bursts, coming up the hill from the vicinity of the village.

There was only one thing going through my mind - I let this guy go, he was shooting up the village, and now I was going to have to go out there after one of our own!

I jumped off the bunker, pulled my .45, and chambered a round - all while still in the air. I hit the ground with a big boom, and inadvertently shot myself in the hand.

I had been wounded on two other occasions, and this was only a flesh wound, but *man* did it hurt! It appears that the palm of my hand was over the muzzle and my finger was on the trigger. When the round chambered, the pistol fired! Stupid, very stupid!

And there was more bad news - the tanker had wounded two civilians in the village. Fortunately for all of us, not too seriously. The good news was I had shot myself in the hand and was unable to go down into the village, which I surely would have done. If I had, who knows what would have happened next.

I have never felt so dumb in my life. Almost a year in

Nam, a Bronze Star, two legitimate Purple Hearts, and only eleven days left in-country…and I had shot myself. I was dumb for not busting this kid, and now I was guilty of a "self-inflicted wound" - a Court Martial offense…

This was one of those areas where we were not allowed to lock & load unless fired upon. This kid was drunk, and had clearly violated regulations. I should have busted him. As a result of my decision that evening myself and two civilians were wounded. This kid was facing a Court Martial, and I could be facing one myself.

It was a Court Martial offense to shoot yourself in the foot to get out of combat. I guess some guys might have been doing that, but the thought had never entered my mind - not ever!

To make matters worse, 2nd Lieutenant Forest Goodwin definitely wanted to write me up for a "self-inflicted wound" and recommend a Court Martial.

Fortunately 1st Lieutenant John Ripley, our acting CO, overrode Goodwin's recommendation for Court Martial, stating that it wasn't very likely that anyone with as little time left as I did, having seen as much action as I had, and pulling easy rear echelon duty at the time, would shoot themselves to get out of Nam - especially when you consider my orders home would have to be *delayed* while I was recuperating from the wound.

Goodwin just wasn't making much sense, and between the Doc and Lieutenant Ripley they convinced him to drop the court martial concept.

The official report was… well, they had to come up with a good story or send me to a Court Martial. So the Navy Doc and Lieutenant Ripley came up with one. The Navy Doctor asked me one question which resolved the whole issue. "What did you do, fall on a broken Coke Bottle when you jumped off the top of that bunker?"

So my official record states that "When the tracers began flying, I dove from the top of the bunker and fell to the bottom, a distance of some eight feet, landed on some broken glass, and cut my hand." I was classified "WIA, Not Evacuated."

The Marine PFC Tanker who had caused all of this mess received Office Hours and was busted to Private. The wounded civilians received a cash bonus, and I received another Purple Heart. Only the Navy Doctor, Lieutenant Goodwin, Lieutenant Ripley and Tom Hoffa (the other Grunt in the bunker with me) knew the truth.

So I shot myself. This was very hard to live with, or even talk about, for a long time. I was still in bandages when I came home, and was thirty-one before I told anyone the real truth about my third Purple Heart. But now you *all* know the truth! I have only really *earned* two of the three Purple Hearts in my Personnel File.

I went on to become an MP, and spent two years at the Norfolk Naval Ship Yard where I qualified Expert with the .45, a real accomplishment considering the slop found in most service pistols due to old age and mismatched parts.

While there I had many more encounters with drunken Jarheads and Sailors – but there were no more accidental shootings!

The author served in Vietnam with Lima 3/3 from 1965 to 1966.

GUTLESS WONDERS

Captain Dave St. John USMCR

"It must be puzzling to our enemies as to how the bravery of the warriors they face in combat can be offset by the cowardly and self-serving behavior those far from harm's way publicly display at every opportunity."
– Captain Dave St. John, USMCR

One of the saddest things I have ever witnessed was Rep. John Murtha condemning as guilty the Marines who had been accused in the Haditha killing – before any evidence had been presented! You would think he, of all people, would want the facts before making such a statement. Whatever happened to 'once a Marine, Always a Marine'? Whatever happened to due process, and 'innocent until proven guilty'? In my opinion Mr. Murtha forfeited the right to refer to himself as a Marine when he threw his 'brothers' under the bus in the name of politics.

As the war in Iraq spooled up and we poured men and equipment into the breach, those on the 'left' compared this conflict with the war we fought in Vietnam. Somehow, the war in Vietnam had become the defining event against which would be judged all of our future conflicts, wars and military interventions - at least by some in our country.

The same dubious outcome, supposedly guaranteed largely by flawed policy and micro-managed execution by incompetent politicians, lent a smug "told you so" sense of importance and overblown wisdom in these matters to these critics.

When I heard their comparisons, I thought that they had

based their commentary upon the military and political components of the war. I disagreed with them then. Sadly, their comparisons may have the appearance of having relevance... but for very different reasons than previously presented.

America must pose a startling paradox to our enemies. Here we are a nation of laws, a representative republic governed by elected civilians who decide the direction, reasons, timing and rules under which brave men and women are sent into harm's way. Our enemies have met the warriors we send to engage them, and know first hand that they are tough, resourceful, compassionate, brave and persistent. They know that our people, our weapons and our war fighting spirit and skills will defeat them time and time again. And yet, they find hope for their causes.

We as Americans know this to be true as well. Time and time again, we see the television clips of interviews and activities dealing with the men and women in the Armed Forces and their commitment to their friends, units, and the mission they were sent to accomplish. We are in awe of them. Even the most jaded politicians are quick to distance themselves from any public hint that they don't support our troops. They know that this is the political kiss of death. No, they are too cowardly for that, so instead they cleverly busy themselves in more subtle activities which are not aimed at our military directly, but nevertheless damn them by association. Their tactics involve such things as redefining our world image, our honor and our sense of fairness in a world apparently devoid of such concepts - if you believe what they tell us.

They demand public reviews in excruciating detail of pictures, accounts and videos showing our abuse of captured prisoners. They lock arms with so called human rights' groups who, with shrill voices and outraged visages, appear on public television decrying our treatment of detainees. They coin the term "insurgent" instead of thug, murderer or even the most generic term, terrorist, as the main descriptor of those whose gun belts are notched with the slaughter of defenseless and innocent civilians day after day after day in Iraq. They are quick to make public our casualty rates when they reach some prearranged level that will call attention to the cost of our involvement over there. They will turn a deaf ear to the repeated pleadings coming from returning Veterans that the full story is *not* being told about what is going on over there. The good things our folks do are not in their best interest to publicize. They even call for a hard date by which we will withdraw from Iraq. Think about that one for a minute.

Yes, it must be puzzling to our enemies as to how the bravery of the warriors they face in combat can be offset by the cowardly and self-serving behavior those far from harm's way publicly display at every opportunity. Who is the *real* American?

So you see, there *is* a comparison to be made between the war in Iraq and the war in Vietnam. The same crowd who broke our national will in Vietnam and turned the selfless acts of so many into alleged "war crimes" for their own ends is at it again.

Haven't we learned our lesson about the destructive influence of this group? Do any of us think that they might be on to something here? Are there those among us who have forgotten the horrific events on September 11? Have we become so disassociated with reality that we can reasonably equate handling a Koran with bare hands with flying a passenger plane into the South Tower?

Some of these folks are going to ask for your vote. "Trust

me, send me back for another term, and I'll clean up that mess in Washington," they will promise. Recognize it for what it is - tough talk from gutless wonders.

Dave St. John is a Captain in the USMCR who served in Chu Lai, RVN 1966-'67. This essay originally appeared in *The American Thinker* on June 15th, 2005.

I WAS THERE LAST NIGHT

Robert Clark

"All gave some, and some gave all. Some stood true for the red, white and blue, and some had to fall. If you ever think of me, think of all your liberties and recall, some gave all." - Billy Ray Cyrus, from the song *'Some Gave All'*

A couple of years ago someone asked me if I still thought about Vietnam. I nearly laughed in their face. How do you *stop* thinking about it? Every day for the last twenty-four years, I wake up with it, and go to bed with it. But this is what I said. "Yea, I think about it. I can't quit thinking about it. I never will. But, I've also learned to live with it. I'm comfortable with the memories. I've learned to stop trying to forget, and learned instead to embrace it. It just doesn't scare me anymore."

A psychologist once told me that *not* being affected by the experience over there would be abnormal. When he told me that, it was like he'd just given me a pardon. It was as if he had said, "Go ahead and feel something about the place, Bob. It ain't going nowhere. You're gonna wear it for the rest of your life. Might as well get to know it."

A lot of my "brothers" haven't been so lucky. For them the memories are too painful, their sense of loss too great. My sister told me of a friend she has whose husband was in the Nam. She asks this guy when he was there. Here's what he said: "Just last night." It took my sister a while to figure out what he was talking about. *Just last night.* Yeah, I was in the Nam. When? *Just last night.* During sex with my wife. And on my way to work this morning. Over my lunch hour.

316

Yeah, I was there.

My sister says I'm not the same brother who went to Vietnam. My wife says I won't let people get close to me, not even her. They are probably both right.

Ask a vet about making friends in Nam. It was risky. Why? Because we were in the business of death, and death was with us all the time. It wasn't the death of, "If I die before I wake." This was the real thing. The kind where boys scream for their mothers. The kind that lingers in your mind, and becomes more real each time you cheat it. You don't want to make a lot of friends when the possibility of dying is that real, that close. When you do, friends become a liability.

A guy named Bob Flanigan was my friend. Bob Flanigan is dead. I put him in a body bag one sunny day, on April 29, 1969. We'd been talking, only a few minutes before he was shot, about what we were going to do when we got back in the world. Now, this was a guy who had come in-country the same time as myself. A guy who was loveable and generous. He had blue eyes and sandy blond hair.

When he talked, it was with a soft drawl. Flanigan was a hick and he knew it. That was part of his charm. He didn't care. Man, I loved this guy like the brother I never had. But, I screwed up. I got too close to him. Maybe I didn't know any better. But I broke one of the unwritten rules of war. *Don't get close to people who are going to die.* But sometimes you can't help it.

You hear vets use the term "buddy" when they refer to a guy they went to war with. "Me and this *buddy* of mine..."

"Friend" sounds too intimate, doesn't it? "Friend" calls up images of being close. If he's a friend, then you are going to be hurt if he dies, and war hurts enough without adding to the pain. Get close; get hurt. It's as simple as that.

In war you learn to keep people at that distance my wife

talks about. You become so good at it that twenty years after the war, you still do it without thinking. You won't allow yourself to be vulnerable again.

My wife knows two people who can get into the soft spots inside me. My daughters. I know it probably bothers her that they can do this. It's not that I don't love my wife. I do. She's put up with a lot from me. She'll tell you that when she signed on for better or worse she had no idea there was going to be so much of the latter. But with my daughters it's different.

My girls are mine. They'll always be my kids. Not marriage, not distance, not even death can change that. They are something on this earth that can never be taken away from me. I belong to them. Nothing can change that. I can have an ex-wife; but my girls can never have an ex-father. There's the difference.

I can still see the faces, though they all seem to have the same eyes. When I think of us I always see a line of "dirty grunts" sitting on a paddy dike. We're caught in the first gray silver between darkness and light. That first moment when we know we've survived another night, and the business of staying alive for one more day is about to begin. There was so much hope in that brief space of time. It's what we used to pray for. "One more day, God. One more day."

And I can hear our conversations as if they'd only just been spoken. I still hear the way we sounded, the hard cynical jokes, our morbid senses of humor. We were scared to death of dying, and trying our best not to show it.

I recall the smells, too. Like the way cordite hangs on the air after a fire-fight. Or the pungent odor of rice paddy mud. So different from the black dirt of Iowa. The mud of Nam smells ancient, somehow. Like it's always been there. And I'll never forget the way blood smells, sticks, and dries on my hands. I spent a long night that way once. That memory isn't going anywhere.

I remember how the night jungle appears almost dreamlike as the pilot of a Cessna buzzes overhead, dropping parachute flares until morning. That artificial sun would flicker and make shadows run through the jungle. It was worse than not being able to see what was out there sometimes. I remember once looking at the man next to me as a flare floated overhead. The shadows around his eyes were so deep that it looked like his eyes were gone. I reached over and touched him on the arm. Without looking at me he touched my hand. "I know man. I know." That's what he said. It was a human moment. Two guys a long way from home and scared shitless.

"I know man." And at that moment he did.

God I loved those guys. I hurt every time one of them died. We all did. Despite our posturing. Despite our desire to stay disconnected, we couldn't help ourselves. I know why Tim O'Brien writes his stories. I know what gives Bruce Weigle the words to create poems so honest I cry at their horrible beauty. It's love. Love for those guys we shared the experience with.

We did our jobs like good soldiers, and we tried our best not to become as hard as our surroundings. We touched each other and said, "I know." Like a mother holding a child in the middle of a nightmare, "It's going to be all right." We tried not to lose touch with our humanity. We tried to walk that line. To be the good boys our parents had raised, and not to give in to that unnamed thing we knew was inside us all.

You want to know what frightening is? It's a nineteen-year-old-boy who's had a sip of that power over life and death that war gives you. It's a boy who, despite all the things he's been taught, knows that he likes it. It's a nineteen-year-old who's just lost a friend, and is angry and scared, and determined that, "Some *@#* is gonna pay." To this day, the thought of that boy can wake me from a sound sleep and leave me staring at the ceiling.

As I write this, I have a picture in front of me. It's of two young men. On their laps are tablets. One is smoking a cigarette. Both stare without expression at the camera. They're writing letters. Staying in touch with places they would rather be. Places and people they hope to see again.

The picture shares space in a frame with one of my wife. She doesn't mind. She knows she's been included in special company. She knows I'll always love those guys who shared that part of my life, a part she never can. And she understands how I feel about the ones I know are out there yet. The ones who still answer the question, "When were you in Vietnam?"

"Hey, man. I was there just last night."

BALLAD OF IRA HAYES

"They battled up Iwo Jima hill, two-hundred and fifty men, but only twenty-seven lived, to walk back down again..." - From *"The Ballad of Ira Hayes"* (Written by Peter LaFarge and recorded by Johnny Cash)

Ira Hayes was a Pima Indian. When he enlisted in the Marine Corps, he had hardly ever been off the Reservation. His Chief told him to be an "Honorable Warrior," and bring honor upon his family. Ira was a dedicated Marine. Quiet and steady, he was admired by the Marines who fought alongside him in three Pacific battles.

When Ira learned that President Roosevelt wanted him and the other survivors of the flag raising to come back to the U.S. to raise money on a "Heroes of Iwo Jima" Bond Tour, he was horrified. To Ira, the heroes of Iwo Jima, those deserving honor, were his "good buddies" who had died there.

At the White House, President Truman told Ira, "You are an American hero." But Ira didn't feel pride. As he later lamented, "How could I feel like a hero when only five men in my platoon of forty-five survived, when only twenty-seven men in my company of two hundred and fifty managed to escape death or injury?"

The Bond Tour was an ordeal for Ira. He couldn't understand or accept the adulation... "It was supposed to be soft duty, but I couldn't take it. Everywhere we went people shoved drinks in our hands and said 'You're a Hero!' We knew we hadn't done that much, but you couldn't tell them that."

Ira went back to the reservation attempting to lead an

anonymous life. But it didn't turn out that way... "I kept getting hundreds of letters. And people would drive through the reservation, walk up to me and ask, 'Are you the Indian who raised the flag on Iwo Jima?'"

Ira tried to drown his "Conflict of Honor" with alcohol. Arrested as drunk and disorderly, his pain was clear... "I was sick. I guess I was about to crack up thinking about all my good buddies. They were better men than me, and they're not coming back. Much less back to the White House, like me."

In 1954, Ira reluctantly attended the dedication of the Iwo Jima monument in Washington. After a ceremony where he was lauded by President Eisenhower as a hero once again, a reporter rushed up to Ira and asked him, "How do you like the pomp and circumstance?"

Ira just hung his head and said, "I don't."

Ira Hayes died three months later after a night of drinking. As he drank his last bottle of whiskey, he was heard crying and mumbling about his "good buddies." He was only thirty-two.

FEELING THANKFUL

Lance Corporal Jessica Kane

Dear Mom and Dad,

I, as most would have thought, was expecting a very homesick Thanksgiving. But, although I wish I could have been home, my Thanksgiving was filled with motivation and inspiration. To start off, the unit got together and the CO said a couple of words. He complemented us for our hard work, and was extremely impressed with the plans we have for the future. We then had lunch with some MRE crackers, popcorn, and SPAM. Afterwards, like we do most days, we prepared for a convoy into the city. It was a good convoy, and all went well.

While we were in the city we were asked to get together, because the General wanted to talk to us. The General being General Casey, the four-star General in the Army who is in charge of all Coalition Forces in Iraq. He again complemented us on the good work and sacrifices we are making. He told us that our hard work had paid off, and that there is no longer a safe haven for insurgents in Iraq. He then said something that would inspire the weakest of heart. He said, "The enemy was willing to die for their cause, and you gave them their wish." He told us that next year, when we are home for Thanksgiving, we will be truly grateful for all the gifts in our life. We can look back at this Thanksgiving and be proud of what we are doing.

Filled with juice and energy, we convoyed back to Camp Fallujah. As we came to the first gate into the camp, I was in shock because a Marine Corps Major was standing post.

Along with the Major was a First Sergeant. I reported to the Major what convoy we were and how many packs we were carrying. He told me to proceed, and to "have a happy Thanksgiving." As we came to the second gate, a Marine Captain and Sergeant Major were standing *that* post. There was not a PFC or Lance Corporal to be found. None of the posts had young Marines at them; Officers and Staff NCOs manned them all. The command had decided that the young Marines were going to have the night off to get some good chow. It was unbelievable, and a wonderful sight. The leadership took charge and took care of the younger Marines. This filled me with a pride I can't describe with words. I am so honored to be a part of an organization like this. Marines taking care of Marines with such unselfishness.

As I went to Thanksgiving chow with my brothers and sisters, the I MEF Commanding General, Lieutenant General Sattler, and the I MEF Sergeant Major were serving chow. The amazing part was they were so enthusiastic about it. Everyone was in a great mood, and ready to take on anything. It makes you think that if a three-star general in the United States Marine Corps can serve turkey to a bunch of 18-20 year old Lance Corporals, then you can suck up whatever you have to do and stop complaining. So, as I went to bed, I felt very thankful and indeed blessed for a great life.

Tomorrow, I am sure, will be full of fighting and disaster, along with the added stress of little sleep, and cold days and even colder nights. But tonight it's Thanksgiving, and everything is okay.

One Motivated Lance Corporal,

Jessica

The author of this letter is Lance Corporal Jessica Kane of I MEF 4th CAG HQ S-6

CAREER DAY

"Liberals are stalwart defenders of civil liberties - provided we're only talking about criminals and terrorists." - Ann Coulter

The poster child for liberal academia is Professor Ward Churchill of the University of Colorado at Boulder. In the wake of 9-11 he wrote: "As for those in the World Trade Center, well, really, let's get a grip here, shall we? True enough, they were civilians of a sort. But innocent? Gimme a break. They formed a technocratic corps at the very heart of America's global financial empire, the 'mighty engine of profit' to which the military dimension of U.S. policy has always been enslaved, and they did so both willingly and knowingly." He then wrote that the victims were... "too busy braying, incessantly and self-importantly, into their cell phones, arranging power lunches and stock transactions, each of which translated, conveniently out of sight, mind and smelling distance, into the starved and rotting flesh of infants. If there was a better, more effective, or in fact any other way of visiting some penalty befitting their participation upon the little Eichmanns inhabiting the sterile sanctuary of the twin towers, I'd really be interested in hearing about it." Well... that pretty well sums up the way liberals think. A good example of the way they <u>act</u> (when they don't get their way) is contained in the following letter from Major Michael V. Samarov, Commanding Officer of Marine Corps Recruiting Station San Francisco, concerning a Career Day held at the University of Southern California's Santa Cruz campus:

"We received word through MEPCOM and U.S. Army CI regarding plans for a 'counter-recruiting' demonstration on the USCS campus. Rick Nee personally received threatening phone calls at the office. Rick arrived on campus at about 1130, and was met by several of his poolees. They told him that several 'student' organizations had staged class walkouts yesterday in preparation for this protest. They also implied that numerous members of the faculty were involved in encouraging and organizing this action. This included, but was not limited to, scheduled classes on civil disobedience.

Rick took the precaution of taking his team to today's career fair in appropriate civilian attire. This proved to be ineffective, because the entire campus was staked out by anarchists with Nextel walkie-talkies. As soon as one of them heard a poolee refer to Rick as 'sir,' the entire group was mobbed by fifteen to twenty protesters.

Rick brought his team into the building. In addition to several civilian employers, there were representatives from the Corrections Department, the U. S. Marshals, the Army, the Navy, and us. Shortly after Rick set up his table, the UCSC Police Dept was overwhelmed. A violent crowd of over one hundred anarchists burst through the police and into the auditorium where the career fair was being held. The crowd assaulted towards the military and government agency tables, grabbing fliers, ripping various materials, and throwing garbage at the government employees and military members. The U.S. Marshals and Corrections Officers quickly fled without taking any of their materials with them. The Navy and the Army quickly followed suit. After them, the campus police also vanished.

At this point, Rick was called aside by the career fair organizers. They requested that he leave. Rick called me and received guidance to hold his ground until and unless he felt himself and his Marines (SSgt Verhoff and SSgt Eichler - outgoing and incoming OSAs) were physically threatened. Rick told the UCSC personnel that he had every right to be there, and reminded them of their stated promise to keep the protests outside of the auditorium. The administrators acknowledged his right and called the City of Santa Cruz Police Department.

The SCPD arrived in full riot gear. By this point most of the other employers had left and the auditorium contained Marines, Marine candidate poolees (linked arm-in-arm defending the table), riot police, and six hundred anarchists. The outside of the auditorium was completely surrounded by an even greater number of rioters. The SCPD began arresting people. At this point, they advised Rick that, in the interest of public safety, they were ordering him to leave. Rick, his Marines, and his poolees were surrounded by a phalanx of riot gear clad SCPD officers who, together, fought their way to a police van that was waiting by the back door of the auditorium. The police took this group to the parking lot that is five miles away from the auditorium. Rick found his GOV (Government Vehicle) with its tires slashed but no further damage. All GOVs that were parked in this lot had sustained similar damage.

Now, here's the question: Does this incident mean these Marines rates an additional star on their Combat Action Ribbons?"

REFLECTIONS
On a Glorious Birthday

Paul Young

The first Marine Corps Birthday I attended was at Subic Bay in the Philippines in November of 1959. I was stationed at Marine Barracks Cubi Point, a dedicated 'post flanker' on my third year in the Corps. It was my seventeenth month in the PI, and I was holding down and serving well the grand rank of Private First Class – I was proud as punch of that stripe!

On previous birthdays I'd pulled duty and only got part of the cake, but none of the party. That night would be the first time I would actually be present and accounted for at a Marine Corps Birthday Party. Anticipation in the off duty section of the barracks was high. Shoes were shined to a high gloss, uniforms pressed, emblems coated, brass polished, piss cutters set at a rakish angle - the Cubi Marines were ready… and damn, we looked good! So off we went.

The party was held mainside at a brand new club, and things started out just peachy. Several of us from Cubi were seated around a table, spiffed to the nines in our Class A tropicals minus ties. San Miguel beer flowed like water, and a dance band played "Smoke Gets in Your Eyes," "As Time Goes By," and the like. Unfortunately there were only about three Filipino women present among roughly one hundred Marines from both Cubi and mainside, so not a whole lot of dancing took place. But the testosterone was there nonetheless.

It wasn't long before we were all pretty mellow and

enjoying a high degree of fellowship and camaraderie. In fact each of us grew more handsome and intelligent with the downing of each beer, and the telling of each sea story.

The cake arrived and was cut by the commanding officer, Colonel Cash, and as the ceremony played out we all enjoyed cake and beer - not an unusual combination at that point in our lives.

Not long into the evening, a fight broke out at one of the tables behind ours. Not to worry, we did a lot of that in the PI, and a fight was generally part of the evening's entertainment in the fair and exotic city of Olongapo. We were quite used to them. It seems some sailors and a couple of Marines were in disagreement, which was not unusual. Nothing to worry about, and when the dust settled, the few sailors who had come were gone.

Then a fight between some Mainside and Cubi Marines broke out. Now things were getting personal. The band sagely struck up the Marines' Hymn, and we all abruptly snapped to attention amid a clutter of broken bottles and puddles of beer. The fighting stopped.

The Hymn ended, and we took our seats and continued downing beer - although a tad on the edgy side. Then another fight started, only this one spread out a bit and involved a few more tables - which began going over with loud crashes. And then a few more tables. More beer bottles flew thru the air. The Marines at Young's table put their backs to the wall and stood their ground, wisely not entering into the fisticuffs and acting only as observers.

By now, the floor of the club was awash in beer and broken bottles as fists continued to fly and Marines cursed and struggled. The band again struck up the Marines' Hymn, and for a brief moment we all came to attention. Then someone threw a bottle at the band. Then some more bottles.

The band quickly decamped, the singer hiking up her evening gown above her knees and sprinting like a cat in high heels for the nearest door.

The fighting grew and spilled out of the club onto a surrounding field. One of Young's buddies was jumped by a mainside Marine, and down they went. Another Marine jumped in, and now it was two on one against a Cubi Marine. Things were really personal now, and a wrong had to be righted!

Young grabbed one of them, and was in turn grabbed from behind by some guy who was strong as an ox and hit like a mule! Down they went, and Young was saved by the fact that he landed on top. He began to hammer on the mule guy with everything he had, and was barely holding his own. The collar got ripped from his shirt, and was left hanging by a thread. Then his lip got fattened, and a gash appeared on his forehead. Young realized that if he let go of the mule and for some reason stopped pounding on him, he would get the beating of his life – so he hung on with everything he had and pounded away, wondering the whole time how in the hell was he going to get out of this mess!

Whistles started blowing from every quarter, and AFP and Shore Patrol raced onto the scene and swung into action with their clubs. They whacked first and asked questions later - which was the norm at the time.

To the sound of thumping billies and much yelling and cursing, the fighting abruptly ended. Young was rescued from his battle with the mule, which at that point was not going well at all! Off we scattered like a bunch of quail.

About that time a sailor staggered out of the dark holding a bleeding head, claiming he'd been hit by a brick. Small pockets of Marines continued to fight out of range of the AFP, as sirens screamed and patrol cars and paddy wagons arrived.

Young and several of his buddies were stopped, shoved inside a paddy wagon and transported to the AFP station near the main gate. The brigs were full, so we sat on benches lining one wall - somewhat sobered and subdued by the evening's events and our new surroundings.

And there was Young in the pokey, bleeding from the head, a fat lip, loose teeth, collar hanging by a thread, trousers grass-stained and muddy, formerly spit-shined shoes scuffed and filthy, brass dull, and aching from head to toe.

And grinning from ear to ear.

It had been a glorious Marine Corps Birthday! My first, and never to be equaled. A *real* Marine Corps Birthday. One to be cherished until my dying day. It had been wonderful, with a fight scene just like in the movies!

We were released at midnight and returned to our barracks, where we were chewed out by a cigar chomping 1st Sergeant by the name of Armond who seemed to mistake every Marine within reach for a "low-down, yellow bellied skunk!"

And that, as they say, was the end of that.

Paul Young is the author of *1st Recon, 2nd to None*.

331

A SWORD
For Corporal Boscovitch

Connie Schultz

"Without a sign, his sword the brave man draws, and asks no omen, but his country's cause." - Homer

The Marine Corps has many strongly held traditions, and the swords carried by our officers and NCOs represent one of the very oldest. The Marine Officer and NCO swords are the oldest weapons still used in the United States Armed Forces. Noncommissioned officers of the Marine Corps hold the distinction of being the only NCOs in any branch of the regular United States Armed Forces who still have the honor of carrying a commissioned officer's weapon. Shortly after the Marine Officers' discontinued the use of the Calvary Sword in favor of the Mameluke, which had been presented to Lieutenant Presley O'Bannon by the Pasha of Tripoli, the Seventh Commandant, Brigadier General Jacob Zeilin, presented it to Marine NCOs and it became known as the 'Marine NCO Sword.' The Commandant did this because of the significant role NCOs play in leading Marines in combat. Prior to this, only officers were issued swords because of its symbolic representation of leadership and authority.

When you love someone who is grieving, you'll do almost anything to bring them a moment's reprieve. For Steve Wright, that meant he had to somehow, some way, find the proper sword to bury with his stepson, Marine Corporal Jeffrey Boskovitch, who had been killed in an ambush in Iraq.

332

It was the Marine NCO sword, shorthand for the ceremonial weapon of the noncommissioned officer. Steve and his wife, Kathy, didn't even know how important it was to Jeffrey until his girlfriend told them he'd always wanted one. As soon as she heard that, Kathy wanted the sword for her son.

But reality trumped yearning, it seemed. Marine NCO swords, which cost more than five hundred dollars, have to be custom-made. Shaped like a saber, the length is based on the Marine's height, and each sword is engraved with the Marine's name.

Wright found out that the Ames Sword Company, a small operation in New London, Ohio, made the exact sword they needed. When he listened to the company's voice-mail message left in response to his query, though, his heart sank. The normal waiting period is eight to ten weeks. Jeffrey would be buried in seven days.

Jeffrey's stepfather, an Air Force veteran, called the company president, Russell Sword (yes, that is his real name). All Sword needed to hear was that a Marine had been killed. "I'll get it to you on Monday," he promised.

"As soon as I talked to him, I knew he'd keep his word," Wright said. What he didn't know was why.

In 1967, nineteen-year-old Russell Sword had escorted the body of his best friend, a fellow Marine, home from Vietnam.

"His name was Davis Jones," Sword said. "He was from Wellington, and he was only twenty years old. I hadn't even shipped out yet. But when his mother asked me to do it, there was no way I could say no."

Sword went to Vietnam the following year, where he earned a Purple Heart and a Bronze Star. And now, thirty-eight years later, the parent of another fallen Marine needed his help. Sword called three employees who would have to work weekend overtime if he were to keep his promise to the grieving family. He knew their answers before he asked.

Marine Vietnam veteran Lewis Collins, the finisher, said he'd be there. Lloyd Yates, the artist, said he'd be there, too. Production manager Keith Bailey didn't hesitate.

"There was never any question we were going to do our best," Sword said. "I know how much I hurt when I lost Davis. We were going to do this, and we were going to do it right."

They worked through the weekend on the 32-inch sword for Jeffrey. At Wright's request, they also made two others with blades they had in stock: a 32-inch and a 28-inch, which Wright also paid for and donated to the 3rd Battalion, 25th Marine Regiment, in Jeffrey's name. Just in case.

Wright said he would pick up the sabers. Sword had another idea. His future son-in-law was a Marine recruiter in Lima.

"I thought, 'I'll bet Chris would do it, and it would mean so much to me if a Marine delivered this.' You know, once a Marine, always a Marine. I'm fifty-six, but no matter what your age, you always trust another Marine."

So he called Marine Staff Sergeant Christopher Mulet, and asked if he could help. Three days later, at around 1 PM on Monday, August 8th, Mulet and Gunnery Sergeant Terranfus Williams, both in dress blues, rang the doorbell at the Wright home. The family was overwhelmed.

"So many people have been so kind to us in the last two weeks," Wright said. "This one really blew us away."

His wife, sitting next to him at the kitchen table, nodded. "This is maybe hard for some to understand, but there have been small blessings since Jeffrey was killed. He's home. He was viewable to the public. Some of the boys come home in

334

pieces. Maybe he was tortured, we'll never know. But he was whole."

And Steve Wright was able to come through for his wife in her darkest hour.

The sword's simple engraving reads: "Corporal Jeffrey A. Boskovitch, USMC."

This first appeared in the *Cleveland Plain Dealer* on August 18, 2005

THE MARINE
As Seen By...

Himself: A Stout, Handsome, Highly-Trained Professional Killer and Female Idol, who wears a star sapphire ring, carries a finely honed K-Bar, is covered with a crisp cammie cover, and is always on time due to the reliability of his Seiko Diver's Watch.

His Wife: A stinking, gross, foul mouthed bum, who arrives home every six months or so with a seabag full of filthy utilities, a huge ugly watch, an oversized knife, a filthy hat, and a hard-on.

Headquarters Marine Corps: A drunken, brawling, HMMWV stealing, women corrupting liar, with a star sapphire ring, Seiko watch, unauthorized K-Bar, and a fuc*ed up cover.

His Commanding Officer: A fine specimen of a drunken, brawling, HMMWV stealing, woman corrupting bullshitter, with a star sapphire ring, fantastically accurate Seiko watch, finely honed razor sharp K-Bar, and a salty cammie cover.

Congress: An over-paid, over-rated tax burden who is, however, indispensable since he will volunteer to go anywhere, at any time, and kill whoever he is told to, as long as he can drink, brawl, steal HMMWVs, corrupt women, kick cats, sing dirty songs, and wear filthy cammies, big sapphire rings, over-sized knives, Seiko watches and really fuc*ed up covers.

336

ABOUT THE AUTHOR

Andy Bufalo retired from the Marine Corps as a Master Sergeant in January of 2000 after more than twenty-five years service. A communicator by trade, he spent most of his career in Reconnaissance and Force Reconnaissance units but also spent time with Amtracs, Combat Engineers, a reserve infantry battalion, and commanded MSG Detachments in the Congo and Australia.

He shares the view of Major Gene Duncan, who once wrote "I'd rather be a Marine private than a civilian executive." Since he is neither, he has taken to writing about the Corps he loves. He currently resides in Tampa, Florida.

Semper Fi!

CPSIA information can be obtained
at www.ICGtesting.com
Printed in the USA
BVOW08s1938180118

505596BV00016B/147/P